"Long George" Francis

"Long George" Francis
Gentleman Outlaw of Montana

Gary A. Wilson

TWODOT®

GUILFORD, CONNECTICUT
HELENA, MONTANA
AN IMPRINT OF THE GLOBE PEQUOT PRESS

B FRANCIS

To buy books in quantity for corporate use
or incentives, call **(800) 962–0973, ext. 4551,**
or e-mail **premiums@GlobePequot.com.**

A · **TWODOT**® · **BOOK**

Text design: Nancy Freeborn

Library of Congress Cataloging-in-Publication Data
Wilson, Gary A.
  "Long George" Francis : gentleman outlaw of Montana / Gary A. Wilson.—1st ed.
     p. cm.
  Includes bibliographical references.
  ISBN 0-7627-3976-2
  1. Francis, George, 1874-1920. 2. Outlaws—Montana—Havre Region—Biography. 3. Cowboys—Montana—Havre Region—Biography. 4. Frontier and pioneer life—Montana—Havre Region. 5. Havre Region (Mont.)—Biography. 6. Havre Region (Mont.)—History. I. Title.
  F739.H36W547 2005
  978.6'14'092—dc22
                                                                              2005014776

Manufactured in the United States of America
First Edition/First Printing

Dedicated to my supportive family: Mike, Jeanne, and Donna; and to the memory of those caring people of northern Montana whom I was honored to know: Mary Almas-Antunes, Rose Faber, Frank Grable, John "Blacky" Lofgren, Alvin "Al" Lucke, Martin Nobel, Hilda Redwing, and Ron Smith, to name just a few.

The barbed wire made the cowpuncher history. The only place he is found now is on paper. The oldtime cowpuncher would run on a band of horses, hold up a stagecoach, work a brand over—maybe notches on his gun, but wouldn't steal milk from a calf.

The few old rawhides that [remain] are found in a blind pig or they hide in the mountains making moon[shine]. They have lived past their prime. They were good cowmen. They might have bragged on their roping and riding, but the moon they made can't be bragged about.

C. M. Russell

> When my old soul hunts range and rest
> Beyond the last divide,
> just plant me in some stretch of West
> That's sunny, lone, and wide.
> Let cattle rub my tombstone down
> And coyotes mourn their kin,
> Let hawses paw and tromp the moun'
> But don't fence it in.

Charles Badger Clark
"The Old Cowman"
from *Sun and Saddle Leather*

Contents

$500.⁰⁰ REWARD

FOR

GEORGE FRANCIS

KNOWN AS

"LONG GEORGE"

———DESCRIPTION———

Height, about 6 feet 6 inches; weight, about 190 pounds; age 45 years very **slender, blue eyes, good teeth, deep dimples on cheeks when smiling,** light **complected. He carries revolver with smooth pearl handle, 45 calibre, nickel plated, all metal parts engraved. Has webb fingers on left hand, deformed nails on same hand; right leg has been broken; wears longer heel on right shoe**

"LONG GEORGE" HAS BEEN PROVEN GUILTY
OF HORSE STEALING AND IS NOW A FUGITIVE
OF JUSTICE

To receive reward, arrest, hold and wire

GEORGE BICKLE

HAVRE,   Sheriff of Hill County, Montana   **MONT**

Foreword

Why a biography of Long George? As a Western bad man Long George Francis rates hardly a line. He robbed no trains. He led no columns of riders, lean and wary, to the storied Hole-in-the-Wall. He carried a revolver, perhaps loaded, but it was an adornment, silver-fluted, with mother-of-pearl stocks; he left no Ringo Kids shot down "in the hot dust of Masquelero" as the pulp writers in *Top Notch* magazine liked to say. He had a fondness for horses, extending perhaps to one or two not strictly his own, but it was hardly the stuff legends are made of.

Long George was a show cowboy, but no William Cody, no Ponca Bill. At rodeos—then called "stampedes" or "roundups" in his part of the country—Long George paraded. He was somebody to look at. Even when he became a fugitive he wanted an audience. Legend has him living in a cabin on Long George peak, or some say on Little Joe Mountain—the author of the following book will probably settle the matter—in the Bear Paws, at most 23 miles from the Hill County jail. But he was lonely, longed for visitors, and was frequently in Box Elder in the poker game, where he was said to scrooch down in his chair at the advent of strangers, an act which made him look, if anything, even taller than he was. His companions were men such as Al Thompson, brother-in-law of the late Senator Cowan, and Harry Green, son of famed U.S. Cavalry Captain Hugh Hamilton Green, intermittently deputy sheriff serving northern Chouteau County. If a sheriff ever seriously went looking for him, it has not been recorded.

Yet Long George became the Milk River country's favorite bad man. Let me pursue this paradox.

When I think of Long George I am likely to recall Jack Mabee (pronounced Maybe), Gildford saloonkeeper, later famed as bartender to the Western stars, Hollywood. The Cushmans lived in Box Elder at the time, and Jack would drive up to Pa's joint on the main street, a row of buildings facing the railroad, in his Hudson Super Six, a mighty car famed for its balanced crankshaft. It was of a flush color, with yellow side curtains, when every other car in town was black. Jack was said to get his Super Six up to 60 miles an hour! And if you stood on the wagon ramp of the Rocky Mountain Elevator, you could see its dust all the way to Big Sandy suspended in the evening air.

Jack liked to go to Big Sandy—where there was plenty of sporting action during cattle-shipping time. Until about 1913, Big Sandy claimed to be the biggest cattle shipper in the nation. Or he could have visited Fort Benton, oldest town in Montana; or Great Falls, with the highest smokestack in the world. ("Are we in it!" Scoop Hersey, editor, liked to write in his *Box Elder Valley Press*, implying we, too, were part of the big action.)

I was sure proud that Jack Mabee always headed for our joint. It showed we amounted to something. Five minutes of joviality, people gathering to look at the Hudson and laugh at the jokes, then off again, slow so as not to run over the chickens, then *boom!* as he gave it the power, to Havre, 25 miles northeast, or Gildford, a cut-across 20, on the Sage Creek road.

It occurs to me that had Jack gone by way of Havre the boom of the engine might have been heard by Long George himself—at his homestead near Burnham, population seven—might have, were he at home.

He had filed on a claim like everyone else, but, being no farmer, tiller of the soil, it seems unlikely. George was a horseman in a land being destroyed, to his lights, by being turned grass side under. At any rate he was soon to join, with others, in a venture to put Havre on the map. They organized the Stampede.

The idea wasn't so original, but the timing! Northern Montana had experienced the last of the great land rushes. The land thereabout had once been part of the Blackfeet Reserve, and after that, hay and grazing for Fort Assinniboine. Later, it was thrown open to settlement in 320-acre homestead plots. Claimants rushed to take it in a few brief seasons. Turned by the plough, its virgin soil, with richness accumulated since the ice age, produced with abundance. It rained, the sun shone, and spring wheat had no trouble getting itself shipped on the railroad at high, wartime prices.

Oh, the crowds that came for the Stampede! We went by train. Not a hotel room was to be found. We slept in a blacksmith shop. Actually it was an extension of Linder & Neilsen's hotel, which they had cleared out and lined with cots, each with fresh white sheets, one dollar per night.

x

Of the Stampede itself I have little recollection. There were always people in the way. I am sure Long George was there, and I saw him in his hat. (Later, when Pa moved to Zurich, where he had a pool hall and dance hall, Long George came and wore his hat, which was memorable. "There's Long George!" people would say. No matter where he went Long George was the most looked-at person there. However it is not my purpose to write Mr. Wilson's book for him.)

At the outset I tried for a scholarly tone by using the word paradox. How was it that Long George, an essentially likeable and non-violent man, came to be, without changing his nature, the Milk River country's favorite outlaw? So here goes, but with a diversion—

In Big Sandy there lived a man called Broncho Billy, and he was about as opposite to Long George as it was possible to be. His real name has not come down through history, although it could probably be found if one went through the old newspaper files. He became "Broncho Billy" because of a resemblance in actions, if not physique, to Broncho Billy Anderson, the first of the Wild West picture stars. Broncho Bill (Anderson) was for a time, 1909 or so, establishing the Golden States picture industry practically single-handed. Turning out as many as two films a week for a company called Essanay, a tempo which left little time for nuance, but plenty for riding and shooting. This suited the Big Sandy audience just fine, and filled the seats at Oliver Tingley's Oliver Opera House, one of the Cowboy Capital's three theaters.

Big Sandy's Broncho Billy was a mule driver, master of the double team. He was an unruly character, perpetually seeking revenge for ills real or suspected. An example will serve. On hearing that several cases of smallpox had been diagnosed and isolated in Havre, Billy traveled thence and secreted himself in the pest house where he was noticed by Dr. Joseph Almas, at that time County physician.

Asked why was he there, didn't he realize he could catch smallpox? he said yes, he did. It was his purpose to catch it, and take it down and give it to all those sons-of-b's in Big Sandy.

Billy's chief hate was Barney Van Alstine, saloonkeeper and proprietor of the historic old Spokane House, a log and frame building just off the main thoroughfare in the center of town. "His time will come, never fear," Billy promised.

An occasion arose one day when Billy was returning, with his two-span and an empty wagon, from Lohse's Ferry, now Judith Ferry, on the Missouri

River. It was cattle-shipping time with herds being held to wait their turn on the average two trains sent daily to South St. Paul, and cowboys left to watch. To keep these men content, so near the fleshpots of Big Sandy, it was common for the owners to furnish them with liquor, and being invited over, as he drove along the road, it came to pass that Billy arrived in town in a condition it generally took him an hour or two to attain.

In fact he was rip-roaring drunk, on an empty stomach, with rested mules, and, topping the slight rise at the end of the main street, Johannes Avenue, wide enough to drive cattle down, with its two- and three-story buildings on both sides, he whipped his teams to a run. "Get out of my way!" he yelled, "I'll deal with you later." This time he was out to settle scores with the big fish himself. "Barney Van Alstine, I'm coming in after you!" and opposite the Spokane House, which sat back from the street, he executed a forty-five degree turn and drove his terrified teams straight across the sidewalk and the old wagon yard, for the front door.

Fortunately the mules recognized the obstruction of a log-and-frame hotel, with front porch, and took a last, frantic haw turn, which saved them, although doing damage to the wagon and the porch, and kept on, terrified, for the street, Billy still at the whip, calling that he'd be back, it was only a sample.

It was of course a busy time, with guests seated on the porch, enjoying the sweet of the afternoon—cattle buyers, auctioneers, traveling men, and poker players from as far away as Denver for the big action; they scattered to save themselves, diving for "what cover could be found, and now emerged, shaken and voluble.

"What kind of an animal do you call that?" was the tenor of their surprise and anger. "Do you put up with creatures like him? I thought this was a civilized place.

"They should take an s-o-b like that out and horsewhip him," etc.

Among the guests was a local rancher, a huge German immigrant, named "Big Hans" Lehfeldt. Seeing Billy, he had taken the newspaper which he was perusing and retired to the lobby, beyond thick whitewashed logs, but as soon as the danger was past he returned and went on reading. Big Hans listened while these strangers gave Billy a very hard time, but finally he felt he should introduce a little equity.

"Vell!" he said, rattling his newspaper to command attention, "dot was choost Broncho Billy. He does those things."

Similarly the paradox of Long George. Nobody supported violence, dishonesty or even flight from the law in serious matters, but for all that they liked things the way they were, it was why they came West. You had to give a little in order not to be hemmed in. They liked it sort of free and easy. Perhaps Long George got hold of the wrong horse. Perhaps he evaded the law. But he was just Long George. He did those things.

Dan Cushman

Publisher's Note:
Dan Cushman, internationally known novelist and historian, spent much of his youth in the north-central Montana communities of Box Elder, Philbert railroad siding, Zurich, Havre, and Big Sandy before settling permanently in Great Falls. He chronicled these experiences in his book, *Plenty of Air and Room.* Cushman is best known for *Stay Away, Joe, The Grand and the Glorious, The Old Copper Collar, Montana—the Gold Frontier, The Great North Trail, The Silver Mountain,* and a famed collection of pioneer recipes, his *Cow-Country Cook Book.*

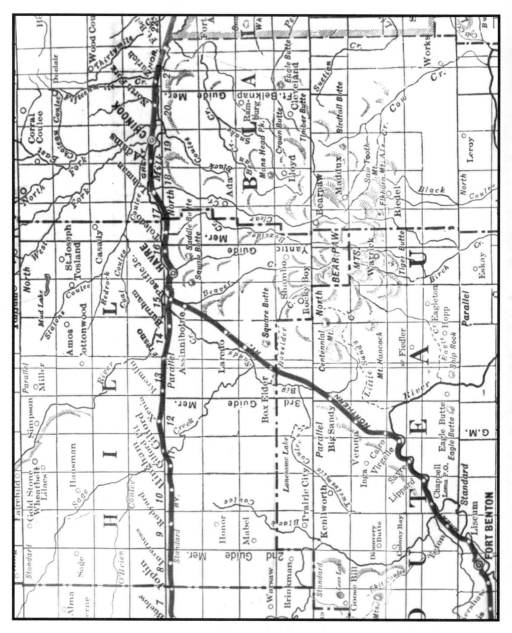

Northcentral Montana map © 1938 by McGill Warner Co., St. Paul Board of R.R. Commissioners.

Introduction

On a cold, clear winter's day in 1898, the tall, rangy, young cowboy dozed on a lumpy, undersized steel-framed bed in his second floor room in Havre's Windsor Hotel. The only light in the drab and sparsely furnished room shone through the engraved glass chimney of a heavy glass kerosene lamp. His right leg was encased in a heavy, hardened mixture of plaster and gauze, and the leg of his black woolen pants was split up the seam to accommodate the bulky cast. He wore a dark blue flannel shirt with a front opening shield fastened by mother-of-pearl buttons; his rough and calloused hands were folded across his chest over a copy of *Ben Hur* by General Lew Wallace. His wide-brimmed Stetson hat and a red neckerchief hung on a small wooden chair, and the beginnings of a hand-woven horsehair rope were looped on its seat. The large bowl of his black bent-stem pipe was still warm as it lay in a heavy, clear glass ashtray filled with the butts of hand-rolled Bull Durham cigarettes. Littering the bare floor nearby were well-worn copies of Sir Walter Scott's *Ivanhoe*, a Porter's of Arizona "Saddles, Accessories and Western Apparel" catalog, a Montgomery Ward and Company catalog—and a not-so-worn copy of the Bible.

Though his senses were dulled by sleep, he became increasingly aware of the smell of smoke. As the air became heavy with the odor, he sat up with a start, glancing around the room. Suddenly from the hallway came the sounds of running feet and voices filled with panic shouting: "Fire!" "Fire!" "The place is on fire!" Only then did he see the smoke seeping under the door, and a cold fear swept over him.

"Surely someone will come to help me," he thought, "they know I'm up here with a busted leg." But as the long minutes went by it was obvious that the hallway, and probably the hotel, was now deserted. He clumsily eased himself off the bed, crammed *Ivanhoe* in his belt, hastily tied on his neckerchief, and jammed on his hat. With his crutches he awkwardly lumbered towards the door, and threw a last glance over his shoulder at his possessions.

Bracing himself, he cautiously opened the door a crack. Peering out, he was met by a blast of intense heat and thick, acrid smoke that took his breath away and burned his eyes and nostrils. Slamming the door shut, he paused to adjust his neckerchief over his nose and mouth, after wetting it in his wash basin; then taking a deep breath, he eased out into the smoke-shrouded hallway.

The dimly visible staircase seemed a long way off as he slowly moved towards it. There was an explosive crash behind him as part of the ceiling's burning timbers collapsed. Abandoning the unwieldy crutches, he sat on the floor and, looking over his shoulder, began pulling himself along with his hands and pushing with his good leg, the cast dragging and bumping as he fought to remain conscious. He felt his strength ebbing as the lack of oxygen, the heat, and the extra effort required to hurry the painful and cumbersome leg along took their toll. His headway had all but stopped.

The cowboy knew that death was close. "What a way for a man of the outdoors to meet his end!" he reflected. And what of his family in Idaho? He hadn't seen them in six years! Too late now. Wait, were those footsteps and voices on the stairway? His heart leapt with hope. Then, "No, my mind is just playing tricks on me," he thought as he passed out.

"There he is!" a choked voice said, as two figures emerged from the smoke and flames. They half-carried, half-dragged the oblivious cowboy down the narrow stairway, through the lobby and outside to the cheering crowd gathered on First Street. Within scant minutes the flimsy wooden structure was completely engulfed in flames, the upper floor gone.

The fresh, cold winter air revived the cowboy after a few minutes, and turning to his rescuers with a grin on his soot-blackened face, he asked them, "Gotta match? Got to have a smoke!" Dr. Joseph Almas and Town Marshall Erick Thorsen, who had just heroically saved him from a very smoky place indeed, just shook their heads.

This cowboy was George Francis, "Long George," who, along with saloon owner Christopher W. "Shorty" Young, was considered the most colorful and controversial individual who ever lived in northern Montana. His local exploits reached the pages of the *New York Herald* and eventually the national airways of major radio stations. Reportedly his life story was once considered movie material—but the close-mouthed locals apparently wouldn't put forth any details to the outsiders from Hollywood.

Francis, a tall and slender man, was 6 feet 6 inches and 190 pounds, with blue eyes, straight white teeth, deeply dimpled cheeks when he smiled, and thinning light brown hair. His fame was a result of his expertise and showmanship as a rodeo horseman, roper, and bulldogger. His trick horse Tony, fancy cowboy dress, and silver-mounted saddle gear were his trademarks. Francis performed in rodeos throughout the Northwest and commanded celebrity status at the 1919 Calgary (Alberta) Stampede. In 1916 he established his own rodeo, The Great Northern Montana Stampede in Havre, Montana, and it was fast becoming a major attraction on the western circuit before his troubles with the law forced him to abandon it.

Though well liked and respected by most, he was both feared and hated by a few who held that he was an outlaw, the rumored leader of a major gang of cattle and horse thieves, and later, supposedly the head of a ring of bootleggers and hijackers. Yet others considered him a Robin Hood-like character: a Jesse James, Sam Bass, or Butch Cassidy type of folk hero or anti hero, who waged wars against the rich and greedy, while helping the poor and impoverished—although he never robbed a bank or train and never shot anyone. Neither viewpoint was accurate, though.

Francis lived in the twilight years of the old West when the wide-open stock ranges from Texas to Montana had nearly vanished, and with them came the demise of the major cattle companies and their large-scale cattle drives and roundups. He also witnessed the appearance of the "detested sheepherders" and the dreaded invasion of the homesteaders. The "fool hoeman" crowded out the cattle, Francis, and cattlemen and cowboys like him, forever changing their way of life.

He became a symbol: Rightly or wrongly he represented the old ways and rebelled at the winds of change that were blowing over the prairies of the last frontier. First went the buffalo, then the Indian, and finally, the free grasslands and the range cowboy. It was inevitable that in the process Francis would lose too.

Ironically, even his horse-stealing conviction partially resulted from the "evidence" of a scar left on a horse's hide by barbed wire, the loathed devil-created instrument of the homesteaders. And his own premature death was caused by another product of the new mechanical and far less romantic age that he opposed—the automobile.[1]

His enemies had hoped that his death would diminish his fame, and although they did their best to tarnish his memory, they only succeeded in emphasizing the mystery and romance surrounding his life; and in a minor way he joined the ranks of such "heroes in defeat" as the legendary bandit Joaquin Murieta, Army Colonel George Custer, Metis revolutionary Louis Riel, and Nez Perce Indian Chief Joseph (Hin-mam-too-pah-lat-kekht).

To this day it is difficult to separate the man from the legend, the good deeds from the bad; and to the chagrin of his enemies' descendants and the delight of his few old living friends and their grown children, the persona of "Long George" Francis is as big as ever.

The Cowboy

GEORGE FRANCIS CAME TO THE MILK RIVER COUNTRY of northern Montana about 1893.

He stepped off the single passenger car of a Utah and Northern cattle train pulled by a Great Northern Railway locomotive on a spring day at Box Elder. He had arrived here after a long, monotonous, and cramped journey from southeastern Idaho over mountains and more mountains. The train carried the remaining stock of the "U" up and "U" down brand of the Warbonnet Livestock Company. No longer welcome on the Fort Hall Indian Reservation near the Snake River and crowded out by the homesteaders elsewhere, these cattle joined the flood of both Shorthorns and Longhorns going to the last virgin open range left in the continental United States. This herd was to be driven to the rolling grasslands of the Clear Creek Valley, just north of the Bear's Paw Mountains[2] and just south of the Milk River.

Boss Robert Anderson, formerly a Wyoming rancher himself, and his cowboys were met by the town's chief and almost only white residents: David and Jane Cowan, their son, William, and daughters, Grace and Minnie. The family owned a trading post, and also did a lucrative business buying buffalo bones from Indians and Métis and shipping them to eastern fertilizer plants. Other than the store, school, post office, and two-story Cowan home, the town consisted of several abandoned tarpapered and unpainted green wood shacks, although more people were beginning to

1

settle the area again. The railroad had tried to establish the farming community of Bremer there a few years earlier, but most of its residents had left because of several poor, rainless growing seasons.

The cowboy crew asked about the Indians camped in canvas lodges on the edge of town.[3] Cowan told them that they were Chippewa, Plains Cree of Canada and Métis[4] (May-tee), who were a mixture of French, English, Scotch, and Indian, principally Chippewa-Cree. The name roughly means "the crossing of customs." Originally from the Saint Lawrence River region, the Chippewa had followed the game westward from the Great Lakes area, through the Northwest Territories of Canada, to the Turtle Mountains of north central North Dakota, and finally to Montana. The warlike Plains Cree, who lived in the area from the northern part of Manitoba Province west to the Saskatchewan River, Cowan further explained, were involved in the Northwest Territories Rebellion of 1885 under the leadership of Louis Riel, Gabriel Dumont, and Cree chiefs Little Pine, Big Bear[5], and Poundmaker—along with the Rattlers Warrior Society principally led by Little Bear, Little Poplar, and Wandering Spirit. Riel had supposedly promised the Cree that the Métis would kill all Canadian whites and then the Americans would come and pay large sums for their lands.

The Métis people had previously attempted to hold territory formerly called Assiniboia, originally in Hudson's Bay Company-controlled Prince Rupert's Land, now part of the province of Manitoba. The land had originally been granted to them by the government of Quebec's New France and later England, but their charters were not recognized as valid by the fledgling Dominion of Canada government.

Poundmaker's and Little Pine's bands attacked the community of Battleford, and Big Bear's band assaulted Frog Lake and Fort Pitt, while the Métis "Red River Cavalry"—in a separate and actually unrelated action—attacked the Duck Lake N.W.M.P. "Mountie" post and the town of Batoche. Many Cree and a few Métis had escaped to Montana after Riel's army's final defeat at the Battle of Batoche and the Army's relentless pursuit of the Cree bands. The refugee Cree in northern Montana were led by Little Bear—"Immassees"—whose father, Big Bear, was now in the Canadian prison at Stony Mountain.

About four years ago, Cowan related, these people had been attacked by a band of Blackfeet from the Two Medicine country west of the mountains. The battle over the Blackfeet's former hunting grounds occurred southeast of Box Elder by Mount Centennial and raged for several days until the trespassers were finally driven away. The defenders suffered few casualties. The townspeople were anxious about the outcome and had armed themselves from Cowan's supply of .44 Winchesters. He said that soldiers could have been summoned from nearby Fort Assinniboine, but as a matter of pride, they wanted no help; besides, the Cree had no recognized legal right to the land either.

Cowan said the Indians had tried to earn their keep by cutting hay and wood for the fort in the valleys of the nearby Bear's Paw Mountains. Unfortunately, the railroad's arrival with cheap, plentiful coal and the increasing scarcity of wood, plus new government conservation measures initiated by Theodore Roosevelt's administration, had badly hurt their means of making a living. The ever-increasing scarcity of game also stopped them from being able to price and sell beaded belts, moccasins, and shirts from pelts. They still gathered what was left of the buffalo bones and sold the horns after polishing them, but because the skeletons were getting harder to find in the tall grass, they set fire to the prairie to uncover them. This, he said, caused some anxious moments, although so far none of the blazes had gotten completely out of control and threatened the town. With their worsened plight, he said, many had been reduced to begging for food around the fort and towns and prostituting their wives and daughters to the soldiers. Looking sad and shaking his head, he stated, "This was bad enough without them becoming prey to the white man's diseases and rotgut whiskey too. If only the government would do something for them."

Once the conversation with Cowan ended, cowhand George Francis observed as an interested newcomer the numerous hardy box elder shade trees along the creek from which the town was named. To the east he saw the formations called Square Butte and Centennial Mountain—but mountains were something he was all too familiar with. It was the open country in the other three directions that he fondly gazed over, for there were miles and miles of relatively flat, open range—prairie sod occupied only by bleached buffalo bones and wildlife.

But taking in more of the idyllic landscape would have to wait: First their horses, personal gear, the chuck wagon, hoodlum (bedding-equipment) wagon, and the cattle had to be unloaded from the various railroad cars.

After buying supplies from Cowan, the crew made camp near the tree-lined creek. The men, their horses, and the cattle were certainly enjoying the escape from the stresses of confinement. The cattle were allowed to spread out and leisurely eat and digest their fill of grass.

Presently, the outfit's pilot, Bill Thackeray, arrived, meaning the crew could pull out at sunrise. Thackeray was the son of Ontario, Canada, transplant William Webster Thackeray, Havre bakery-confectionery store owner and major town property owner. The family had first lived in the shack town north of Fort Assinniboine on Beaver Creek. Bill wasn't the city type and preferred the outdoors life. Walking behind a plow and horses, he had helped carve the first G.N.R. right-of-way fire break between Fort Assinniboine and Great Falls, delivered mail for the fort, and worked as a cowhand for the Conrad Circle Cattle Ranch. Thackeray, like most of the local cowboys, became a good friend of Francis's; and he adhered to the frontier code of loyalty: Once a favor was done or a friendship made, it was never forgotten or gone back on.

When asked about Havre, Thackeray said it was located about 13 miles to the northeast and had been established about three years earlier. He told them it came into being when the Great Northern Railway moved its shops and station, located about two miles northwest of Fort Assinniboine, to a site on the Milk River near Bullhook Creek. He said it was a wide-open town where violence was commonplace around the many saloons and dance halls.

Soon darkness fell, and the boys turned in for their first good sleep since before they boarded the cramped train's quarters. The night passed quickly, and as the first rays of light broke over the mountain slopes, the camp became a beehive of activity. The cowboys responded to the cook's "come-and-get-it," the gear was picked up, the horses fed and saddled, and the herd pointed out.

Soon, the train trip with its many stops for coal, water, and tending to the cattles' needs was forgotten. The animals were now strung out for three-quarters of a mile. Bringing up the rear were the wagons and remuda man with the extra horses. Thackeray and Anderson rode point, directing the course of the herd. On each side were two swing men, who kept the flanks of the main herd from wandering too wide; and at the rear were the two drag men or tail riders.

Their job required much riding to and fro while making occasional whiplike thrusts with their lariats, and the unlimited use of blasphemy to prevent the lazy and reluctant beasts from deserting the procession or refusing to walk any further.

On the rider's lariat was spliced a long buckskin popper, and with an underhand throw and a snap of his wrist, he could "shoot" the popper and 20 feet of rope at an indolent cow's hide.

4

Bringing up the drag, riding a horse outfitted with the longest stirrups available on a saddle because of his long-legged frame, was George Francis, a beanpoled kid of eighteen. His instant love of the country made his job of eating dust, inhaling the foul smells, and tolerating the noise of thousands of hooves striking the hard ground almost enjoyable. Others on the crew included brothers Fred and George Aldous and their cousin, Fred "Kid" Aldous, who were to remain friends with Francis.

The trail led southeast, passing just east of Big Sandy, one of the last major cattle shipping centers in the Old West. Eventually they caught the old Cow Island Trail, which went from Cow Island Creek Landing on the Missouri River to Big Sandy and then down the Culbertson Road to Fort Benton. The trail had been traveled by hundreds of wagons with thousands of pounds of freight since the beginning of the gold rush days in 1862. On the left towered the ever-present snowcapped Bear's Paw Mountains of volcanic and glacial origin and their prominent peak: Bald Mountain—also called Mount Bear's Paw, Bear Pole, or just plain "Baldy"—rising 4,000 feet above the plains.[6]

They learned from Thackeray that the naming of the mountains was sometimes credited to an unknown group of Indians from the early nineteenth century who had climbed to the summit and envisioned the shape of the ridges below as the huge paw of a bear.

All this country as far as the eye could see, they learned, was part of the over ten-million-acre Chouteau County. It was once larger than the combined states of Connecticut, Massachusetts, and New Hampshire. Until 1893, when Teton County was carved from its western border, Chouteau County was one of the largest ever created in the United States. Fort Benton, with 600 people and located on the Missouri River, was county seat.

Sources of water were certainly no problem here, with all the creeks running off the mountains—quite a contrast to the often harsh, waterless lava rock desert areas of southern Idaho. Those emptying into the Missouri even contained trout. They passed creek after creek: Box Elder, Duck, Camp, Gorman, Big Sandy, Godfrey, and Little Sandy. Ahead were Eagle, Dog, Little Birch, and Birch.

The cattle drovers made good time, covering a good distance before making their late afternoon camp in the shelter of low trees by the bank of a small stream in view of Mount Hancock. With the chores completed and the animals bedded down for the night, the boys had some free time.

Instead of engaging in the usual card game or tall-tale swapping, or contests reciting or singing the labels of canned foods from memory, Francis gazed pensively at the blended blues and lavenders, oranges and yellows of the sunset, merging with the darkening horizon. He stretched out on his bedroll, leisurely puffing on his pipe while watching the shadow-shapes of the cattle beyond the glowing embers of the campfires. They were scattered on all sides for a mile or so.

The darkness held so many sounds: the lowing of cattle, the murmuring of the creek, the peaceful silence of the prairie occasionally broken by the yelping of a roving coyote, the snapping of a dry twig by a restless steer, the whinnying of one of the picketed horses, or the music of one of the cowboys on night herd duty giving his best "E-string" rendition of "The Ballad of Sam Bass."

Francis liked this country; there was no doubt. He was determined to make a success of himself and be his own boss and have his own ranch. He would make his family back in McCammon proud—and show his father . . .

His peaceful sleep was cut short since it was his turn to do the last two hours of night herding duty and to rouse the camp to begin another day. That day and the following went by quickly.

The journey was nearly over when they reached Birch Creek and turned north paralleling it. Soon they passed the Warrick post office, operated by the owners of the NL Horse Ranch. They left Birch Creek, with Mount Baldy in the foreground, when they turned northeast and crossed through an unnamed divide[7] that led into Clear Creek.

Through another divide to the east was Lloyd, located on Bean and Snake Creeks. Lloyd was an island of humanity in a sea of cattle, serving as the cattlemen's headquarters with its saloon, post office, blacksmith shop, and general store.

Thackeray pointed out to Anderson that on Snake Creek in October of 1877, the remnants of several non-treaty bands of Idaho and Oregon Nez Perce Indians fought their last desperate battle with pursuing army units. They were trying to reach the safety of Canada. Though defeated, some did escape across the border. He said they should visit the battlefield and view the rifle and shelter pits that the Indians dug on the east side of the creek bank.

The cattle were now pointed northward, soon to be turned loose to merge with the thousands already on the plains.

This was the end of one trail for Francis, yet the beginning of another, more arduous path. Later, when public attention was focused on his controversial life, his early beginnings received little attention; yet after his death, many inaccurate stories were told of his earlier life.

Life began for George Mortimer Francis not in Colorado, as once popularly believed, but at Camp Floyd, Cedar Valley, Utah, on September 21, 1874,[8] the third child of William and Sarah (Hickman) Francis. His father's family came from Kentucky and Virginia. William, son of a Baptist minister, left home at an early age to join an overland freighting outfit, possibly from Missouri, following the Oregon and California trails to the Sacramento area during the gold rush days. He stayed in the freighting business, however, instead of becoming a placer gold miner. He continued making trips across the and plains of Utah through Fort Hall, Idaho, and along the Humboldt River of Nevada and over the Sierra Madre Mountains to the Sacramento Valley.

At North Ogden, in the Salt Lake Valley, Wiliam Francis became acquainted with William Hickman, a fellow Kentuckian, with whom he had several cattle and horse tradings. Hickman's family and that of his wife, Minerva Wade, had come west led by Brigham Young, successor to the slain Joseph Smith, in the Mormon Church's 1840s migration to escape religious persecution in Illinois and Missouri. Hickman was a trusted lieutenant of the Mormon leader. The 28-year-old Francis also became fast friends with the Hickmans' 16-year-old, Salt Lake City-born daughter, Sarah.

On one of his return wagon trips to North Ogden he proposed; they were married on November 18, 1867, in the Utah Hotel, and left the next day for California's Sacramento Valley. They may have been engaged in farming, missionary work, or prospecting—or all three.

Sarah returned to her family at North Ogden in the spring of 1869 to await the arrival of their first child. After William's birth in October, the new father returned, and he moved the family to Camp Floyd, located 40 miles southwest of Salt Lake City, where he worked a mining claim.

Camp Floyd was a former military post built during the bloodless, but grim, so-called "Mormon War" of 1857–58. It had housed the 3,000-man army invasion force under General Albert Johnston, sent to oversee the newly negotiated peace between the Utah territorial and religious L.D.S. leaders and the federal government representatives, including a new governor to replace Brigham Young. Because of a bad winter and a surprise attack by Mormon cavalry that destroyed their supplies along the Green River, the Union force at Fort Bridger was not able to cross the Wasatch Mountains to enter Utah. This delayed and prevented a clash between the federal troops and the 6,000-man Nauvoo Legion. During the time when the Mormon Deseret forces were being marshaled, east-west travelers were prevented from crossing Utah. A wagon train with the Fancher party had tried and met with destruction. Fortunately, no further major violence occurred and an uneasy peace settled over the area, once the federal contingent arrived.

The post (present-day Fairfield) was abandoned in 1861 because of the War Between the States; it also served as a freighting headquarters for the firm of Russell, Majors, and Waddell and a stage stop. But all this was of little concern to James, the newest member of the Francis family, born there in 1872, and his brother George, born two years later.

William sold his mining claim in 1877 and moved the family back to North Ogden, where he purchased livestock to begin ranching further north, near the North Promontory Mountain Range. There a rugged peninsula extends southward from Promontory Summit for 35 miles into the Great Salt Lake. Here a daughter, Frances, was born in 1877.

Perhaps they lived in the mostly abandoned railroad camp of Promontory: it had served as the Union Pacific's railroad construction headquarters. Wherever they lived, it was certain that the Francis boys got their first real exposure to tending livestock over the rocky, barren peninsula.

In 1880 the nomadic Francis family joined the major northward Mormon migration to the southeastern corner of the Idaho Territory. They settled just west of McCammon in the northern end of Marsh Creek Valley, 26 miles south of present-day Pocatello. Marsh Creek parallels the Portneuf River, which winds north through a sparsely vegetated, narrow mountain gorge. The walls on either side of the gorge were colorful with red and white quartz, sandstone, the greys and blacks of shale and flint, and the muted whites of limestone and phosphate. The canyon extends for about 11 miles until it widens out again at present-day Inkom, where Marsh Creek empties into it.

One of the first settlers, an Irishman named Murphy, charged a toll for the use of his swampy private road. He probably did quite well because it was on the main supply route between Corinne and Ogden to Fort Hall on the Snake River and north across Monida Pass to Virginia City, Helena, and beyond.

Previously the location of the Harkness stage stop, McCammon originated as a railroad construction camp for the Utah and Northern Railroad in 1875. The Ogden-based line was reaching north to connect all the

Mormon settlements. Shortly after the Francis family arrived, the Oregon Short Line built a branch line from the main U.P.R. tracks at Granger, Wyoming, to the newly founded town of Pocatello, Idaho. Hence, McCammon became a hub for two railroads.

Here William Francis at last found his niche in the Great Basin Region on the fringe of the desert, a place with narrow valleys, mountain ramparts, and basin floors of sand, gravel, and volcanic soil. He engaged in irrigated farming, the raising of livestock—especially draft horses—and some trapping. He also did fancy decorative silver work on saddles, bridles, etc. George and his brothers learned these trades as they worked beside him.

And during this time Sarah gave birth to five more children: Ella, Frederick, Warren, John, and Henry. When Sarah wasn't bearing her own children, she acted as a midwife for others.

George often said he felt more at home in a saddle at the age of six than on the ground. When not on a horse, hunting and fishing were no doubt major preoccupations and probably necessary to supplement the Francis larder. Marsh Valley and the nearby Bannock Mountains to the west supported various kinds of game, fish, and waterfowl.

In their play time the tall Francis boys probably explored for relics on the older branch of the Overland (Oregon) Trail and made forays into the Portneuf Canyon and the old McCammon stage station on the Government Trail where a stage coach was robbed of gold and its occupants murdered. Perhaps they even imagined they found the Robbers Roost at the big elbow of the river. The railroad roundhouse in town with its steam-belching, fire-breathing iron horses surely competed for their time, too. They frequently came into contact with friendly, helpful local Indians, probably Shoshone.

While George was learning the ways of the great outdoors, his formal education was neglected. Consequently, at the age of eleven he journeyed to Utah, perhaps with an older brother, and stayed with Grandmother Hickman at North Ogden while attending school. With help from Mrs. Hickman, he could handle a third-year reader, write an acceptable letter, and do elementary mathematics by the end of the school year.

At school, George had a rough time with the other boys because he was tall, skinny, and ignorant of book learnin'. Western author Walt Coburn, who knew Francis personally,[9] described him as "a sunburnt, sandy complected, blue-eyed kid with deep dimples in his cheeks. An easy-going and good-natured kid who grinned a lot." Coburn related that George's

9

schoolmates ribbed him about his facial features and deformed left hand fingers: "The web-handed frawg with girl dimples." Coburn wrote that his scrawny appearance was the cause of much kidding too: "How's the weather up there? You growed so fast you left your brains in the seat of your breeches!"

Through the many fistfights, wrestling matches, and exchanges of angry words, George endured. In fact looks were deceiving; he was strong and held his own in the school yard battles. The hurt feelings were the hardest to cope with. No doubt these experiences helped account for his later reputation of being snobbish and arrogant. He really was shy and only warmed up to those he knew well and trusted.

He never returned to school, but years later in Havre he taught himself the ways of finance and bookkeeping so he could properly run his horse business and rodeo interests. He had learned a love of reading, though, and constantly had his nose in books that included the classics.

But unfortunately, he didn't attack his work projects at the family place with the same vigor, which didn't exactly endear him to his impatient father. As a result, his father confronted him with harsh discipline on several occasions. His younger brothers suffered the same fate, but endured. This, combined with the rather crowded living conditions of the homestead shack, convinced him that it was time to move on. In a bitter mood, he departed in June of 1890 at the age of sixteen, glad to be leaving a stern father who continually told him he wouldn't amount to anything, but sad to leave his loving mother and brothers and sisters behind.

George's friend, Marie Gibson, wrote in her memoirs (quoting his mother) that "George never could get along with his father so he decided to leave. I pleaded with him and so did his sister but he said goodbye and left." He didn't leave immediately for Montana—it probably wasn't even in his thoughts—instead he worked as a cowhand for the biggest and one of the most powerful cattle ranches in Idaho, the Warbonnet, bossed by "Cheyenne Bill" or "Bilious Bill" McDaniels, who had the reputation of being a rock-hard character.

The Boston and English-owned cattle company, originally from Nebraska,[10] came to the Fort Hall Bottoms area from Cheyenne, Wyoming, in the late 1870s. The Bottoms, located between the Snake and Portneuf Rivers, was their winter headquarters. This land, in contrast to the volcanic cones, domes, and lava beds of the nearby Snake River Plain, was considered one of the best natural livestock feeding areas of grass and white sage in the Idaho Territory. In winter months the area received just enough snow to fill water holes but not cover the grass.

In the spring the herds moved eastward to the vicinity of the Blackfoot and Portneuf Rivers. During the summer months, the Warbonnet cattle ranged the whole country between the Snake and Bear Rivers with their summer headquarters at both Carrol Creek near Chesterfield and Cranes Flat near Grays Lake. Overshadowing and surrounding this vast and lush grazing range of the middle Rocky Mountain region were eight mountain ranges with many basins, plentiful streams and brooks, plateaus, and valleys.

The cowboy's summer recreation spot was the town of Soda Springs, while the winter diversion was at Blackfoot. A former cowpuncher of the Warbonnet remembered when the entire outfit went to Blackfoot to celebrate the Fourth of July. A train carrying a band of musicians stopped for water and band members gave the cowboys a free concert. The boys enjoyed the music so much that they drew their six-shooters and detained the train, forcing the band to play all day. When the county sheriff arrived, the captors scattered for more distant places.

Francis wrote of none of this to his family; in fact he apparently never wrote at all until one of his mother's letters found him. In a letter postmarked June 8, 1890, George wrote from Bingham County, where Blackfoot is the county seat; in it he acknowledged he was working there, but didn't want the rest of his belongings sent. He also wrote of the availability of good land there and made reference to having seen a rodeo, perhaps his first. He replied to a letter from brother James sent two years later. It was postmarked from Ross Fork, now in the southern part of the Fort Hall Indian Reservation. George wrote James that he didn't have any money to send and that he wasn't sure of his future work plans, that perhaps he would go away for the summer and return for the fall roundup.

Other facts his family surely didn't know about George's employer was that the company had a virtual monopoly on the country, and it was said they were not adverse to "sweeping in" cattle from the smaller herds of local, mostly Mormon, settlers. Trail herds could be doubled this way. When their cattle were sold, it was further said that the animals being counted traveled past and around a knoll several times, making the herd even bigger.

Another story told of a deal that backfired on the greedy owners. It seems they bought a herd of cattle on deferred payment. The Mexican seller, named Carmen, and his crew, came for the overdue money. They met such reluctance that they had to collect at gunpoint, at the same time trying to convince the Warbonnet to stop claiming calves belonging to settlers.

Obviously large cattle companies like the Warbonnet didn't always recognize the rights of competing outfits and didn't welcome settlers along the streams or bottom lands. Sheep were not welcome either, and their herders held in contempt, considered unmanly for roaming the claimed cattle ranges on foot. Some cattlemen maintained from ignorance and prejudice that the woolies had a gland located between their two-toed hooves that secreted a foul-smelling fluid. Anywhere the sheep traveled—including water holes—the cattle wouldn't go; and it was claimed that they cropped the grass at the root, destroying what was left with their sharp hooves. Actually, whether cow, horse, or sheep, too many of any animal would cause the destruction of the range grass. There was room for all under proper range management, but the cattlemen just didn't want any more animals or settlers, period. A more legitimate enemy was the rustler, who did a booming business. Large numbers of stock from the Warbonnet and other ranches were stolen and disposed of in several ways: They might be driven to the Jackson Hole country of Wyoming or up Montana way; or transported by railroad to all points west from Pocatello or south to Corinne, Utah; or hidden in any of the several nearby box canyons for future transport to market.

Young Francis may have joined in the guarded excitement of pursuing some of the thieves. Regardless, he certainly received an education during his brief time with the Warbonnet that farming couldn't give. So did his coworkers, the three Aldous boys from Downey, who were possible distant cousins of Francis.

One of the bits of philosophy that the shy and impressionable teenager learned was that "might was right." He worked for a company that was a law unto itself. Stealing was all right (and profitable) for the ranch, but no one else could get away with it. Sheepherders were bad, the scum of the earth, and settlers were in the way of the cattle and had no rights and weren't to be tolerated. It wasn't unusual for ranchers throughout the West to pay their hands $5.00 per maverick brought into the herd, no questions asked. And it went unsaid to be sure when eating beef on the range that it was someone else's brand.

This prevailing attitude, combined with his bad school experiences and the impatience and orneriness of his father and the religious training from his mother, contributed to his many-faceted but sometimes incongruous philosophy—a kind of outlaw code combined with dignity, honor, and pride.

Two future Milk River neighbors of his showed this in their opinion of him. One said, "He had a perverted sense of pride and a mistaken sense of greatness in his chosen way of life." The other said, "I always felt he loved to pit his energies against anyone smart enough not to be afraid of him in a (livestock) deal; he considered them a direct challenge to his cunning and an adversary worth beating. He would go to silly, daring means to attain his way short of getting caught. He wasn't as ruthless as some others . . . and could always carry off a situation in a chivalrous manner. He was quietly accused lots of times (of rustling) and preyed on rich and poor alike, too many were victims of his greed."

While the many cowboy friends he had—including several lawmen—just laughed off that "he got a little careless concerning livestock that didn't belong to him," another said that the nonviolent Francis "was a piker in comparison to Montana's real badmen, and his worst traits were stealing cattle and horses."

Thus people's future fascination with him wasn't generated just because he was tall and friendly, wore fancy clothes, and was a rodeo celebrity; but the fascination some had was for a man of action who often acted on his own private crusades and dealings according to his own personal moral code. A true anti-hero.

But the Idaho education that helped mold his future was over, for the day of the large cattle companies in the Northwest was over. Drought, hard winters, cattle rustlers, mismanaged ranges, poor economic times, and crowding from incoming settlers had all contributed to their end.

And lastly the government stopped the winter grazing of cattle on the Fort Hall Indian Reservation. The large ranchers were being replaced by stockman-farmers, who raised their own hay and oats for their livestock on smaller ranges behind barbed wire. And yes, they even milked cows!

Former Warbonnet cowboy Tom Bond said of those days: "They held their last roundup on their headquarters at the Portneuf and Blackfoot rivers in 1894. A herd of an estimated 20,000 cattle had dwindled to less than 3,000. At one time they had branded that many calves at the fall roundup."

This left the choice of either selling the cattle in the good markets of Wyoming and the Dakotas, or moving them to the newly opened grass-lands of northern Montana. The Warbonnet owners chose the latter. Now all that remains of the Warbonnet in Idaho is an annual rodeo in the Black-foot River country called the Warbonnet Roundup.

Thus the cattle and the cowboys, including newcomer foreman Bob Anderson, George Francis, and friends, boarded a Utah and Northern train, beginning their journey to the last frontier of the great old American West.

All aboard!

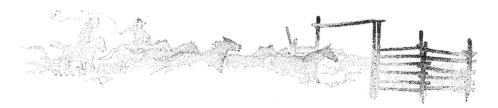

The Land

THE LONGER FRANCIS LIVED AND WORKED in the Clear Creek area of the Milk River Country and adjoining valleys, the more he knew this was to be his permanent home. It compared favorably to the Blackfoot Valley of Idaho before it filled up with farmers. Its mountains, buttes, foothills, and smaller, more shallow valleys and coulees provided protection against the harsh winter storms and accompanying arcticlike winds. Here was the abundance of the rich, knee-high mixture of bluejoint wheat and needle grasses, along with the shorter gramma and buffalo grasses on the rolling prairie, needed to feed thousands of Texas Longhorns. It was considered by locals to be one of the best range-raising areas in the United States, ranking in grass production with the Sand Hills of Nebraska.

The Longhorn brought to this country was the result of crossbreeding of the black Moorish and brown Castilian Spanish cattle, and its coloration possibilities ranged from solid black to combinations of black, blue, brown, or yellow. It is a big, rawboned, rangy animal with hairy, thick-slabbed sides and a squarish look; it has long legs with the huge forequarters making the front legs seem shorter. The shaggy head is large and long, giving its buffalo-like eyes a widespaced appearance, while the neck is short and stocky. Their average weight is 1,200 pounds, and their horns can grow to a possible 9 feet. They have a fearless disposition, amazing physical stamina, and a resistance to disease that no sissy Hereford or Durham could equal.

Clear Creek provided not only a fairly stable supply of mountain water, but higher up, it also offered brush and trees along its banks: aspen, box elder, cottonwood, chokecherry, and willow that provided the cattle with both summer shade and winter shelter. The frequent westerly chinook winds brought brief warmings, clearing the range of crusted snow and giving the cattle better access to the grass beneath.

Clear Creek, as Francis discovered, begins on the northern mountain slopes, fed by both the winter snowpack and the smaller streams and springs. The creek flows north through the windswept prairie for some 40 miles, roughly paralleling Little Box Elder Creek and emptying into the Milk River just beyond Yantic, the Great Northern train stop and section house. The river was named by Meriwether Lewis of the federally sponsored Lewis and Clark Expedition of 1805, because the explorer noticed its water possessed a peculiar whiteness, being about the color of a cup of tea with a tablespoon of milk added.

The Milk River begins on the glacial peaks of the northern Rocky Mountains with its two forks flowing northeast and merging once in the Dominion of Canada. The river then runs parallel to the border for about 100 miles until it once again enters northern Montana, flowing south and east for some 60 miles until it reaches present-day Havre. For the waterway's last 200 miles eastward, it roughly parallels the Great Northern tracks until it empties into the Missouri River just below the small community of Nashua, on the western boundary of the Fort Peck Indian Reservation. It was an unstable source of water, however, at times alternating between flooding and hardly flowing. Flourishing in the area were over 150 varieties of wildflowers. In early spring came yellow bells and buttercups, lavender crocuses and shooting stars, followed by pink wild roses, yellow sweetpeas, purple lupine, and pink and white geraniums—the hills seemed carpeted with them. Growing on the higher ground were varieties of chokecherries, raspberries, service berries, gooseberries, and wild strawberries.

North of the Milk River was the vast open stretch of unfenced range that went beyond the "Medicine Line" to the Cypress Hills of Canada. While bison and black, brown, and grizzly bears no longer roamed, still in evidence were prairie wolves, foxes and coyotes, cougars and bobcats, antelope and elk, mule and white-tailed deer, and mountain sheep. Along the brushy thickets of the beaver-occupied river, creeks, and coulees were prairie chickens, pinnate and sharp-tailed grouse, Hungarian partridges, Chinese pheasants, mallard, teal, pintail and spoonbill ducks, and Canadian honker geese; while sage hens shared the prairie flats with white-tailed jackrabbits, black-tailed gophers, yellow-bellied marmots—and a full complement of porcupines, skunks, and rattlesnakes.

But the main occupants were now the steers, cows, and calves. In 1891, according to the Fort Benton River Press, an estimated 114,000 cattle and 10,860 horses populated Chouteau County with hundreds of wolves and some cougars threatening their safety.

The large cattle owners in the valley were organized under the new banner of the Bear Paw Cattle Pool, which combined about 50 brands and 50,000 animals that had forded or had been ferried across the Missouri River in the very dry year of 1890. They mostly came from the depleted, fire-blackened, and overcrowded grasslands of the Judith River Basin in the western half of Fergus County and the Musselshell River drainage in both Fergus and Dawson counties. Thieves and predators had also taken their toll.

The cattle pool's headquarters was at foreman L. B. Taylor's ranch on Bean Creek near Lloyd. The Shonkin Stock Association Pool, with about 20,000 cattle, headquartered in Fort Benton and bossed by Charlie Williams, came from a region roughly bordered by the Missouri River, the Arrow River, the Highwood Mountains, and the Belt River. The pool now extended north of the Milk River into Canada. Other later ranches, like the Matador of Texas, leased land to the east on the Fort Belknap Indian Reservation. The new northern Montana cattle country, supporting perhaps a million beef cattle, stretched eastward through adjoining Valley County to the Dakota line, representing companies from at least twenty-one states, the Northwest Territories of Canada, and the British Isles.

Francis and his friends probably journeyed to Chinook before they ever saw rip-roaring Havre. Chinook was once the headquarters of the Assiniboine and Gros Ventre-populated Fort Belknap Agency, which had been moved 25 miles east to near Harlem after part of the reservation had been opened to settlers in 1888. Indian agency trader Thomas O'Hanlon brought in the first cattle and sheep ten years earlier. The community of about 1,000, located near the Milk River, was about 15 miles north of Lloyd. It had the usual businesses, including several saloons and the "White House" of painted ladies located across from the Methodist Church. A tri-weekly mail and stage company serviced the nearby smaller communities to the south. Two town regulars were cowboy artist Charlie Russell and gunman Harvey "Kid Curry" Logan; both were acquaintances of Francis. Russell and Logan traded at the A. S. Lohman general store.

When the Bear Paw Pool wanted supplies, they often sent Russell, who liked to draw sketches on the order sheet margins. Since they were thrown away after the list was filled, the Lohmans unknowingly had a small fortune pass through their hands. Russell drifted in and out of Chinook between 1890 and 1893, working for his old brand, the Bar R of Stadler and Kaufman, which originally was from the Judith River Basin, where its headquarters had been at Utica, Montana. Russell was of medium height and build with yellow hair, blue eyes, and heavy eyebrows. Although from St. Louis, he wore the traditional red waist sash of the Spanish vaquero, Texas cowboy, and Red River Métis. During the terrible livestock-killing winter of 1886-87, the 22-year-old Russell sent his boss in Helena a handpainted postcard depicting the emaciated condition of his cattle. Titled "Waiting for a Chinook," it showed a skeletal, starved Bar R cow on a snow-covered prairie surrounded by wolves.

Russell wrote ". . . it was the hardest winter the open range ever saw. An awful lot of cattle died. The cattle would go in the brush and hump up and die there. They weren't rustlers. A horse would paw and get grass, but a cow won't. Then the wolves fattened on cattle."

During those years Russell developed his dislike for sheepmen and for homesteaders. They crowded the range and fenced it with barbed wire. This even extended to the railroads that attracted and transported them. Whenever Russell came to Chinook, he tied his horse to the hitching rail by Mrs. Cook's Chinook House, across from the Lohman general store. He sat cross-legged on the porch rail, working with modeling clay. He would make a bear, horse, or steer, ball it up and start another figure. He attracted children, who were fascinated with his talent, and they usually came away with a nickel or dime to buy candy. He befriended one little girl named Laura, whose working mother put her and her dog on a leash tied to a wagon. Russell would cut the girl's leash and amuse her.

During the usual winter layoff, Russell rode the grubline from ranch to ranch. He wasn't much for doing chores, but he did do watercolor portraits and outdoor scenes for his keep. He was also an expert at telling colorful tall tales. Once, though, he met his storytelling match in Warbonnet foreman Bob Anderson. They matched wits while Anderson was visiting a lady friend who boarded at the Alex Ross ranch.

Russell spent his last winter in town, holed up in a log cabin owned by and located behind the Lohmans. He, Con Price, Al Mallison, Tony Crawford, John Thompson, and Slim Trumbel, along with either Bob Stuart,

Ambrose "Kid Amby" Cheney, Billy Weaver, or Curley Robinson, were dubbed "The Hungry Seven" by Chinook Opinion editor W. C. Kester.[11]

They had little food or money. Their cabin was so cold at times that they wore heavy arctic German socks and lined mittens to even cook and eat—". . . and nearly froze at that." Russell started a credit account at Lohman's general store to ease the situation. The men kept their gear in the store's basement, too, giving them an excuse to enter and appropriate such food items as bacon, ham, and potatoes. Thus, more time was probably spent in the rear of the store in front of the potbelly stove, where they made Mrs. Lohman unhappy because of the language they used. When Charlie wanted to obtain something, he would hold up one finger to indicate to the owner that it went on the tab. But finally, he had charged too much, prompting Mr. Lohman to say, "Russell, that finger of yours is too long already." Angry, Charlie returned to the cabin and painted a picture that netted enough to pay the bill. They then shifted their business to the rival, O'Hanlon's store. With Con Price acting as his agent, Russell began to paint more often to buy them food and liquor, sometimes selling pictures for only $2.00 each. Russell remembered: "I had to paint fast in those days, for the boys had to have lots of licker."

Price and Russell tried running a saloon for a short time in the Clark Building, across the street diagonally from the Lohmans. Mrs. Lohman said that at night the cowboys rode in and shot the bar's ceiling full of holes—she didn't mention whether anyone attempted to live upstairs. The cowboys loved the place and drank their share, but they didn't have much cash for it. And even though the sheepherders did have money and were drinkers too, the cowboys kept booting them out. Russell had no trouble dispensing beer, shots of whiskey, or ditches, but once when a customer asked for a mixed drink, Charlie was baffled over the recipe. So he just poured from various bottles, topping it off with a lemon slice. The man took one healthy swig and left the remainder. Russell laughingly said, "Maybe he went to the Milk River to put out the fire an' bogged down in quicksand!"

The Hungry Seven had other methods of putting food on the table: they became proficient chicken thieves, acquiring them from the coop or loose in the yard. In fact newspaper editor Kester's hen house was a favorite. They tried all kinds of trapping methods, including whiskey-soaked corn and lines with baited fishhooks thrown over fences. Once, after raiding a chicken coop, and with the bird cooking, someone knocked at the door. To their chagrin, there was the sheriff. But before they could confess and ask for mercy, they found he only wanted them to testify at a trial. On another occasion, Con Price received an invitation to dine at the "White House," with the provision that he bring the chicken, which he did. They dined on the freshly butchered chicken, and the next morning when the Madam stepped out to feed her little flock, they were gone. By spring, it was said that Chinook's chicken population had all but disappeared. Those darned foxes!

Wanting a better and more stable existence, Russell decided to give up on the cowboy life and turn to full-time painting in both Cascade and Great Falls. Obviously, the Old West was at its trail's end; at least he could capture it on canvas. He did return often to the Milk River Country to visit and sketch pictures; he also later bought half ownership in Con Price's Lazy KY ranch near the Sweetgrass Hills to keep one foot in the outdoors, and maintained a lodge in Glacier Park on Lake MacDonald.

While Russell rose to national prominence as a Western artist, his fellow cowboy, Harvey Logan, known as "Kid Curry," rose to national notoriety as one of the West's most wanted outlaws and cold-blooded killers. At this time, though, Curry was supposedly legitimately ranching with his brothers and comrade, Jim Thornhill, on the southern edge of the Little Rockies. Later Curry became part of a major outlaw gang known as the Wild Bunch. They operated from a ranch within the red canyon walls of the Hole-in-the-Wall of Wyoming's Powder River Country. Obviously, he was not a man to fool with.

Curry was always polite in his dealings with Andrew and Lillian Lohman, although he didn't exactly put them at ease. He was a medium-sized man, perhaps 5 feet 7 inches, 150 pounds, of partial Welsh heritage, described as having dark skin, dark brown hair, fierce black eyes, a fleshy prominent nose, and thick mustache and tobacco-stained teeth. The Kid was a reserved man who spoke in a soft Kentucky drawl, drank heavily, moved slowly and deliberately, yet he could become violent if his hair-trigger temper was aroused. The only ones who were said to have exercised any control over him were his now-deceased brother, Henry, and outlaw leader Butch Cassidy. One day Curry decided that he wanted to buy Mrs. Lohman's buggy and team. She tried to refuse in a calm and polite manner, explaining that they had been a cherished gift from her husband. But Curry wouldn't accept no for an answer, and finally, afraid of angering him, she quoted him a high price—which he paid promptly and without protest.

Then, in 1894, when Curry shot and killed the much bigger, but older, Powell "Pike" Landusky in "Jew Jake" Harris's Landusky saloon, he fled south on the outlaw trail, rejoining the Flat Nose George Currie gang in their commission of robberies of banks, express offices, company payrolls, and the like. Landusky was the retired, uncrowned saloon brawling champion of Montana, and a killer himself. It was done in self–defense, but Landusky carried a deputy sheriff's badge and owned the town and a prosperous gold mine.

Probably many settlers and townspeople, including the Lohmans, breathed a sigh of relief when the Kid left. But not so among the cowboys such as Long George Francis and rancher Robert Coburn and sons. He was well-liked and missed—perhaps even hero-worshipped by some, along with the likes of Sam Bass, Billy the Kid, Jesse James, et al. Probably his friend and partner, Jim Thornhill, shared the letters he received from him.

Kid Curry's younger brother Lorenzo (or Lonny, Lonnie, or Lonie) was a horse of another color. Described as friendly, handsome, mischievous, outgoing, and a ladies man, he and cousin Bob Lee, who called himself Bob Curry, operated the Curry Brothers Club Saloon in Harlem sometime after the Currys' Little Rockies ranch was sold. Business was good; furthermore, Lorenzo was always in demand to play fiddle at local dances and to entertain the young ladies and widows. To match his new status, he grew a mustache and shed his cowboy clothes for business suits. With his wife and two children, he lived in the former Washburn residence.

This new successful life ended abruptly when Louis and his cousin both hurriedly boarded a train at nearby Zurich to avoid arrest. They had been warned of their impending arrest by Pinkerton detectives for their involvement in the Union Pacific train robbery in Wyoming with the "Flat Nose" George Currie gang. Lorenzo Curry died in a shootout with officers at Lee's home in Dodson, Missouri, in 1900. Even a Havre newspaper lamented his death. Kid Curry returned the following year, robbed the G.N.R. train at Exeter siding, near Wagner, and killed rancher Jim Winters at Landusky. Winters had killed another of Curry's brothers, Johnny, in self-defense during a land ownership dispute. Kid Curry went on from there with his outlaw career, killing at least fifteen men before being captured and jailed for trial in Knoxville, Tennessee. He escaped, possibly because of bribe money supplied to certain officials by Thornhill. Soon after, he supposedly robbed a train in Colorado, where he was "killed." Oops! Wrong man. Then he turned up in South America, continuing his outlaw career, and was "killed" again.[12]

Chinook had more than just the cowboy element, however. The business community had held hopes that a mining boom would develop. In 1888 (and earlier) when the Indian reservation opened, it brought hundreds of miners stampeding into the Bear's Paw Mountains, but they left as quickly as they came, empty handed.

An earlier and illegal mine shaft—called the Black Diamond—was dug between Snake and Peoples Creeks by an "old man" named Lloyd. It, like later mines, including the one in the White Pine Gulch, showed only traces of copper, gold, lead, and silver. O. (Oliver) Peter and Milton Zortman operated the Lloyd general store and bar from 1894 to 1896. They were farm boys from Harrisburg, Pennsylvania, who had been prospecting in the Black Hills of South Dakota before coming to Clear Creek. It was said they first came to Montana in 1869 to help construct the Fort Browning agency post near present-day Dodson. They explored the area for precious minerals, always maintaining that it had potential.

Pete found his pot of gold at the rainbow's end in the Little Rocky Mountains: He named the Alder Gulch mine "The Alabama." He built a 100-ton capacity crushing mill in the town of Zortman and took gold out to the 100-foot level. It yielded over $600,000. He sold out, and with his new schoolteacher bride, apparently returned to Pennsylvania, but not before establishing a mine and stamp mill near Bellevue, Idaho. The new owners called it "The Ruby" and struck a rich new vein at the 500-foot level. Pete's unlucky brother, Milton, had previously returned home before the strike instead of prospecting further.

Contrary to Zortman's optimism, gold in any quantity was never found in the greater Clear Creek area. Coal, grass, lumber, and water constituted the valley's main assets.

Besides the cattle and mining interests, the bottoms around Bean, Clear, and Snake Creeks supported several sheep ranches. Much to the cattlemen's chagrin, Chouteau County had 291,000 sheep in 1891. Since the sheep shared the grazing lands with the cattle, it was only a matter of time before their respective owners clashed.

The Sprinkle brothers and their brother-in-law, Washington Connel Blackwood, were among the earliest and largest sheep ranchers. Bob, Charles, and James "Les" came from Granville, Missouri, where the well-educated family had a large and prosperous farm. Before arriving on Clear Creek, the Sprinkles had a cordwood business in the Butte area. Blackwood, a second generation Scotchman, was married to Linnie Sprinkle, and he previously was an expert carpenter, millwright, and co-owner in a flour mill. When the mill failed, Blackwood moved here, taking up the John Collier homestead. He began expanding the two-room cabin and building a house for the Sprinkles on Bean Creek. The brothers' original dugout became a root cellar and the original log house, a pig pen. They eventually owned four ranch sites. Blackwood wintered their sheep until he could afford to build up his own herd of 3,500 Spanish Merino sheep, known for their finely textured wool. After a few more moves, Blackwood acquired the homestead of Orrie "Kid" Tibbets, expanding the garden, fruit trees, and house, turning the latter into a richly furnished and spacious two-story Victorian house. A teacher was brought from Missouri for the six children and lived in the Blackwood house for three years until a school was built at Lloyd. And also, the family was attended by "Pat," a black servant—a unique situation.

Other major sheep owners included Brown, Kuhr, Mattheson, Miller, Putnam, Ross, and the Northwest Sheep Company. Some had both cattle and sheep, proving that the animals could be compatible with proper range planning.

While animosity developed between some of the cattlemen and sheepmen, the cowboys developed a camaraderie among themselves. George Francis's outfit was no exception. Camped next to his Warbonnet U up and U down employer was Colen Hunter's YT Cattle Company from Cheyenne, Wyoming, under Texas foreman Jim McCoy. Working for the YT as night horse wrangler was Canadian-born Irishman John Ambrose Joseph "Jack" Ryan. He and his brothers, Ben and Will, came to the area from Minnesota. They built a log house on Little Box Elder Creek, west of Clear Creek, for their families, and a second house for their parents and widowed sister, Anne, and her children. Jack's family consisted of wife Delia, daughter Honora "Hilda," seven; John, five; and Bernard, one. Besides cattle ranching, the brothers herded sheep and cut and sold logs from the mountains. The lives of the Jack Ryans and George Francis would soon become very much entwined.

The cattle outfits that employed Francis and the Ryan brothers decided to have a contest one evening. A bet was made as to which crew could build a roaring stove fire the fastest. The cowboys raced around setting up the stoves outside the cooking tents and gathering wood. The YT boys had theirs assembled first with wood in place, but because of a poor chimney draught, theirs refused to ignite. So Ben Ryan quickly grabbed the stovepipe and placed it back through the tent stovepipe hole and lit some grass and sticks under it. Hence, they made the first smoke.

In November, when some beef was shipped to market and the rest wintered, most of the cowboys were out of work until spring; so they went on the "grubline"—going wherever they could bum a meal and a bed.

Francis, now known as the "Long Kid," and his four out-of-work friends were said to have spent one unemployed winter trapping in Wyoming, perhaps in the Big Horn mountain and river basin country. On their way south, they applied for work at the Custer Cattle Company, which was wintering its stock on the Crow Indian Reservation. There they first met young cowhand Andy Avery. He was a chunky 5 feet 10 inches and later was known as "Cod Belly" to his friends.

The following spring, they stopped by the Custer outfit before heading back to work at the Warbonnet. Unfortunately, furs had not brought a good price, and they suffered accordingly. Avery described them as "the worst-looking bunch I ever saw." They apparently had nothing but the ragged clothes on their backs and were dirty, haggard, and hairy. Avery said that about two years later he met Warbonnet foreman Bob Anderson and asked him how Francis and his friends were doing. Anderson replied that after a season's work, Francis, the Aldoes, and George Fleming had established a ranch of their own in the Bear's Paw Mountains and that they called themselves the "Wild Bunch," apparently in honor of the Butch Cassidy-Kid Curry gang. They established the ranch in about 1898. After the Warbonnet Company ceased business in 1895, Francis worked the next three years for the YT, perhaps the last two in a supervisory position. Their ranch was located to the west of the Clear Creek and Little Box Elder divides in Saw Mill Gulch of Beaver Creek Valley. Their cabin was situated at the head of the large gulch, which generally ran east and west. The area's west boundary was Beaver Creek; Sucker Creek was on the south emptying into Beaver Creek, and Mount Reynolds was on the east. They probably had nothing more than squatter's rights, if that. In fact it was on the fringes of the Fort Assinniboine Federal Reservation. It was named Saw Mill Gulch because an Army contractor had originally had a horse-powered wood-cutting operation there.

The animals they "owned" were mostly unbranded stock: "maverick" calves and "slick" colts and fillies. Picking up unbranded stock was a common practice and was usually not condemned by other ranchers if it took place in the late fall after the roundup. It was almost an unwritten law that if a rancher didn't care enough about his stock to have it branded, he deserved to lose it—and finders, keepers.

Francis reportedly earned a good living at it, inducing some envy and jealousy among his fellow ranchers. He was able to catch the best horses because of his expertise with a 100-foot rope. On the other hand his detractors said he caught so many mavericks and slicks because he went out before the roundup crews gathered all the animals to brand. In fact, they said, Francis had at times been blackballed from these roundups because of his reputation as a professional livestock thief.

Bill Nye, a Wyoming humorist, told of how one young rancher got his start perhaps as Francis did: "Three years ago a guileless tenderfoot came into Wyoming, leading a single Texas steer and carrying a branding iron; now he is the opulent possessor of 600 head of fine cattle—the ostensible progeny of one steer."

Francis was rumored to have had a second place towards the upper end of Clear Creek in a secluded aspen-filled gulch near Wind Mountain and Creek. It was located about 1½ miles southeast of John "Bearpaw" Griffin's Diamond-Bar Ranch. Supposedly, here concealed corrals were used to brand strayed young stock, or to rebrand older stock with a running iron made from a cinch ring, broken horseshoe, or the side bar of a riding bit. Green sticks made excellent handles for the improvised branding irons. Brands could be made to look old by "blotching": putting a wet blanket or cowhide between the iron and the animal's hide, or the animals could be left long enough for the new brand to heal.

Another method, less hazardous, was to delay branding the calves, colts, or fillies picked up before the roundups in the fall. Then, if spotted, they were given back with the excuse that he just hadn't gotten around to notifying the owner yet. One temporary measure was to brand lightly so just the hair was scorched or the skin was reddened, using a bogus or "sleeper brand," and then brand permanently later. Another method was to barely apply the rancher's own brand and change after the roundup. If the rustler's operation wasn't discovered, it was a nice supplement to cowhand pay.

During the roundup season from about May to October, Francis and friends also worked for the likes of the YT, P-Cross, and Diamond B of the Bear Paw Cattle Pool. In the spring, approximately forty cowboys rounded up all the cattle that had drifted all over the countryside, branded all the calves, and castrated all the young steers.

Branding time meant the smell of sweating cattle and cowboys, combined with campfire smoke and the odor of singed hair and seared flesh that resulted in a more offensive odor than the smell of sheep. (But this the cowboy wouldn't admit.) A tally man was selected to keep count of each rancher's number of branded animals. The cattle were then driven across the Milk River at Cypress Landing and perhaps across the international border into the Cypress Hills for summer grazing.

In the fall they were rounded up again and driven back to the Bear's Paw Mountain country; there, any of those that escaped the spring branding were marked. And lastly began the cutting-out process of the selected older animals to be shipped to market at Chinook and other local railroad shipping points, depending upon the supply of cattle cars. Before a local railroad existed, they were driven to the U.P.R. railhead at Cheyenne, Wyoming, and later east to Devils Lake, Dakota Territory, where the "Manitoba Road" (future G.N.R.) building had started.

During the roundups the men usually worked one section of range per day until it had all been covered. It required long, dry, hot, and dusty hours in the saddle with little rest. The cowboy spent so much time in the saddle that he was said to have left his fingerprints on the saddle horn. Each man needed four horses, three resting while one was being ridden. The boys lived better and made more money than their counterparts who drove herds up the Texas Trail. Usually they had tents to sleep in and plenty of sowbelly or bacon, beef, breadstuffs, coffee, beans, dried apples, and canned tomatoes. When not on horseback, they sometimes put up with rain-soaked or dirty beds, cold or poor food, alkali-water coffee, and on a dry range, sometimes had to drink water that was standing in the cattle tracks. The cowboy's dream was going to town for good food, perhaps a bath, drinks, and female companionship. Of course, some townspeople liked the cowboy on the range where he was thought to be relatively harmless, as opposed to in town where he got liquored-up, used foul and blasphemous language, and was considered lecherous and utterly corrupt.

The roundup, branding, and castration of bulls wasn't the end of the work. The cowboys had to play doctor and watch for any open wounds on the cattle where blow flies laid eggs and three-quarter inch maggots hatched. Then carbolic acid salve had to be applied to kill the maggots, followed by persylic ointment for healing.

Axle grease was another general all-purpose medication. Besides good grass and water, salt had to be provided. But no matter how well or not-so-well they lived during the roundup seasons, the majority of the men lost their jobs in the late fall when the remainder of the herds were turned loose (all but the bulls, which were tended by only a handful of the very best of the cowhands, unless the lesser were relatives, of course).

Depending on the severity of the weather, the men attempted to keep the animals' iced-over water holes open, and had to prevent the cattle from drifting into dead-end ravines where snow could block their exit and result in starvation. Also, if the stock ran into a natural barrier, the herd's momentum carried them forward and the frozen animals stacked up like a pile of cordwood. The hands tried to pull, push, or prod weak calves and emaciated cows from the frozen ground to prevent their death. Another menace they dealt with were the packs of big, gray lobos for which they set traps when they became too numerous. They were baited with strychnine applied to carcasses.

When the blizzards came and visibility was zero, sometimes the cowboys were confined to the bunkhouse and line shacks, and the stock had to fend for themselves until a lull in the storm. The men repaired harnesses and saddles and read old magazines and newspapers, played cards, or made music on guitars and harmonicas and sang songs composed from canned food labels set to music—and all the while wondered how many animals were dying.

The winter of 1893-94 was one of the worst in the Milk River Country, but the following years the ranchers brought in even more cattle. *The Fort Benton Record* stated that the ranges in northern Montana were badly overcrowded in 1895, despite the large number of wolves and coyotes. In November over 1,400 wolves and 3,900 coyotes were brought in for the $3.00 bounty in Chouteau County.[13]

During that period the Bear Paw Cattle Pool, along with other cattle and sheep ranchers, suffered devastating losses, as long winter storms kept the grasses covered and little hay was available.

Stock drifted ahead of the blizzards, searching for food as the snow piled higher over the prairie and in the coulees. Streams froze deep as the temperatures fell to minus forty-five degrees in January of 1893. By spring the ranges were strewn with the carcasses of hundreds, maybe thousands of cattle and sheep. Some sheep owners quit, while the big cattle companies became smaller and less in number. In fact only about seven major cattle companies remained locally.

It was obvious that the Spanish system of leaving a herd to fend for itself on native grass would have to be replaced by smaller combination farm-ranches that raised their own feed—and, yes, fences might even be necessary.

The Warbonnet held on until the winter of 1895, when Anderson took the remaining cattle and drove them—presumably with Francis along to help him—to their new owners at Glasgow (Montana). It was so cold that the company had to hire replacement riders when the frozen ones dropped out in the towns along the way. Afterwards, Anderson went to the Chicago stockyards, working as a Montana state stock inspector. He returned in 1901 to establish a homestead on Little Box Elder Creek with his new wife, Mary Street, a local schoolteacher.

With the big outfits' decline, the smaller cattlemen now took over and organized the Bear Paw Cattle Association for any rancher having 500 or more cattle. An even broader cattlemen's group was formed: the Northern Montana Roundup Association. It included cattle pools and individual ranchers from areas including the Milk, Missouri, and Sun Rivers and the Bear's Paw, Judith Basin, Little Rockies, and the Larb Hills east to the Dakota border.

Each member of the local ranchers association had to contribute a cowboy and a string of ten horses. A foreman was hired and the cost of the group's supplies was defrayed by selling stray mavericks. Anyone having a smaller herd of cattle could have them gathered, branded, and shipped for a small fee. Their animals ranged as far southwest as Fort Benton and the Missouri River, west to Chester, north to the Canadian line, and east to Glasgow.

Some of the small-time cattlemen formed the Ranchers Stock Association.

The depletion of the rangelands from the bad winters, dry summers, and plain mismanagement certainly didn't help the hard feelings between some cattlemen and sheepmen. A major problem facing the cattlemen was the moving of sheep into their traditional winter range on Beaver and Clear Creeks during the summer while the cattle were grazing north across the Milk and into Canada. The major clashes of the cattlemen were said to have been with the Sprinkle brothers and Connel Blackwood.

The stories still persist today that George Francis was the leader of the resistance; when the woolies moved into the forbidden zone, his group stopped the herders, ordered them down, and burned their wagons. Also, herders were either shot at or offered large quantities of whiskey. Usually the cowboys wore gunny sacks over their heads, but Francis would still stand out. If this is true, Francis's Idaho cowboy days had certainly prepared him. To quote one authoritative source, "There were bitterness between the sheepmen and cowmen, and many unfortunate incidents occurred among them in the early days."

The homesteader's arrival forced the two factions closer together on an even smaller range. Luckily, hostility never reached the intensity of the clashes happening in such places as Arizona, Colorado, or Wyoming, where dozens of sheepmen caught "hemp fever" and many thousands of sheep were killed between 1888 and 1909.

At least, in the early years, Beaver Creek Valley was peaceful. The only authorized civilians and cattle herds on the Fort Assinniboine military reservation were those employed by the post trading company and the Diamond-B cattle brand, owned jointly by "Colonel" C. A. Broadwater, R. L. McCullogh, and A. G. Wilder. Broadwater had been a partner and superintendent in the Diamond-R freighting lines and, later, president of the Montana Central Railroad, a subsidiary of the soon-to-be Great Northern Railway. Broadwater also won a similar post trader contract for the construction of Fort Maginnis with future state senator C. J. McNamara of Big Sandy. It was to be built near the Judith Mountains on Ford's Creek. After Broadwater's death, McNamara and Broadwater's nephew, Thomas Marlow, operated the 125,000-acre McNamara and Marlow IX ranch near Big Sandy, and a general store and warehouse in Big Sandy.

Fort Assinniboine was established in 1879 due to the fears of the War Department's commanding officer, General William Sherman, and the Division of the Missouri leader, General Phil Sheridan, that further Indian wars would occur. The overwhelming defeat of Brevet General Custer's Seventh Cavalry Regiment by Sioux and Northern Cheyenne under Crazy Horse, Gall, Two Moons, and Sitting Bull in the Valley of the Little Big Horn River in 1876 was serious enough, plus the 1877 attempted flight to Canada of several nontreaty bands of Oregon and Idaho Nez Perce under Looking Glass, Chief Joseph White Bird, et. al. Added to this were the several thousand hungry, fugitive Sioux and Cheyenne Indians under Teton Sioux political and medicine man Sitting Bull and some twenty subchiefs, just across the Canadian border, who were attracted by the plentiful game of northern Montana; and the Canadian Cree, who raided reservations in northern, Montana. The area was populated with about

14,000 Indians of several tribes—as well as ranches further south. All these added to the previous attacks on the freight companies' wagons journeying along the Milk River by several tribes, including the Blackfeet confederation, fed their fears.

The combined sale of alcohol and guns by prominent local traders added fuel to the fire, too. The troops assigned to police these problems came from Fort Shaw on the Sun River, Fort Ellis near Bozeman, or Fort Keogh near Miles City, but they were usually too far away to intercept raiding parties.

The post's name, Fort Assinniboine (misspelled by the army with an additional "n"), came from a Siouan Indian tribe that had formerly been part of the Yanktonai Sioux who had lived on the Canadian plains and southward to the Milk River. The name in Chippewa meant "stone boilers" or "stone cookers," because the Jesuit priests observed them cooking their food with heated stones. Nicknamed the "Stoneys," they actually called themselves the Nakota, meaning "the generous ones."

The occupation began when the 18th Infantry under Colonel Thomas Ruger arrived in May of 1879, from Atlanta, Georgia, with 200 green recruits and a small force of regulars. They were joined by two troops of the 2nd Cavalry from Fort Custer, Montana. In a five-day march of some 40 miles, they reached the construction site after debarking from steamboats at Coal Banks Landing on the Missouri River. The uneventful advance came to a complete halt near Square Butte (now called Box Elder) when they were ambushed by a large party of Cree Indians—thought at the time to be Crows—upon the butte. Unbeknownst to the soldiers, a number of warriors were killed while the soldiers suffered no casualties.

A tent city north of the construction site on Beaver Creek was established for the crew of 500 Métis, 350 civilian workers, and the soldiers. Workers dug clay and sand, carried hod, drove mule team wagons hauling bricks, and fired bricks in the kilns. Two brickyards produced 25,000 bricks a day. The workers and soldiers were initially somewhat nervous with the news that almost continual Indian battles between the Cree and Sioux raged at Cree Crossing near the big bend of the Milk River, near present-day Malta, 100 miles to the east. During the nights gunfire was heard as the nervous sentries fired at shadows.

At its peak the post had ten companies—both cavalry and infantry—numbering about 500, with 150 packers and Helena-based teamsters and

50 Assiniboine and Gros Ventre scouts. It was one of the largest forts and military reservations in the United States.

The fort "rose out of the ground" between hunting journeys, as the Indians said. Some 100 buildings were eventually constructed. Some had battlements that resembled a Scottish castle more than a Montana Territorial fort. The outer stockade-less post was laid out in the form of a rectangle, using the points of a compass laid nearly northeast and southwest. A North Dakota newspaper gave the following description:

> To come suddenly upon Fort Assinniboine with its rows of mansard roofs, bay windows, etc., after a weeks ride through the boundless prairie is like coming upon an oasis in the desert. It is a city and every building is of an architectural design, a beauty in itself.

The fort, like a good-sized city, seemed to supply everything necessary to man or beast. A traders complex was built to serve the post soldiers and civilians, consisting of a general store, hotel, barbershop, post office, stagecoach terminal, restaurant, storeroom, two warehouses, officers club, and a large saloon. Francis and his friends were said to have been frequent visitors, and continued to visit with the caretaker even after the post closed.

The company operated a stage line between there and Fort Benton and Fort Belknap. An Indian trading house was built near the general store, which from 1882 to 1884 yielded 1,260 buffalo hides and after that, none. By 1888 there was a camp of about 100 lodges nearby on Beaver Creek. Those approaching the camp met with an unusual sight: many lengths of colorful fabric draped through the trees, hung there by the Indians to provide strong medicine for the Sun Thirst dances. When Broadwater died, his partner Robert McCullogh became post trader. Devlin supervised the store, slaughterhouse, and meat-processing operation, while Simon Pepin, a former Diamond-R wagonmaster, was in charge of the cattle herds. Pepin brought his three nephews—Adolph, Exor, and Zeal—to work at the fort; likewise, Colonel Broadwater put to work his cousins from Missouri—Art, Ed, and Will.

Several companies, including Broadwater's, alternated as suppliers of hay, wood, corn, and oats to the post. At times, according to one source, the graft and payoffs became so bad that the same load of hay was "delivered" several times and wheels had to be "greased" often to prevent lockup. Also, some cattle traveled in a circle, being counted several times over. When caught, one guilty contract officer received a five-year prison term, but no names were revealed, and he reaped a large reward for being close-mouthed.

When this business was terminated by the government, Devlin, Pepin, and the three Broadwater brothers established the Pioneer Meat Market of the P-Cross ranch in Havre and moved their slaughterhouse operation to the southwest edge of Havre on the Post Road, now part of Montana University–Northern campus.

The soldiers had their share of animal problems, too. During the construction period, when the soldiers lived in tents, they hung meat in trees to keep it safe. Two companies lost their meat and each blamed the other; it was all settled a few days later when a 1,100-pound brown bear was killed, caught in the act.

Although game and wood were plentiful in Beaver Creek Valley, its creek was devoid of fish. Only the streams emptying into the Missouri had them. So, some 18th Infantry army officers transplanted fish from Eagle to Beaver Creek. Henceforth, their permanent recreational camp at Dillon's bottoms provided fishing, too.

The recreation, at least for the officers, their families, and civilian dignitaries, was probably more exciting than the fort functions, patrol duties, and manning outposts on Coal Banks Landing, Sucker Creek wood camp, and the Sweetgrass Hills at the base of East Butte near Corral Creek. In the Officers' Amusement Hall, amateur theatricals were performed with such "stars" as First Lieutenant John J. Pershing, who loved to kiss his female costars—even during practices—which wasn't done in those days.

Though the fort was a magnificent structure, its troops had no major battles to fight except with yearlong boredom, mosquitoes in the summer, and frozen water closets in the winter, until the troops left for the Spanish-American War in 1898. No Indian attacks ever came, although the troops were on constant patrol, keeping the Blackfeet, Sioux, Crow, and Canadian Indians from raiding the reservations and the ranches to the south. The local Assiniboine-Gros Ventre Indian Wars were over before the post was finished, but skirmishes continued into the 1800s with other tribes.

Most casualties resulted from accidents in the field and on post, disease, alcoholism, desertion, fights among soldiers, and suicides. Some soldiers were wounded on patrol, but reportedly there were no direct combat deaths.

Temporary excitement resulted from a short tour of duty in the Little Rockies on the Fort Belknap Indian Reservation during the gold strikes of 1884, but the miners were impossible to stop, short of shooting them. The Métis Northwest Territories Rebellion of 1885 caused worry, yet brought no enemy, just many Cree and Métis refugees. A Cree Indian leader, Little Poplar, wanted in connection with the Frog Lake-Fort Pitt murders of the rebellion, was killed near the fort, but not by the Army. The killer was a Métis civilian named James Ward, whose rifle was more accurate than the Indian's revolver in settling a horse-ownership dispute. In 1890 some of the fort's soldiers were temporarily garrisoned at the Fort Peck Indian Agency during the Ghost Dance religious upheaval at the Pine Ridge Indian Reservation on Wounded Knee Creek in South Dakota, but they experienced no trouble.

Seemingly to justify their existence in later years, troops oversaw and harassed the already poorly off Cree, Métis, and Chippewa peoples, who were of little threat to anyone: they just wanted life as it should be and a home of their own, instead of subsisting on wastes from garbage dumps and slaughterhouses. But at the time the lands in north central Montana belonged to the Gros Ventre. The restrictive policy was hot and cold, however. Some commanders, such as Colonel E. S. Otis, ignored their illegally built cabins and even tried to provide food and work for them, while under other commanders, the cabins were burned and the refugee people marched back to Canada. This happened as early as 1881 and as late as 1896.

In the May 1896 roundup to Canada, Pershing's troop spent two months and went as far south as Great Falls. The 253 Cree people and some legal residents of other tribes were sent in railroad cars to Canada. Another troop collected "renegades" around Chinook. Pershing is remembered because he rose to the status of general and commanded U.S. troops in World War I.

Perhaps one of the more exciting experiences the troopers had was the ceremony held for the arrival of James J. Hill's "Manitoba Road" Railroad. Held on the 8th of September in 1887, the band played and banners flew. Hill had bought the bankrupt Minnesota and Pacific Railroad in 1877, and with his Canadian, European, and American backers, he reorganized it and eventually started west.

He first viewed Montana at the insistence of old St. Paul friend Paris Gibson, who at the time headed the Cataract Flour Milling Company. Gibson, now a successful sheepman near Fort Benton, wanted to build a city at the head of the falls of the Missouri River, to be called Great Falls, and to bring Hill's railroad there. Its westward progress stopped then at Devil's Lake in Dakota Territory. Former territorial representative and lobbyist Major Martin Maginnis was pressing Hill, too. Maginnis had been instrumental in securing congressional funding for Forts Assinniboine and Maginnis. Finally, after four years of Gibson's insistent letters, Hill came to Montana in 1884.

Once having viewed the area, he agreed with Gibson that it had much potential for agricultural, coal mining, and water power development, and he returned immediately to make plans.

His detractors said, "The old man has met his Waterloo," when he announced his westward intentions. They said he was building into a desert that would never amount to anything.

The construction began again, only to be stopped 120 miles west at the new Minot siding. President Grover Cleveland, perhaps pressured by rival railroad officials, refused to grant the railroad access through the vast Indian reservations. Finally, Hill and his political allies won the battle and were granted a 75-foot wide right-of-way and small station plots every ten miles or so, for 50 cents a mile.

Rail construction resumed in April of 1887, completing approximately 643 miles of track, reaching Bull Hook on September 6, Fort Assinniboine on September 8, Great Falls on October 15, and Helena on November 18, It was the most track ever laid by a single railroad in one construction season, starting from only one end of track. During the hot, dry, mosquito-infested month of August, crews laid 116 miles of track, averaging over 3½ miles per day. An all-time record of eight miles of track was laid in one day near present-day Saco. The chief contractor responsible for the rapid construction was D. C. Shepard of St. Paul.

The crew building the railroad numbered about 9,000 men, with about 7,000 horses, mules, and oxen. First came the bridge builders, then the grading gang followed by the roadbed builders, the tote teams, and the tie-laying gang. The graders employed six oxen pulling wooden scrapers across the virgin prairie that made two parallel strips, each about 6 feet wide and separated by an untouched strip of the same width. Behind them, workers with shovels and wheelbarrows heaped the resulting topsoil about 3 feet high on the median strip and ditched it out for about 20 yards on either side. Freighters brought them supplies, dropping them at certain intervals at the makeshift camps.

On the next day came the men unloading and hauling the heaps of rails, spikes, and ties from the small work train. Hours behind were the tie layers, measuring 2-foot intervals, laying the ties and each pair of rails on top of them, and hammering the spikes into the fishplates that fastened rail to tie. The foremen constantly rode, urging them, on and inspecting their work. These men were housed in double-deck rail bunk cars with attached cook cars.

Just west of the Fort Assinniboine terminus, the railroad built a passenger station, section house, small restaurant, roundhouse, and train yard. Passengers were transported from the station to the fort in Army ambulances. This location became the railroad's western divisional headquarters.

The soon-to-be orderly city of Great Falls, under the auspices of the Great Falls Power and Townsite Company, never experienced the boom-town atmosphere of Bull Hook railroad siding.

The railroad soon moved its headquarters from Fort Assinniboine to the Bull Hook bottoms because of the undependable nature of the Beaver Creek water supply. The bottoms was situated in a shallow valley of the Milk River, with three streams of Bull Hook Creek flowing through the land to the Milk River. Its wells produced an abundant source of water for the belching, thunderous, iron steam horses. The bottoms had been a favorite camping and hunting place for Indian and white travelers, and it was a major wagon and freight train road from Minnesota to Fort Benton.

Almost immediately, it became the scene of a huge, 6-block-long construction and material yard for the expansion of the railroad west to Everett, Washington, over the newly discovered Marias Pass on the Continental Divide.

In October of 1891 the newly named Great Northern Railway built a laborers boarding camp, roundhouse, and boxcar depot at Bull Hook siding, now called Havre. They were located on the north side of the tracks, where a tent city had been previously established.

The land claimed by Ed Broadwater and Simon Pepin was donated to Hill with the understanding that on it would be built the railroad's western divisional headquarters. However, the St. Paul railroad officials wanted a classier name for the town. So the new property owners, former Diamond R and P-Cross men, gathered to talk about it. The discussion started calmly, but soon tempers flared and blows were exchanged. Meeting adjourned!

The next meeting was more subdued. It was decided to have only the original five landowners vote.[14] Since most were of French (Canadian) heritage, a French name was naturally favored. Joe Demars's suggestion of naming it simply "France" was turned down, but Gus Decelles's idea of calling it Havre, after his family's seaport home of Le Havre, was carried three to two.

Along with the railroad came the vice element from Cypress, a tent town that had been located near the northerly confluence of Big Sandy Creek and the Milk River, just off the military reservation. It was built to give the soldiers all the comforts of home—and more. The town's land coincidentally was owned by post trade store employee Ole Olson. The town became too rough and was declared off-limits to soldiers. But that didn't matter to the "girls," who apparently just moved their business closer to the post. Entertainment was also available at the Spaulding—"Ma Plaz" Pleasant Resort, with dugout cribs behind the main building, and at the Lakeview Resort halfway house on the post road across from Half Way Lake, as the road turned east towards Havre. It was run by former soldiers Baily and Purnell. Soon the merchants were all settled in saloons, dancehalls, and gambling houses in the bustling railroad settlement of Havre. They, of course, were joined by the legitimate merchants, too.

Soon, this crude frontier town had a business district with general stores, hotels, restaurants, bakeries, livery barns, barbers, blacksmiths, etc., and about seventeen saloons, with a mix of railroad laborers, soldiers, cowboys, and Indians selling their wares.

Newly arrived schoolteacher, Mrs. C. Gallows, described the scene as "a cluster of tents, log cabins and tiny wooden cottages set down in the midst of barren brown hills." She also observed that the only green in sight was the cottonwood thicket along the river, north of town, between the shiny new rails and the river, where a cluster of shacks marked the spot where the town had first been located.

The cowboys, she continued, "used to come to town and rope the chairs off the porch of the (Windsor) hotel. Saturday nights, they would get wilder and dash their ponies up and down the streets while they let out a few blood-curdling yells and shot off their guns for a little more realistic noise."

The town soon gained a reputation that spread from Seattle to Chicago, and as one writer put it, "Havre was a particularly seething cauldron because its clientele was made up of violent and conflicting elements such as soldiers from Fort Assinniboine, (coal) miners, railroad workers and range riders (cowboys). Shorty Young's temple of divertissement (the Honky Tonk) catered to them all and there was never a dull moment."

The Honky Tonk was made up of the Montana Hotel building with a bar, stage and dancehall, gambling room, and adjoining cribs and Parlour House. The place was always fitted with every kind of gambling device and card game. Young's first saloon, called the Montana Beer Hall, and restaurant annex run by O. R. D. Wellbourne, steak chef supreme, was nicknamed the Bucket of Blood. Even Texan historian Ramon Adams had heard of Young and his tough establishment. Adams said "most of these places were so low that a rattlesnake would be ashamed to meet his mother there."

Young, originally from Buffalo, New York, stepped off a boxcar from Fargo and proceeded to work his way from the position of saloon employee to being the owner of the Honky Tonk complex, another deluxe bar and restaurant called The Mint, and several houses of prostitution. He had a large ranch and coal mine just west of the city on the valley hillside, where the fairgrounds are now located.

George Francis apparently became a good friend of his, and both loved Havre and the surrounding area, each for his diverse reasons. The two of them—for better or worse—became the most memorable, notorious, and colorful individuals that ever emerged from the Milk River Country.

The People

IT WASN'T TOO LONG BEFORE GEORGE FRANCIS VISITED Havre, particularly since he now resided south of town in Beaver Creek Valley and at times worked for the Havre-based P-Cross Cattle Company along with Fred and George Aldous. In fact he became somewhat of a fixture in town, especially during the winter months. He didn't acquire the handle of "Long George" right away. The first with that nickname was George Hossack, a fellow P-Cross cowboy and a township constable. Francis was first called the "Gobbler," perhaps because he was a fast and greedy eater. Contrasting in size was "Sawed-off" or "Short George" Card, also a P-Cross cowhand.

Another colorful cowboy was 400-pound "Sleepy Tom" Conant. A native of Canada and a P-Cross employee, he had worked previously at Simon Pepin's Bear Creek, Alberta, ranch before moving to the Havre-area ranch as foreman. Conant was appointed first town marshal by unofficial mayor Pepin before formal city officials were elected, but quit because he felt he made a large and slow-moving target.

Conant was noted for his sharp memory and joke-telling abilities. He got his nickname from taking many naps on the prairie, usually after meals. One day the boys received a report that a dead steer was lying in the bushes behind one of the tents. Checking out the report, they found Conant "snoring away like a hog." Waking him, they all drew their knives as if to skin him. For once the big man moved fast and the boys scattered. Later, after regaining his composure, Conant decided it was humorous after all—so the boys ventured within talking distance again.

One cowboy who worked for Conant at the ranch was Bert Davey, who was described as a large man with only one hand. In about 1890 he was racing across the prairie, trying to overtake the roundup crew. Before crossing the flood-swollen Sage Creek, he tied his clothes to the saddle and led the animal through the water. Once across, the horse bolted, leaving Davey afoot and otherwise naked! Soon the mosquitoes descended upon him and he rolled in any available waterhole or mud puddle to avoid them. He finally walked the 10 miles to the Dayton railroad station, near present-day Gildford. He crossed the railroad bridge and hid behind a pile of railroad ties by the section house. Finally at sunrise a woman appeared, who was tending the flower beds while the railroaders ate. The desperate cowboy called to the woman, but she was scared and hurried back inside, informing them there was a crazy nude man outside. The men came out, and the embarrassed Bert explained to them his obvious predicament.

Since he was a big man, all the trousers they possessed were too small. So they put an old skirt on him with a swallow-tailed coat and a high silk hat. After eating breakfast, Bert caught the next freight train back to Havre. When he entered the Pepin and Broadwater general store building, clerk Ed Broadwater thought Davey was a crazy man too. After another explanation Broadwater sold him some clothes on credit.

The following year Davey had more problems. Riding east of Havre, this time to another roundup, he took two horses—one carrying his gear. About dusk, near Chinook, the pack slipped and startled the horse. The skittish animal started bucking, kicking, and going in circles. The offending pack finally fell free of the horse, with feathers from a trampled pillow drifting in its wake. Davey caught the beast after a chase of a mile or so. But when he dismounted, both horses bolted. The unlucky Davey had trailed the horses for about 5 miles when he came upon an encampment of Indians. Luckily they had captured his horses, and with their directions, he found the cowboy camp. Later, though, when he rode back for the remains of his pack, he found only the feathers. Perhaps after that he changed occupations.

Tom Conant found a new job; he moved to Vernon, British Columbia, just north of the Washington-Oregon line, where he operated a livery barn. One day a dirty, unshaven man—an apparent hobo—drifted in and asked for work. The unkempt stranger said he was good with horses, so Tom hired him. He drew his money every day and drank it up at night. The man had a familiar look that puzzled Tom, yet he couldn't place him. Drunker than usual one night, the "hobo" opened up and told Tom about many things that happened in Montana in the early days. The next morning he was gone. On thinking over his rambling stories, Tom believed he had finally resolved the mystery: the "hobo" must have been Kid Curry, Harvey Logan.

If this was indeed Curry, the year would have been about 1904. In 1903, he had escaped from the Knoxville County jail with the sheriff's horse and seemingly disappeared into thin air. It was rumored (and believed by the Pinkerton Detective Agency) that he had taken a ship from the West Coast to South America and rejoined the remaining gang members.

Perhaps one incident could be passed off as mistaken identity, but when another Havre area man had a similar experience, it made one wonder . . .

In September of 1903 Yantic rancher James T. Moran was approached by a stranger, who asked to buy a saddle horse. As with Conant's experience, the man was dressed as a roughrow hobo. His shoes were even toeless. However, this "hobo" was well armed and carried "a roll of greenbacks as large around as a man's leg." The stranger spoke of all his old friends in Havre and the saloons he had just visited; he also mentioned the fact that Moran had moved his residence across the river since he had been in the area last.

Moran wasn't positive about the man's identity since he had never known Harvey well, although Moran had known other brothers who resembled him.

Law enforcement officers scoffed at the idea, but the Great Northern Railway officials apparently took it seriously and investigated.

Another northern Montana cowboy who would have recognized Kid Curry was Louis "Louie" Chambeau, a 5 feet 8 inches stocky blond with blue eyes, who was probably among the first cowboys to the area; it was said he first visited here with a party of Métis people hunting buffalo in the 1860s.

Born in Louisiana of French parentage in 1846, he traveled to St. Paul, Minnesota, with his family in 1852. He learned horsemanship early. He and his older sister Mary rode an Indian pony, purchased by their father, to the distant parochial school. Chambeau, however, decided by age 12 that the West was bigger than the St. Paul area; hence he left home on his new pony, riding bareback with only a hackamore for reins.

From there on, his life reads like a Hollywood movie script, although seemingly contradictory datewise, at times. The young adventurer obviously became interested in his Indian brothers as he then visited and was befriended by a band of Chippewas. He found them quite friendly and industrious and apparently stayed with them for some time. After absorbing their way of life and language, he moved westward to the Turtle Mountain region of the Dakota Territory, where he supposedly lived with a band of Sioux. Chambeau moved on with them into eastern Montana for years, coming in contact with other tribes—such as Assiniboine and, of course, Métis people.

By then he was quite conversant in Indian customs and languages and the hunting of buffalo and other game with both the bow and rifle. It is believed he next moved on to visit the Crow of the Big Horn River country, the Cheyenne, and the Shoshone of Wyoming and Colorado.

While the Indians were always friendly and treated him well, Chambeau said that the whites seemed to get bigger, rougher, and tougher the further west he went.

Chambeau also laid claim to having used his Indian knowledge to become an Army scout with Luther "Yellowstone" Kelly under General Crook in the 1871-76 Sioux War of the Yellowstone River Valley and southern tributaries.[15] He then rode as a scout for Miles at the 1877 Battle of the Bear's Paw on Snake Creek. Here most of the fleeing Nez Perce of eastern Oregon and southern Idaho were finally stopped from their attempted flight to Canada to join Chief Sitting Bull's band.

He commanded one of the scouting parties with six Cheyenne braves, discovering the Nez Perce camp at about 6:00 A.M. on September 29, Soon Miles arrived with the main body of troops, and they charged the camp. Chambeau's horse was riddled with bullets so he used it as cover until its odor from repeated hits drove him to a new position. He moved to behind a rock with Corporal John Haddo and Yellowstone Kelly. Haddo was killed, while Chambeau said he killed about nine enemy before he escaped with Kelly at nightfall. About twenty-two soldiers and twenty-four Nez Perce died as a result of the battle.

Chambeau later said of his adversaries: "Those Indians were the best shots I ever saw. I would put a small stone on the top of my rock and they would get it every time." (The Nez Perce were said to be one of the few tribes to understand the fine techniques of rifle sighting.) Not only did he have respect for their fighting abilities, but he was divided in his loyalties: he respected the Indian people and thought the white man had treated them unfairly, yet he served under the Army and even killed them. He often said, though, that he wasn't proud of that duty.

Next he said he scouted for Lt. Colonel Brooke and his Fort Shaw troops as they looked for a new post site in the Milk River Country. Once Fort Assinniboine was built, he worked both as a scout and courier carrying the payroll and secret military documents. His first government check was issued to Louis Shambo and the new spelling stuck.

He left the service and worked on a cattle ranch in northern Nevada, probably along the Humboldt River, which was a major cattle raising and shipping area with Winnemucca being the main cowtown. He and some cowhands took a brief excursion to California, but didn't like it and returned to the ranch.

The young adventurer got his chance to return to Montana in about 1885 when delivering some cattle to the Howell Harris ranch near Fort Benton. The following year he helped drive another herd to Montana, this time to Broadwater-McCullogh & Company at Fort Assinniboine. Louie, Charles Harvey, and Tom McDevitt accompanied the Diamond B wranglers bossed by John Kinsella, Lawrence Devlin's nephew. This time they stayed and worked for the traders' cattle company with Shambo becoming their chief horse wrangler.

Kinsella homesteaded on Saw Mill Gulch in 1891, apparently just east of where George Francis and friends located seven years later. Besides cattle, Kinsella raised Belgian draft horses.

When not working as a cowboy, Shambo, a teetotaler, served drinks, first for George Bickle at the almost-deserted Cypress camp saloon, and later for ex-soldiers John Bailey and George Parnell in Havre.

He tried the domestic life, marrying a Gros Ventre woman from Fort Belknap, but she tired of the lonely life in their little Havre rental house, with Shambo always working, and returned to the reservation with their five children to live with her parents.

Shambo spent his last years working on Bickle's Beaver Creek ranch in the summers and living in town during the winters, socializing with old friends. He briefly had a homestead on the newly opened military reservation, raising horses until his death. He was once offered $1,500 by a visiting newspaperman for his life story, but without any hesitation, he refused—not once, but several times. Save for Charles Harvey's daughter, Vina, none of his life would have been recorded.

Another colorful cowboy was Texan Jim McCoy, boss of the YT Cattle Company. McCoy was considered an expert roper—and probably equal to or better than George Francis.

He first brought cattle up the Chisholm Trail from the Lone Star state to Abilene, Kansas, in 1876 at the age of fifteen. He ventured further north in 1883, helping drive a herd to Fort Benton, and brought the YT outfit to the Clear Creek area about 1893 from Cheyenne, Wyoming, by way of Miles City. McCoy was one of the few men of the region to always wear a revolver. Unlike George Francis, he was a conservative dresser, clothed in a light-colored stiff-brimmed Stetson hat, a white neckerchief with polka dots, and light jacket with tan trousers. He always wore suspenders and his Sunbelt, plus he carried a notebook to keep notes about the cattle under his care. Nothing has been recorded about his physical features except that he wore a handlebar mustache. After selling out the ranch holdings, he settled in Chinook, marrying Mina Dowen of Fort Benton and working as a deputy stock inspector and town marshal.

With cowboys like McCoy, as opposed to what the movies portray, the beard was not popular because it was too warm during good weather, became grimy from sweat chewing tobacco, and housed too many four-to-six-legged varmits. Francis even shaved his mustache off after arriving here.

During those early years, the few letters Francis did write home were brief, and he wrote little of the people he met. The earliest appears to have been written on March 12, 1895, from the settlement of Lloyd.[16] The young cowboy was out of work for the winter and awaiting the spring roundup. He noted that he spent his spare time practicing with his lasso, that he was healthy and was up to 190 pounds. The following September, the family got a letter postmarked Big Sandy in which he wrote: "Been here since last April. The outfit sent me to Wyoming and I just got back. Times are tough and I am sick with a bad cold. I will send you a bill (banknote) now. Address in Chinook." The "outfit" was probably the YT, and the trip was most likely to bring back additional cattle.

In March of 1896, again writing from Lloyd, Francis extolled the virtues of the Clear Creek country, but said that the wolves would eat a rancher out of existence unless he stood over them with a gun; also that horses were scarce and could be traded for good ranch land. The remainder of the letter related: " 'Pap' and I have been making big medicine in regards to ranches on Green River. [Live]Stock winters out[side] and it is handy to everything." He said that they were about 200 miles from the railroad and cattle were easily obtainable. The "Pap" mentioned was possibly one of the Aldous clan.

43

The Green River he wrote of flows through Wyoming, Utah, and Colorado. The upper Wyoming valley of the river, being 100 miles long and 50 miles wide, was recognized as one of the finest grazing fields in the Rockies. The Green River Basin was described as having "meadows of native hay, threaded by tree-lined streams." At Green River, Wyoming, were the Union Pacific Railroad yards.

In an undated note, Francis said he and Pap could start at the YT if nothing else happened job-wise. And in December of 1896, he again wrote home, sounding happy, and planning to settle down and get a ranch with some cows.[17] His tone still changed when he mentioned his father: "I would hate to be around Dad if he is just as mean as ever. I can just see and hear him growling."

The same month he wrote his sister, Frances, or "Fannie" as she was called. Replying to her letter, he apologized for taking so long and said he had a felon (deep inflammation) on his thumb. He expressed the wish to come home, but begged off because it was too far away. Lastly he mentioned the possibility of going to Colorado and working the following spring and summer for $60.00 a month, and an unidentified company wanted him to bring a herd of cattle back. He closed with ". . . having a good winter and will send photo."

The final (known) letter of that particular time period was postmarked from Havre in November of 1897. In it he told his family that he was still working as a cowhand, although he had obtained some land, had ten cattle on it, and intended to build a house on it in the spring. Commenting on the weather, he said that the winters were warmer than Idaho but had more snow, that it wasn't necessary to raise cattle feed, but stock sheds were needed.

In the fall of 1897, Francis was breaking horses for Archie Smith, a neighbor on Sucker Creek. Perhaps this is the job he spoke of in his letter. He probably made about $5.00 a horse.

Horses being broken were usually kept in a corral at night and handled during the day with just a saddle and hackamore—a leather basal ring around the head immediately above the mouth with reins attached. The hackamore didn't give the rider much physical control; its rider ruled the horse more by his personality than by mechanical means. Later a bit and halter would be introduced. Being a horse lover, Francis was probably more interested in gentling the horses than breaking them with "quirting a-plenty" or "shoveling in the steel," particularly since it could result in a spoiled or mean horse. However, the beasts all learned respect for the rope when the rider initially lassoed and threw them to the ground.

But in one case Francis was bested. A bronc must have reared up and rolled over on its side with Francis still aboard. He was unable to kick free, resulting in his right leg being broken in several places. He spent the beginnings of winter convalescing at the Windsor Hotel, where he almost died when the hotel burned down. The tall cowboy was rescued from the top floor just before the building was engulfed in flames. Both he and Art Decker, the 300-pound hotel manager and city councilman, had to find new housing. By spring Francis had graduated to crutches and by summer he had returned to the saddle. The only visible reminder was the necessity of having a longer heel on his right boot.

Besides ranching the "Long Kid" and the Aldous clan worked hauling supplies to Fort Assinniboine. In 1898 the fort's rail and telegraph station had been abandoned, making it necessary to use horse and mule-drawn wagons (and sleds in the winter) to haul supplies from the Havre railhead. They also rounded up wild horses for the Army in the vicinities of the Sweetgrass Hills, Little Rockies, and Missouri Breaks. George Aldous worked for the Sprinkle Brothers, tending their cattle on the Fort Belknap Indian Reservation. In 1903, the Aldous boys helped dig up the soldiers' remains from the Snake Creek battlefield and moved them to Fort Assinniboine for reburial. Reportedly, Fred Aldous soon returned to the Downey, Idaho, farm when his father became ill, leaving brother George and cousin "Fred the Kid."

There seemed to be no end to their work activities. One of George Aldous's sons believes Francis accompanied his dad on at least one cattle drive from Texas, while Aldous brought up another herd for the H. H. Barrott ranch, becoming their foreman. And too, he established his own EA brand. They also did work on a Wyoming ranch, as Francis related in a letter home.

Aldous also told the story of a Wyoming sheepherder who ran his woolies through their cattle camp and how they opened fire, seriously frightening him if not creasing him a time or two. Charlie Russell—a cattleman, himself—thought that funny and made a sketch of it. Only he spelled Aldous, "Aldoes," and that's the way it stayed.

It took some cattlemen many years to see (and some never did) that sheep were a good cash crop, augmenting the cattle business with two yearly products: lambs and wool. In fact, in later years Charlie Russell and W. C. Blackwood became friends. Both Blackwood and the Sprinkles had become wealthy from their sheep businesses while many cattlemen had gone broke.

Not only did Wyoming suffer from rancher-sheepman animosity, but the large ranchers who belonged to the Wyoming Stock Growers Association were determined to keep both their ranch hands and the homesteaders out of the cattle business and off THEIR open range. The banning of cowhands from owning cattle only worsened the situation, resulting in the big ranches suffering heavy stock losses; the rustlers were bitter cowboys who were backed by the small ranchers and sympathetic townspeople and courts of northern Wyoming. When the cattle kings couldn't get convictions, they resorted to vigilante action with the result being shootings and lynchings. Most incidents were said to have never reached the pages of recorded history.

Some ranchers, such as Bob Anderson, Warbonnet foreman, left the state, not because of drought or range overcrowding, but because of the many corpses swinging in the breeze from trees.

The trafficking of cattle and horses from southern Idaho to Wyoming was a major business. The mountain-rimmed valley of Jackson Hole, alone, had been the refuge of a large band of outlaws led by Harvey Gleason—alias Teton Jackson.

Known only to a few outsiders, George Francis and his friends had stolen stock from Idaho and sold it in Wyoming. Reportedly, once Francis felt cheated on the price gotten for some horses and stole them back. Eventually they had prices on their heads and apparently couldn't return to either state for a while.

From then on, Francis and company concentrated on the Sucker Creek ranch. And by 1901, the area was filling up. Two years earlier, Jack Ryan built a home north of the Francis place. Ryan, succumbing to wanderlust, had previously sold his homestead on Little Box Elder Creek, operated a combination general store and post office at the Yantic railroad stop by Lohman, and moved the family to a house in Havre on First Street by Bull Hook Creek. He left the family there and joined the Klondike-Yukon Territory gold rush, staked by saloon owners John Bailey and George Purnell.

46

Not finding a bonanza, he returned shortly and worked as a machinist's helper at the G.N.R. roundhouse.

At the same time Ryan built up a dairy herd, with the family doing the milking and delivering. Next, after building a house, they moved four miles southwest of Havre to wife Delia's homestead claim near Squaw Butte.[18] He added a barn, bought more cows, and built up their Havre-area milk business. For delivery purposes, he built a frame on the wagon to hold the five- and ten-gallon milk cans to keep them from spilling, and daughter Hilda splashed buckets of cold spring water over the canvas top to keep the liquid cool for the trip to town.

Jack and his brother Will must have felt grass was beginning to grow under their feet, because after an abortive attempt to move to Maple Creek, Saskatchewan, in which the wagons were way overloaded, they spent the winter in the old homestead into which Ben Ryan had already moved. Meanwhile, Jack procured a 640-acre homestead in Beaver Creek Valley through the Desert Land Act and built a new house. The family stayed in a nearby one-room log house and tents until 1901, when the new place was completed. The old Squaw Butte place was sold to John W. Clack, a recent arrival from Texas.

Along with having cattle, the Ryans planted mainly oats to sell at the town livery barns with Hilda operating the hayrake (mowing machine) to gather the alfalfa crop for winter stock feed—plus they had a garden to supply their own food needs. Their cattle often "strayed" onto the nearby Fort Assinniboine military reservation. The soldiers would drive them off with the Ryans' help, but as soon as they left, the family drove them back on the federal lands.

The new two-story house was home to three boys and one girl (one girl, Delia, had died, and a son, Frank, was added) and was quite a contrast from the usual one-room log cabins in the valley, according to local historian, Robert C. Lucke. The spacious home had a kitchen, living room, and three bedrooms down and two up. It was one of the first to have indoor plumbing; the water was hydraulically pumped from the nearby spring to a holding tank on the second floor and piped around the rooms. The logs for the structure were both notched and dovetailed for an exacting fit.

The house became a very popular meeting place for parties and dances because of its location and size; it also became a halfway place for people going back and forth from the mountains and Havre. Cowboys on the grubline—including George Francis—stopped for meals.

Ryan hired Francis, Fred Aldoes, and George Fleming to tend his cattle that first winter. Apparently they did a poor job because Ryan wasn't happy with the condition of his herd the following spring, but he continued to employ them through the summer while the Ryans built their new house. In the fall, sixteen-year-old Honora "Hilda" Matilda Ryan met George Francis for the first time. She described him as being very shy and very tall, not particularly handsome, but nice-looking. Hilda said that he was always clean and neatly dressed, always wearing a white shirt with a stiff collar when dressed up. The horses he rode were always of the best quality too. He first had a mustache, but shaved it off—perhaps at her insistence.

In comparison to Francis's 6 feet 6 inches, 190-pound frame, Hilda stood 5 feet 3 inches and weighed 125. She had dark brown wavy hair and brown eyes. Her mother, Delia, was about three inches shorter, whereas Dad was about 5 feet 5 inches and stocky.

The following spring and summer, George lived and worked at the Ryan ranch, putting up hay. He was very candid with Jack and Delia about his prior life, including the theft of some horses taken from Idaho and sold at Sheridan, Wyoming. (This revelation later proved to be a mistake.) He even let Delia read the letters he received from girlfriends; where they were from is not known.[19] Hilda apparently overheard many of these conversations. The fall of 1902, Hilda attended school in Havre, and George returned to his Sucker Creek place, though sometimes he rode with her to town.

Soon another man was to come into her life. Five miles north of the Ryans on Bull Hook Creek was the Ed Redwing homestead; it formerly belonged to "Long George" Hossack. It consisted of a one-room log cabin, plus a crude corral and a few cattle. Redwing (the name was "Americanized" from Rodvong) came of Norwegian stock from Fillmore County, Minnesota. He stood about 6 feet and weighed approximately 210 pounds; he had blue eyes and thinning light brown hair.

Redwing came to Havre in 1890. From the age of fifteen, he had worked on his brother Andrew's farm in North Dakota. He initially traveled here to visit with friend, Andy Holean, who worked for the railroad at the fort. He decided he liked the country and found work at the roundhouse as a wiper and assistant hostler—starting the boiler fires in the steam engines. Redwing moved with the railroad to their new operation at Bull Hook siding and worked as a fireman shoveling coal into the red-hot bellies of the engines to maintain their top speed of 25 miles per hour. Ed continued on the railroad until January of 1894, having worked on locomotives running from Spokane, Washington, to Minot, North Dakota, and Havre to Great Falls, Helena, and Butte.

Cattle now became his main line of work. The previous spring he and fellow railroaders Al Rehburg and John "Baldy" Thompson ordered fifty heifers and fifty steers from the Thuet Brothers Livestock Commission Merchants of South St. Paul, Minnesota, for $11.00 a head. The Lazy-P-Connecting-N-branded cattle ranged on land at the head of Bull Hook Creek, presumably on Redwing's land, since Rehburg's homestead was east of the Ryans, and Thompson would not file on Little Box Elder Valley property until 1896. Rehburg and Thompson apparently financed the operation, and Redwing ran it.

Soon Rehburg became disenchanted with the business and decided he wanted out. In fact he told Thompson that he thought Redwing was cheating them by taking more than his share of the profits. Rehburg quit the partnership and reportedly said that he would shoot Redwing if he ever saw him again. Rehburg promptly stopped blustering, but Redwing didn't forget it. Subsequently, one day Rehburg was dove hunting when Redwing happened along; when he fired at a bird, Redwing thought he was being ambushed and vamoosed!

Rehburg, along with several other settlers, sold out to Simon Pepin for his new ranch in the mountain meadows of Beaver Creek. Before railroading, the Silver City, Montana, native had worked on a ranch near Cascade and had been a horse wrangler at Fort Assinniboine and a bronc-buster for the P-Cross. He eventually settled in Billings, building a lodgepole pine house and acquiring a large dairy herd. He counted as a good friend western art painter, J. K. Ralston.

His former partner, John Thompson, decided to separate from Redwing in 1898; at the same time, he quit the railroad and settled on his new ranch. His good friend, George Francis, helped inventory and put a value on the cattle, since he considered Thompson a novice about the cattle business and wanted him to get his fair share. Francis frequently stayed in his bunkhouse and read from Thompson's extensive library. In return Francis did work around the place and even made some furniture which is still a prized possession of the family today.

Thompson stayed a bachelor until he was about fifty years old. Self-sufficient from a young age in Ontario, he had previously been in the Canadian Army, and had worked for the Canadian Pacific Railway. In Montana he herded sheep and worked at the Great Falls smelter before moving to Havre.

For inspired entertainment he and neighbor Wait Brown, Diamond-Bar ranch owner from just across the divide, got together and recited Shakespeare. Francis may have participated, or at least was an amused observer.

The division of assets was finally settled in district court in 1901. Not deterred, Redwing continued to add to his cattle interests.

Long George ran a wholesale calf business—even though he had only a few cattle of his own—and it was reported that he always delivered as many animals as the customers wanted. Thus it was whispered that he "dragged a long rope with a maverick-hungry loop" and that he was a "brand artist" who ran a "maverick factory."

A cowboy and later a railroader, Dan O'Neil, rode on one trip to Canada with Francis when they brought back 250 calves; how obtained, he didn't reveal. Perhaps they were American cattle grazing on leased pastures in the Cypress Hills. They were supposedly sold to Redwing. He was said to have stocked Redwing's place "with more cattle than any ranch in northern Montana." Reportedly at times law officers tried to follow Francis and many times came close to catching him; but he always eluded them. On one such trip he was warned that federal officers were hiding in a certain barn along his route. So George rode on ahead of the cattle, located the barn and barred the door. After Francis had driven the cattle by, either someone released them or they finally broke out on their own. Actually it isn't clear whether he had stolen the animals or just wasn't paying duty on legitimately bought animals.

Along with the Sucker Creek ranch, it was believed that Francis and friends had a remote place with a cabin and corrals on what is now the northeast side of the Rocky Boy Indian Reservation.[20] A mountain there is officially designated Long George Peak by the Department of the Interior. The isolated outcamp was located above Brough's Coulee near the present Indian reservation boundary. Like the Clear Creek hideout, stolen cattle and horses were supposedly brought here to be either branded or their brands altered.

Francis was almost arrested for stealing a horse that the owner was being cruel to. Before any legal action could be taken, Redwing fixed things up with the owners, probably with coin of the realm.

Regardless of how well their livestock partnership worked, it was certain that their good friendship (as asserted by Hilda Ryan) was going to turn into a bitter feud because of their mutual attraction for the Ryan girl.

Francis, following his stay at the Ryan home, began writing notes to Hilda, which he placed under one of the stones that dammed a spring east of the Ryan home. He knew Hilda came by the spot on her way to an aunt and uncle's home. Soon they were exchanging letters and placing them in a rotten fence post on the Ed Lawlor ranch northeast of the Ryans. They also had a secret meeting place in a grove of pine trees somewhere in the valley. This occurred between the autumns of 1902 and 1903.

Francis wasn't her only suitor though; Redwing was showing considerable interest, too, and the Ryans reportedly felt that Ed was a more satisfactory beau. It is said that Jack Ryan wasn't a fan of either man, but Redwing did have the beginnings of a cattle ranch, while Francis had very little. Since Francis was supposedly such an accomplished rustler, his poor financial condition seems contradictory. Perhaps his fancy clothes, card-playing at the Honky Tonk (he was not a drinker), or sending money home accounts for it.

In addition to the apparent negative attitude of Hilda's parents, the weather seemed foreboding too. In the fall of 1902, there was a big fire on Beaver Creek; and in May of 1903 a major snowstorm struck. Jack Ryan rushed over to Walt Brown's ranch with his horse-drawn V-shaped plank snowplow to help free his trapped sheep. This left the remaining Ryans to dig through several inches of snow to free their turkey hens. Luckily Louis Shambo and George Francis stopped there during a lull in the storm. When the snowing and blowing began again, the coulees filled with snow and landmarks blended with the drifts. Francis and Shambo, now marooned, helped free a young steer stuck in a snowdrift and helped put calves in part of the kitchen. Some other critters tried to escape: One eerie recollection was of rattlesnakes crawling on top of the snow.

Yet nothing would deter Francis: He was quite serious about marrying Hilda. His letters expressed his love and admiration for her. "I would fight the world for you if I knew you liked me," he wrote. George confessed to her that he had a "hard name," but that he was really a gentleman at heart like his parents had taught him to be. In another letter he expressed his sorrow that her folks had turned against him. "I am a good man, but not rich so they didn't take a fancy to me." A subsequent note expressed the same bitterness against her parents, adding: "Say Hilda, there are lots of men in the world as good as I am—but there is no girl in the world as good as you are . . . it is the highest honor that a man could pay to a lady . . . to tell her that he loves her."

Happily for Francis, Hilda replied to his letters. She affirmed that she cared for him, but "friends" were saying bad things about him. He replied immediately that his dreams had been answered by a true friend. He apparently had a love poem published both in a Havre and Great Falls newspaper, captioned: "To My Dear little sweetheart girl." In September he wrote, "We must remain true to each other" and that he had found work in a Havre saddle shop, making $3.25 a day, besides hunting horses to break and sell.

At that point the Ryans stepped in. The last three letters George wrote to Hilda expressed further resentment towards her parents for the abuse given her for caring about him. They had been apparently caught together by the Ryans and told in no uncertain terms not to see each other again. Francis acknowledged they probably wouldn't be able to see each other for a while, realizing that Hilda wasn't going to go against her parents' wishes. Yet, with hope, he wrote her that in two years he would have a good home and an education, although not directly asking her to wait. In further acknowledgement of defeat, he penned that she would probably date Redwing now.

And she did. They courted and were married with her parents' blessing on June 27, 1904, during an 8:00 Mass at Havre's St. Jude's Catholic Church. They moved into Ed's new two-room frame house on Bull Hook Creek. Jack helped to add two more rooms and a pantry. The old log cabin became the bunkhouse.

Nobody made a better friend than George Francis, and conversely nobody made a worse enemy. Francis had helped make Redwing a prosperous rancher, and now he took an oath to break him by whatever means necessary.

The devastated cowboy wrote her another poem in October of 1904, expressing his utter sadness. It told of their secret meetings, love promised but unfulfilled, and of his being turned away for being poor. But he declared that his love for her would never die. The fifth and last stanza went:

Now all this world, Looks dark to me.

And in my dreams, No girl shall ever be.

Though ever yet my thoughts incline,

May God forgive,

Mrs. Hilda *Ryan*.

The second was addressed more generally and was entitled "*Over the Big Divide*," signed only, "Cow Thief, Coolie (sic), Montana, November 1, 1904." The point of the verse was the hypocrisy of some of the other ranchers of the area calling him a thief. The old kettle calling the pot black.[21] Reportedly the Montana Stockgrowers Association showed interest in it and obtained copies.

Francis left the mountain and foothills country he loved for the town of Havre—although his presence would be evident at times.

The Town

ACTUALLY IN ONE SENSE GEORGE FRANCIS'S MOVING to Havre in about the fall of 1903 wasn't a big change of life for him. He had already spent winters there—only this time it was different: All his dreams, hopes, and plans of marrying Hilda and having children had been smashed. Of course he could have stayed at the Sucker Creek place, but it was probably just too close for comfort to the Ryans and Redwings; besides, he may have outworn his welcome on someone else's property since he was believed to have been only a squatter.

Along with getting revenge against Redwing, he intended to show them all that he was a worthwhile individual, which was ironic since his moral code was ambiguous.

What he did immediately for money is not definitely known. Probably he continued to work for the unnamed saddle shop he had written Hilda about. For living quarters he at one time had a bunk either in the office or tack room of Ed "Dogie" Thomas's livery barn near Second Avenue at Second Street West.[22] The smells of straw, manure, and leather certainly wouldn't have bothered him. Perhaps he was night caretaker in exchange. Young Bill LaSalle hung around or even worked at the stables and fondly remembered witnessing Francis and George Herron singing and playing their guitars together. LaSalle also tagged along when Francis went to Brundage's pool hall each night about 7:00 P.M. when he was in town.

A little later, as his financial condition improved, he lived in a boarding house operated by a Mrs. Martin. She was the widow of a railroader and had several children to raise. Later he rented a cabin behind businessman Joseph Gussenhoven's brick and sandstone three-story house on the west end.[23]

Gussenhoven, in partnership with Adolph Pepin, built the town's first two-story brick building in 1900, merging his steam laundry and general merchandise business. He originally had two partners in a combination clothing, grocery, hardware, and liquor business. The partnership broke up literally; Gussenhoven knocked one partner through a wall, obviously espousing the axiom that action speaks louder than words. He kept the hardware and liquor business, putting in an 8-foot bar with a barrel of whiskey and card table in the backroom. Customers such as Doc Almas, Orrie "Kid" Tibbets, and Emma "Dutch Em" McDevitt played seven-up for drinks. He soon had a major beer, wine, liquor, and cigar wholesale business. Gussenhoven also owned coal mines, a brickyard, natural gas wells, and a sawmill in northwestern Montana at Fortine.

The Gussenhoven home was just west of H. (Henry) Earl and Margaret Clack's new brown sandstone home, built mainly by Clack himself. Clack's children reportedly watched Francis pass by on horseback to and from his small white house just up the alley. Clack was in the coal, dray, feed, and grain business and did his business from a warehouse of Gussenhoven's. A brother, Phil, initially worked for him.

Long George and H. Earl were eventually to become bitter enemies, a rivalry which was perhaps even worse than that with Redwing, if such was possible.

The town where Francis went to lick his wounds was called one of the coldest, the driest, and the toughest in the U.S., but locally the newspaper proclaimed it "The Sunburst City of the New West." It must have been fairly tough if the following story is true. Supposedly there was a farmer who lived just across the Canadian border. He had his ranch hand burn down the barn for the insurance money. In reflection the hired hand decided he wanted more money after doing the job. The farmer replied: "Why should I pay you $500 more when I can hire someone from Havre to kill you for $50?"

Thanks to being the divisional point for the G.N.R. in Montana, with its surrounding ranch and farm industries, coal mines, and the partial resurgence of Fort Assinniboine shortly after the Spanish-American War, Havre was booming. In size it had passed Fort Benton, the county seat of Chouteau County—80 miles to the southwest on the Missouri River. Fort Benton still had the only medical facility in northern Montana with the St. Clare Hospital. Havre's population had grown from 300 in 1892 to 800 in 1901, and to 3,500 in 1904. E. C. Carruth acted as a one-man chamber of commerce: He managed the Havre Hotel and was secretary-treasurer of the second hotel's owning corporation and also operated an insurance, land locator, loan, and real estate office. "Ask Carruth, he knows," was his slogan. Carruth also owned a large farm just west of Kremlin, Montana, a homestead town he helped establish.

But all was not roses! One of the local papers was skeptical of the city government. The editor thought the hotels had too many prostitutes rooming in them, there was too much shooting in the saloons, and there were no open town council meetings being held. The editor believed the city fathers would accomplish more by spending less time in the houses of ill repute and more time at work and home.

However, with the coming of the new year, there was an air of optimism about the future growth of Havre. Several new business blocks were planned and a new waterworks was being contemplated. Mother Nature, however, radically changed those plans.

The town was definitely experiencing growing pains. It stood halfway between the ways of a frontier town and the progressiveness of a modern-day city. Fire protection was poor and consisted of little more than a few sprinkling cans, as the *Havre Plaindealer* sarcastically put it. Fire departments were commonly more social organizations than serious fire-fighting teams. Even the fire bell at city hall was defective. Garbage and debris were collecting in the alleys and behind buildings; the town was ripe for fire.

On the evening of January 13, a strong chinook wind blew through Havre, consuming what little snow had been on the ground. About midnight, some men of mixed descent were thrown out of the Bank Saloon for being drunken troublemakers. They left the saloon and proceeded east in the alley between First and Second streets. They stopped behind Gross and Lebert's general store, which also served as the undertaking parlor in the rear. It is said that in revenge they broke in and poured kerosene on the floor and ignited it. Police officer George Bickle had observed these vagrants drinking behind the store, but he thought it looked harmless enough at the time.

About 1:00 A.M., the westbound train arrived with Eric V. Hauser on board, who was just returning from his home in St. Paul. Hauser owned the electric and telephone companies and the steam heating plant, and leased the (first) Havre Hotel from the Broadwater and Pepin Company. On hand to greet the businessman was E. C. Carruth, his hotel manager. As the two walked south on Third Avenue, Carruth remarked about the smell of smoke in the air.

Moments later they heard someone yell, "Fire!" The shouts seemed to come from the vicinity of First Street and Second Avenue. Carruth dashed into Charley Carroll's saloon next to the two-story log city hall, phoning the power plant operator to blow the fire whistle.

The volunteer fire department rolled out with only their hand-drawn portable piston pump and 500-foot hose-reel cart to fight the now almost block-long flames. The town's well, next to city hall, was soon pumped dry because it was plugged with trash and debris. Fortunately the hoses attached to the railroad's wells and Havre Laundry Building tanks had an ample supply of water.

Because of the high winds, wood shingle roofs, and the debris and rubbish in the alleys, the blaze's progress was hastened.

Unfortunately, several buildings contained gunpowder and ammunition; hence the crowds viewed a perilous and bizarre winter fireworks display.

The momentum of the fire was broken about 4:00 A.M. by the heroic efforts of firemen and a citizens' bucket brigade—and a developing cold northwest wind.

The entire south side of the Broadwater and Pepin 200 block on First Street plus of the 100 block was consumed, while the north side of First to Main Streets saved by the railroaders' hoses.

With the coming of daylight, the exhausted firefighters turned in while citizens patrolled the streets, putting out the last of the hot spots, and watching for any new outbreaks.

All seemed well until about noon the next day when M. J. Kechler, a clerk at Stringfellow's drug and variety story at 300 First Street, decided to check the basement for some items. Upon opening the trap door, he was greeted by a thick cloud of smoke. The building was soon consumed, and the fire, fueled by a gale force wind, burned until it had run its course. In the end, sixty businesses over a 5-block area were destroyed. Only the walls of the Bank Saloon, the tall, spire-like chimneys of Havre Hotel, the electric power plant, and the newly built Security State Bank building with thick firewalls remained. There was some looting, but it was stopped when Army captains McDonald, French, and Rice arrived from Fort Assinniboine with a detachment of forty handpicked men and threw a patrol around the ruins.

It was said the sparks that kindled the drugstore must have blown under the wooden sidewalk, though some maintained that the fire had been carried through the steam tunnel system that traversed the town's First and Main Streets. The power plant had put a steam pipe through the tunnels to heat buildings with the waste product of the generators. Later, the tunnels had a more nefarious purpose during Prohibition.

George Francis witnessed and probably helped fight the fire. It must have given him an eerie feeling because of his close call of only a few years before in the Windsor Hotel. This time, on the same site, the Havre Hotel was destroyed; the three-story, sixty-room brick building with gas lighting, steam heat, and porcelain baths had been the best and most modern hotel in northern Montana.

When it became evident that the hotel's bar and the saloons couldn't be saved, their doors were thrown open to the public. Unfortunately some of the exhausted, overheated firefighters—including volunteers and burned-out merchants—had developed a powerful thirst, and in the process of quenching it, some got drunk! It was probably a good thing that additional firemen and equipment arrived from as far away as Great Falls and that additional soldiers and lawmen came, too. Francis, of course, had to write a poem about it, naming names.[24]

As an interesting sidelight local gambler K. "Hy" Hinote decided that Great Falls was a safer place to live. Hinote gambled routinely all night, slept through the morning, and then put on his best suit for a walk. Havre's version of Beau Brummel, he always had a fresh flower in his buttonhole. He always attended the local dances and was known as the "pumper": His and his partner's arms went up high and down low like the action of a water pump. Things went poorly for him in the "Electric City," however. He was arrested in 1917 for being the leader of a major burglary ring that had been plaguing the city. His listed occupation at the time of his arrest was bartender at the Cream City Bar. He had been better off in Havre after all.

While the fire wasn't personal progress for Hinote, it was for Havre and other frontier towns. The now-educated city fathers passed a new building code, allowing the construction of only brick and masonry structures with at least 8-inch thick walls. The still-standing Security State Bank, surrounded by rubble, certainly proved the validity of the new code. The false-front wood and log frontier buildings were now part of Havre's past.

However, not everyone wanted to follow the building code. The editor of the *Havre Plaindealer* pointed out that the new Broadwater-Pepin Block wasn't being built to conform to the new requirements. In response Pepin promptly evicted the newspaper from his rental building. But the editor had the last word: In his next edition he pointed out that Pepin had accumulated large areas of public domain, illegally fenced it, and wrongfully gained land from the government. He also hinted about a certain illegal trade that his former landlord had engaged in with the Indians of northern Montana.

Pepin by now was a very powerful individual, but generally regarded as a well-mannered, friendly, and kind-hearted person who did much for Havre, whether donating land for the cemetery or land and money for the Catholic Church or a new hospital. He was always willing to give cowboys on the rough row a meal. In 1895 the P-Cross encompassed about 19,000 acres with his three ranch sites: one at Bear Creek, Alberta, in the Cypress Hills; another about 2 miles northeast of Havre; and a third, newly founded in Beaver Creek Valley. In looks, Pepin was about 5 foot 5 inches tall with a medium frame, blue eyes, and salt-and-pepper hair. He had a ramrod-straight posture and walked quickly with perhaps a slight limp.

In town and elsewhere, together with three of the Broadwater brothers, he owned a drugstore, two banks and general stores, a hotel, a meat market, and ten acres of the Havre townsite. Because of poor reading and writing abilities, he carried a large amount of cash so he could make business deals on-the-spot and left the paperwork for accountant Ed Broadwater to do later.

He lived in a large, three-story, French-accented mansion with a barn and corrals on the eastern edge of town, spending his leisure time at the ranches checking on his cattle or in his Havre house, being a homebody in his rocking chair. Sharing the home was Rose, their daughter Elizabeth, and Vina Harvey, daughter of his deceased foreman, Charles Harvey. He had assumed responsibility for her, too, when her mother died. Various nieces and nephews and their families occupied the house also, perhaps making up for the Pepins' other four children who had not survived.

While Pepin was happy with Havre, James J. Hill was not. He felt Havre's evil environment was not the place to bring his workers or attract the families he wanted to populate its surrounding plains with farms. In an

1899 *Minneapolis Journal* article, he expressed his intention of either bringing morality to Havre or moving his railroad shops 5 miles further west to Pacific junction. He wrote such a warning letter to Havre's town officials. Apparently he thought that would suffice, as he took no further action. Perhaps he received assurances that all would change. It didn't. For insurance, it was said, all the train dispatchers for miles along the G.N.R., east and west of town, were put on a special payroll to advise the townsfolk when Hill's train was coming.

It is further popularly believed that when he did arrive all the semblances of disorder and lawlessness disappeared; the gunmen left town, the lights went out in the worst of the saloons, the dance hall girls donned respectable dresses, and Havre's red blood turned to water—until Hill left again.

If this system was indeed in effect, it broke down in the spring of 1904, following the fire, when Hill brought some of the G.N.R.'s major investors to Havre in his own personal railroad car. He planned to show them the new, modern city that was being built from the ruins of the old.

The train arrived without advance notice, and the proud Hill probably first took the gentlemen on a tour of the recently built machine shop, steam power plant, and roundhouse. The complex had been moved further south and east to get away from the frequently high waters of the Milk River. (The Milk also caused a local north Havre dairyman trouble. With no bridge, he had to ford the river with his wagonload of milk. It was said when the waters were high, his customers sometimes found minnows in their milk!)

The new roundhouse contained twenty-three locomotive stalls, and the machine shop accommodated eighteen steam engines in the 70-foot-long pits. (Twice the locomotives' length.) The new installation had been built at a cost of over $400,000 and was constructed with over 1.5 million bricks. The skylight in the machine shop cost $7,800 alone. It was the best arranged and equipped railroad yard on its entire line from Chicago to Seattle, employing 200 men.

With the railroad inspection complete, Hill's group probably now started down the streets of Havre. What they saw then was like the new silent western movies or a throwback to the Dodge City of old. They saw every kind of fight through saloon doors and on the streets: men fighting with fists and boots, guns, knives, and razors. Nothing had changed in ten years!

Reportedly Mayor William Swanton and the town council were summoned to Hill's railroad car, where the touring group had retreated. The angry, embarrassed, and humiliated "Empire Builder" gave them one more chance: clean up the town quickly or the railroad goes.

In response a mayoral ticket with railroad lunchstand owner Louis "Shorty" Newman as the candidate for the Citizens Reform Party was formed. Newman had also been associated in the ownership of a grocery store with Pete DesRosier, managed the McIntyre Opera House, and had been city recorder and alderman, among other things. He won the election, 271 to 101, against Citizen's Party candidate James Auld, livery barn owner, rancher, and friend of George Francis. Francis often visited Auld's ranch at Toledo, east of Havre, and cowboyed with son Johnny.

Newman had won the election against serious opposition from the vice element, led by "Shorty" Young, the saloon-brothel owners, and the cowboys. Among the election observers was H. Earl Clack. He had several individuals arrested for voting irregularities. No cemetery occupants voted that day! Apparently the vice crowd didn't believe that Hill meant to pull out after making such a big investment—and perhaps they were right. Besides, the saloons could always follow.

One of Newman's first acts was to increase the size of the police department to convince people that the lawless boom was over and that a more conservative way of life was about to begin. Instead of one town marshal and a night constable, there was the new fearless police chief, George Bickle, a former patrolman and a good man with either his fists or pistol, and three patrolmen, two just temporary. Assisting Bickle were George Hall, formerly a lawman in Texas and Wyoming and currently a stock inspector, plus George Gilliam and Fred Stevens. Hall was a crack shot with a revolver and had won many state trophies.

The new force closed up about ten of the worst saloons in the first month—leaving about fourteen—and forcing their owners to leave town. One of those who left was Patsy W. Dyer, a gambler and gunman-killer from Gilt Edge, Montana. Dyer was given a necktie party by the state of Nevada for more killings.

Bickle wiped up the floor with one saloon owner who sneered at the idea of reform, while Hall winged another proprietor who drew on him. Actually there was a fifth officer of sorts: George Francis was special officer in charge of the animal pound and garbage ordinance enforcer at $60 a month. Dogs on the loose were as much a nuisance as the illegally dumped garbage. One story goes that Francis was so successful at catching wild or branded horses that he was recommended for the job by Simon

Pepin, hoping to keep him off the range, yet his lack of wealth with which to impress the Ryan family would seem to discredit this bit of folklore.

Francis became a regular police officer when Fred Stevens was killed trying to apprehend the burglar of Chestnut's saloon on Third Street at Second Avenue. The shootout occurred on the eastern edge of town. The killer, Joseph Lenhard, had escaped from the Kalispell, Montana, jail; he went on a crime spree that finally ended in the Midwest. Stevens was the half-brother of local merchant Henry Gross, whose building had been the first ignited in the Havre fire.

Francis probably spent some part of his shift keeping peace among the soldiers, cowboys, coal miners, and other rowdies who frequented C. W. "Shorty" Young's Honky-Tonk, officially known as the Montana European Hotel and Grill. Located on the western outskirts of town, it housed a hotel, vaudeville theater, dancehall, gambling room, bar, and Chinese restaurant. Next to it was "crib row" and the Parlour House. The buildings were all connected by passages above and below ground and built in an open "U" around a large court-like area adorned with trees, vines, and a pond.[25]

Francis's old comrade, George Aldoes, worked behind the bar. Around him were the "leg shows": women clad in gaudy, abbreviated evening dresses, acting as both waitresses and entertainers. They mounted tables to dance or sing coarse songs to the accompaniment of a tinny piano. Traveling vaudeville and burlesque acts performed smutty comic and straight or talking woman routines, dramatic monologues, recitations, singing, and acrobatics. Actually, compared to today's hardcore vice districts in big cities, the goings-on were relatively tame.

The Honky Tonk had a color line separating the black "buffalo" soldiers from the white civilians and troopers. When one or the other stepped over, the shooting began, besides other disputes that the bouncers could usually handle. Francis spent some of his off-duty time there at the gambling tables.

In time he and Shorty Young became friends. They had probably first met when Young ran a roulette wheel at the Windsor Hotel bar. Young had a ranch just out of the valley to the west, and their mutual love of horses gave them a common bond. Shorty spent time hunting at John Kinsella's Saw Mill Gulch ranch near where Francis had lived before moving to town. Among Young's other holdings were a cabin on Wild Horse Lake north of Havre near the border, where Francis may have hunted for horses, and another bar/restaurant called The Mint, a more deluxe saloon compared to the frontier-type Honky Tonk. The second floor contained apartments.

The new vice-king-by-default was having trouble with the reform organization of Mayor Louis Newman. Under J. J. Hill's sponsorship, Newman was trying to clean up the town as promised. He kept stepping on Young's toes with new regulations concerning gambling, prostitution, bar hours, etc. One such proposed regulation, "the social evil law," placed prostitutes under close police scrutiny, requiring physicals and a special-levied fine system. This he thought necessary because of an "alarming spread of disease."

Besides Young's and other saloons, officer Francis had to contend with a high burglary rate and further arson fires. Because the city hall had burned down, a red light was placed at Judd's Cafe on First Street between Third and Second Avenues to summon police when a call came in.

Little information remains of the events that transpired during Francis's time as night marshal. He served an arrest warrant signed by Hill County Justice Court Judge W. B. Pyper to a George Andrews for petit larceny in March of 1905. He received $1.50 for serving the warrant, and the city paid $2.00 for mileage and $4.00 for hiring a team.[26]

In another incident, recorded by the Havre newspapers, two men fought over the pleasures of a woman at a private residence at Second Avenue and Third Street. One man cut the other from behind, twice on the head and once on the neck, and nearly cut his coat off too. The wounded man tried to flee down the street with the knife bearer close behind. Just then officer Francis came on the scene and the suspect fled. He fired warning shots, choosing not to hit him, and he got away.

Also recorded: Francis nabbed a razor-wielding man on the train from Chinook once the local skiddoo stopped in Havre—no specifics on victims, if any, or how much difficulty he encountered in the capture. In another, a domestic disturbance, a wife shot three times at her husband, who was being entertained by another woman. The husband was taken to jail by Francis and given thirty days by the judge for "vagrancy" to cool things off.

Once, probably after breaking up a fight at the Honky Tonk between the black troops and civilians or after ordering some out of the bar for being drunk and disorderly, some of the buffalo soldiers followed him down the street, giving him verbal abuse. Finally Francis stopped at the Bank Saloon and procured several empty whiskey bottles. He launched an artillery attack, pitching the glass missiles at them. The "enemy" retreated.

And lastly, at Newman's urging, Bickle and Francis together raided several opium dens in the underworld city where Chinese and whites alike smoked the 2-foot-long bamboo pipe in dimly lit rooms by flickering, smoky kerosene lamps. Those arrested received thirty days in jail or were allowed to leave town. On a more positive note, Francis probably helped distribute the clothing, food, and gift baskets for the needy made up by the girls at the Honky Tonk and other saloons.

Francis himself was arrested on a warrant sworn out by Stock Inspector and temporary Havre officer George Hall, charging him with horse stealing. He appeared before Judge Pyper, and a continuance was granted to the prosecution until more evidence could be accumulated, but none apparently was. He claimed the horse he sold to L. K. Devlin was purchased from an Indian. Perhaps the matter was settled with the return of the horse to its rightful owner.

During this period of time in October of 1904, he wrote home again. "Still working on the police force and having a fine time. I have a good job and want to keep it for a year or two. I felt pretty bad when I learned that Pop was dying. Although I knew he never treated me right. I am a different man from what he always said I would be—there isn't a man any place that has more friends than I have. I haven't heard from any of the folks for a long time. Ask Ella if she ever tried writing to me. When is Bill going to get married? Jim was talking of coming here this fall.[27] I will send you one of my photos dressed in police uniform when I get some taken. I wanted something from home—only brought a horse that Bill gave me. Tell all to write. Election is coming on and I am pretty busy—am working nights now."

His father had collapsed while working on Dempsey Creek near the Idaho town of Lava Hot Springs, which was west of McCammon on the Portneuf River. The elder Francis had died from ptomaine poisoning after eating a can of tomatoes and was buried there. After all the Francis boys moved their mother to a house in Downey, two of the brothers moved the horses from the old property, to their new home in Jackson Hole, Wyoming. The remaining four followed in the 1920s.

It had been fourteen years since George had left home. He missed his family although he wouldn't or couldn't go home. And he had lost his girl: She was soon to bear Ed his first daughter, who they would name Delia Meryl. His life at this point must have been depressing, lonely and lacking in purpose, even though as the letter said, he did have many friends and kept busy.

One friend he may not have bragged about was Harvey (Kid Curry) Logan. Francis, no doubt, had visited the Coburn ranch in the Little Rockies country and perhaps the Logan ranch, too. He very likely saw the Kid and the Coburns at Lonnie Curry's Club Saloon in Harlem or at S. D. Cushman's Zurich bar between Harlem and Chinook. Wherever, Francis appeared one day at Black's jewelry store in the Havre Hotel building with a cufflink that needed repairing; it had the initial " H. L." Francis also had the locking clasp of a stolen mail bag from a Great Northern train robbery that took place near Wagner, Montana, on July 3, 1901, and had been committed by the Kid and associates. He gave this memento to a Chester, Montana, farmer, Ed "Slim" Wigen.[28] Since no questions were asked, one can only speculate.

Francis wasn't much for wearing jewelry, yet as described by Walt Coburn, he certainly liked "fancy cowboy garb, shop-made, made-to-measure high heeled boots, with his pant legs tucked into the fancy stitched tops, gay colored shirts and the best beaver hat made by John B. Stetson. . . ." He further wrote that Francis was an imposing figure, having the reputation for being the best-dressed cowboy in the [Milk River] country. He packed a factory nickel-plated, single-action Colt .45, with a mother-of-pearl handle and 5-inch barrel for show, but carried a standard issue six-gun on the range.

One merchant who got to know him well was the popular Lou Lucke, proprietor of the busy Lou Lucke Company. He and August Mund began with a shoe and boot sales and repair shop in 1903, and when Lucke became the family majority partner in 1908, he added clothing. He moved to the permanent location at 114 Third Avenue in 1911 from the Gussenhoven Building on First Street. Lucke was married to Harriett Thackeray, daughter of Havre businessman William Thackeray, a family Francis knew well.

A regular stop George made was the Hub Clothing store and Louis Halverson's cigar store and factory in the basement of the Liberty Hotel. Halverson made three varieties: the 25-cent Revora, the 10-cent Major Reno, and the 5-cent Little Master. "Ma Plaz," Alice Pleasant, was another good customer. Francis probably ate some of his meals at her Home Restaurant and boarding house at 215 First Street. The 200-pound, cigar-smoking, gin-drinking black woman was well known for her scrumptious steak and chicken dinners. She also dressed the ducks shot by Shorty Young and friends at Wild Horse Lake, Chain of Lakes, etc. Reportedly she brought in possum as a special treat.

"Ma's" husband, Tolliver, had evidently been a sergeant at Fort Assinniboine, and when he died, she was left with three children to support: John, Sis, and Albert. She had previously been involved in the management of a soldier's resort[29] with a two-sister team on Beaver Creek, just northwest of the present-day Beaver Creek Golf Course overpass. She loved the saloons, politicking, horse racing, and gambling houses. It was said that she was the only woman to frequent the saloons other than the dance hall girls. She also loved children, giving a nickel to the parents of newborn babies.

Francis frequently ate downtown at the Grill Cafe located at 315 First Street. Alice Hall, later the wife of Weaver Clack, worked there as a waitress and said that Francis wouldn't accept pennies in change. Perhaps he refused because of a superstition, or maybe he didn't want his pockets weighted with the bothersome coins.

A favorite place of George's to lounge was the lobby of the Havre Hotel. Here he visited with many friends and acquaintances, including the manager, E. C. Carruth. The adjacent hotel bar was probably a favorite for socializing, too. Pat Yeon ran it along with several other saloons in town, including the Board of Trade; there he kept a small zoo of sorts, including such animals as bears, an alligator (which drew a large crowd at its once-a-day feeding of hamburger), a mountain lion, a badger, a monkey, a coyote, and others. The Board of Trade was a workingman's saloon and claimed to have catered to one of the largest trades in Montana. It sported a 60-foot bar and featured a lunch counter specializing in a merchant's hot lunch of roast beef, brown gravy, and potatoes. Yeon kept pencil and paper there and encouraged his patrons to write home to mother. The food and animal smells must have been a strange blend, though.

Along with tending to his stomach's needs, Francis may have sought "culture," since he was an avid reader of the classics, by attending the opera house and seeing such plays as "Uncle Tom's Cabin" and "A Doll's House." Perhaps he took dates to the many dances held in private homes, barns, community halls, or schools. Square dancing, the two-step, and the schottische were the main attraction with a few waltzes and minuets thrown in to complicate things. Of course, there were always the silent movies—especially the westerns.

Francis no doubt missed the large number of cowboys who used to come to town on the weekends and race up and down First Street, letting out war whoops and shooting off their six-shooters. It was sad for him to realize that the era of big ranches was almost gone and was being replaced by smaller, combination farm-ranches. It wouldn't be far in the future that the Old West would be represented by one individual, posing for incoming tourists at the Havre train station. dressed in a colorful neckerchief, sombrero, vest, woolly chaps, flashy boots. and jangling spurs and packing fancy revolvers.

Although he worked as a police officer and lounged around the local businesses, Francis also kept his hand in the livestock trade. He and George Bickle, John Bicher, the Collier brothers, Henry Fastje, George Herron, and Frank Swartz purchased a Belgian black stallion called Cyrus. The draft horse was bought from a Chicago firm for $3,500. They surely hoped to eventually make a profit through breeding, perhaps statewide.

He dabbled with inventing, along with his continued interest in the livestock business. Earlier, probably while at the Ryan place, he and young Bernard Ryan had worked on a simplified stock-gate fastener. It featured a push button spring and arm that connected to a rachet to elevate the bolt. They applied for a patent in 1903 and received patent No. 52,217 in February of 1904.[30] Bernard died in 1910 at nineteen years young from pneumonia. By that time the Ryans had moved to Chinook where they had a livery barn.

Francis made two working models of the gate fastener, putting one at the William Thackeray ranch northwest of town on the North Milk River Road, and the other at John "Bearpaw" Griffin's Diamond Bar ranch on the western edge of Clear Creek Valley. Francis eventually sold the invention to a Minnesota company and received a good price for it, according to family sources in Idaho.

Apparently being a police officer, stockman, and inventor was enough for Francis, because there is no evidence that he participated in the copper rush to Bull Hook Creek on Saddle Butte, but he probably was already aware that it would be a bust. The country had pretty well been looked over by prospectors since the 1870s.

Further excitement was generated by the city election of 1906 in which Mayor Newman survived, assuring Francis of continued employment. His opponents were J. S. Carnel of the Taxpayer's Party and B. Ryan of the Socialist Party. Newman defeated them rather handily; 260 to 142 and 26 respectively. Even though Newman was attempting to reform Havre, he had two critics: The Reverends Francis Poole of the Methodist church and W. B. Young of the Presbyterian church. They told the mayor that his administration was not as moral as the campaign rhetoric suggested. They believed the red-light district was spreading to the downtown and into the respectable hotels and not decreasing in size as promised.

Perhaps Mother Nature was against Newman, too. Shortly after the election, a violent storm—perhaps a tornado—with strange-colored clouds struck Havre with high winds and 4-inch hailstones. In just a few minutes it ripped the roof off the Havre Commercial department store and several other buildings, wrecked smaller ones, and blew out most of the glass windows in town. The damage totaled over $50,000. Much livestock was destroyed, too. This was in addition to the continuing arson fires and vice problems.

While Newman was caught in a crossfire between the moralists and the vice elements, George Francis was seemingly being drawn into a collision course with H. Earl Clack. Clack was becoming a major businessman in the city and had taken a stand in supporting moral reform along with Newman.

Clack, a husky 6-footer, couldn't be faulted for not being a hard worker. With only $30—said to have been borrowed from Simon Pepin—the former cowhand and construction hod carrier had started and operated successfully a growing drayline business hauling coal, feed, grain, and hay. Half-brother Philip, also previously a cowboy, helped for the first five years, but opted for farming, raising registered Shorthorn cattle, and operating an ice business. This was in spite of Philip's being small in stature at about 5 feet 3 inches and having a deformed 3-inch-shorter leg, but not lacking in strength to lug heavy ice blocks around.

Yet Francis saw aspects of H. Earl's personality he didn't like. Perhaps he thought it arrogant of Clack to dump garbage in Gussenhoven's yard, adjacent to where Francis lived, or felt resentment for Clack suing Shorty Young and neighbors over their use of Beaver Creek water.

This resentment perhaps turned to anger because Francis thought Clack's handling of his horses was inhumane. For instance, one day in town, many witnessed the brutal beating of a sulky delivery wagon horse. This temper was sometimes unleashed on people. In May of 1906 Clack was arrested—perhaps by Francis—upon the complaint of P. H. Brader. Brader, the former Fort Assinniboine engineer, operated a general repair shop on West Second Street, doing plumbing and well and irrigation equipment work; he also offered steamfitting, heating, welding, and small engine/automobile sales and service—among other services. It is believed he was the main contractor in the building of Havre's sewers and waterlines using a ditch-digging machine powered by a gasoline engine. He and his family were well known to Francis.

The trouble began when Clack disputed a bill for hay and oats sold to him to feed his horses.

Brader then seized a cow of Clack's and locked it up. Instead of paying the bill, Clack forcibly entered "Mr. Brader's premises and released the cow." They later met on a downtown street, and after a heated verbal exchange, fists started flying. The battle escalated when the bigger and stronger Clack grabbed an iron pipe and struck Brader, rendering him unconscious. Brader eventually recovered, although it was feared originally he would die.

Clack was arraigned before Justice of the Peace Allen and released on his own recognizance until Brader recovered sufficiently to testify on his own behalf. The case was finally tried in Fort Benton after a successful change of venue plea by Clack's lawyer, signifying that there was anti-Clack sentiment over the incident. He was convicted and fined $100 and damages; he appealed, and it continued in district court. The final outcome is buried in the files of the Chouteau County courthouse.

The Clacks' farm-ranch holdings were located just southwest of Havre. The area became known as the "Texas Flats" because of the three transplanted Texas families headed by Ray Sands, John Clack, and Joseph Timmons.

Ray Sands came to the area first with his parents' family, arriving in Harlem in 1888, after the railroad had built as far west as Fort Assinniboine. Brother W. B. Sands became a Chinook attorney, and Ray came to Havre because his sister was married to clothing store owner, Thad Raymond. Ray then worked as a surveyor for the G.N.R.'s western extension from Havre to, roughly, Marias Pass on the Continental Divide. This stretch of rails was the original "Hi-Line." The name originates from the railway having been the most northerly railroad in the state or the "high line" as opposed to the more southerly Northern Pacific and Milwaukee Road lines. Eventually, the name extended as far east as Williston, North Dakota. From surveyor he graduated to brakeman and finally became a young conductor. He established a 272-acre ranch beginning just south of the Havre-Fort Assinniboine road.

Maude Clack, daughter of John Clack of Fort Worth, Texas, came to Havre in 1894 to visit with friends, one of whose fathers was the chief dispatcher for the railroad. She met Ray Sands, and they were married the following year. "She was responsible for the whole Clack family moving up here," said only child Gordon Sands in a 1981 newspaper interview. Phil and H. Earl Clack soon came along, followed by John and Clara with young son Weaver. John bought the homestead previously owned by Delia Ryan.

The thirteen-member Timmons family came a little later from a cattle ranch at Graham, Texas, and settled on 705 acres about 4½ miles southwest of Havre near the Clack holdings. Phil Clack married their daughter, Cornelia, in 1902.

The Clack clan, combined, had 2,500 acres with 1,500 under irrigation. The family had built the Havre Irrigation Canal, which was 9 miles long, and 20 feet wide and its main source of water was Beaver Creek. It culminated on the Sands property in an artificial lake. Apparently they purchased their water rights from the military. All three families had shares in the company.

The canal and its dam brought George Francis into dispute with the Clacks because it seriously restricted the flow of Beaver Creek water to the Herrons. Army Quartermaster Sergeant Frank and Mary Courteny-Herron operated a 186-acre farm-ranch just north of Fort Assinniboine. They were originally squatters along with other fort workers who built shacks there. They were given the land by an act of U.S. President William Taft for supplying the fort with dairy products and farm commodities, especially at the height of frigid, snowbound winter periods. When Frank died, Mary and sons George, Francis, and Pat ran the farm and Jersey Dairy. George Herron was also a county road supervisor and co-owner of a Havre livery stable and local stage line to the fort and Oldham on the Wild Horse Trail at the border. Later he served as a Havre police chief, brand inspector, and deputy sheriff. He and Francis were good friends, which was somewhat strange in that Herron was strictly an honest person.

Since the irrigation company owners refused to release more water, the Herrons took more direct action, probably with Francis's help: They dynamited the dam. It was rebuilt. It was blasted again. The process may have been repeated once again before the water rights battle finally reached the courts, and the Herrons' water rights were once again safeguarded.

Likewise, George's old adversary, Ed Redwing, intruded on the Herrons' space. Redwing was cutting their fences to let his cattle graze. Finally Francis lay in wait and fired over his head. He had a good laugh over it when Redwing quickly cleared out. Perhaps such an encounter with Redwing helped to remind Francis that he hadn't made his fortune because, in

April of 1907, he resigned from the police department, replaced by former Chouteau County undersheriff, Charles Crawford. The newspapers had only words of praise for him; one article stated that he wanted to devote full time to stock raising.

However, all was not well on the cattle and horse ranges. The previous long, subzero, snow-laden winter was possibly the worst since 1886 and 1893. Add to that further hot, dry summers and more of the large cattle companies folded. The new farmers and small ranchers had filed on and fenced in most of the waterholes or choice land where natural hay grasses grew. Adding insult to injury, they sometimes lived off the cattlemen's beef—or "slow elk" as they called it. Those larger ranchers that survived either had large legal land holdings or had their cowboys file on homesteads, which were then sold back to the company. Immigrants were also brought in and paid to do the same thing.

The P-Cross, Diamond Bar, and Miller Brothers were about the last of the large ranches in the Milk River Country, although the Shonkin Stock Association survived for a few more years north of the river and the McNamara and Marlow NL ranch carried on to the south of the Bear's Paw Mountains. The small farmer and rancher now prevailed.

A February 1907 edition of the (Glasgow, Montana) *Valley County News* predicted: "The cowboy with woolly chaps, big spurs and the ability to ride bad horses will be supplanted by fellas who milk cows and follow the plow."

Con Price wrote the following bleak words about that period: "But when I saw those farmers raising 50 bushels of wheat per acre on that virgin soil, I knew it was time for an ol' hoss like me to move on."

The Fort Assinniboine military reservation provided some cattle-grazing relief, although the authorities had trouble keeping the cattlemen's and sheepmen's animals apart. Finally friction was reduced by having the sheep graze on the lower ground and the cattle on the upper part of Beaver Creek Valley.

Yet none of this seemed to affect Francis. He formed a partnership with local businessman Frank Reichel, continuing until about 1910. Reichel had assumed ownership of the Merchant Hotel across from the train depot after E. C. Shelton's bankruptcy and sold it in 1900 to George Hannah, under whose ownership it became known as the Boston House. He also operated a transfer business, a saloon, and later established a liquor store, a grocery store, and finally a bottling supply works and a farm supply store.

Reichel had a homestead north of town where the wild horses they rounded up from the Missouri River Breaks country were possibly broken for saddle and buggy use. They also had cattle. Their livestock ranged from Sage Creek beginning in the Sweetgrass Hills, southeast to Big Sandy Creek and the Bear's Paw Mountains. They used about eight different brands, including Francis's Pot Hook or Flying V and another similar to Ed Redwing's brand—a coincidence, of course.

The 1908 Havre city directory listed George Francis and Frank Reichel as living at the same west-end address. The partnership evidently ended when Reichel married in 1910, moving Francis out and Elizabeth in. Francis must have operated the livestock business alone during the previous year because of Reichel being hospitalized in Helena with a severe aneurism, an enlarged artery of the brain. He survived what is still considered a serious operation. Lacking his own residence, Francis now spent the winter in the Bear's Paw Mountains with friends, according to one local paper. One of such residences was with John Ryan, Hilda's younger brother. He had a homestead in the vicinity of the Ryan place. John wasn't a fan of George's; he didn't like dishonest people. But that was okay; he didn't like Redwing either. Perhaps the embarrassment of Francis lessened with the Ryan family now living in Chinook, running a livery barn and boarding house. Chinook harness and saddle maker A.B. Duke now lived in the Ryan house. What sport Redwing made of Francis's predicament can only be guessed at.

Francis was probably glad to leave behind the Havre political wars between Mayor Newman and Shorty Young and enjoy the freedom of the range and fresh air of the mountains. George Bickle soon followed suit, moving to Fort Benton and becoming Chouteau County sheriff. George Herron became police chief, selling his and *Plaindealer* editor R. X. Lewis's share of the livery barn to Ontario, Canada-born Bruce Clyde, an agricultural college graduate and foreman of the C. M. Jacobs ranch on Clear Creek. Clyde would marry Vina Harvey five years later. Since leaving the Pepin home and attending school at Fort Shaw, Vina worked as a domestic servant, Chinook laundry worker, and maid at Havre's Park Hotel.

In leaving, Bickle and Francis missed the rising political heat. The stakes were now higher since Hill had increased his commitment to Havre in 1907 by enlarging the railroad facilities once again. He built a new freight and passenger car repair shop, enlarged the machine shop and roundhouse, and added a second story to the freight depot for use as division offices. With the railroad's payroll increasing, the showdown with the vice element couldn't help but escalate.

In 1908 Newman said that the mayoral election would decide who was running the city: the people or Shorty Young. At this point Newman was trying to shut down or at least curtail Young's and similar saloon operations with a wine room ordinance. However, his support seemed to be eroding because of his recent strong stands against boxing and gambling. To many people's embarrassment, Havre's own state middleweight champion, "Kid Lee," had to fight Stan Ketchel for the title in Helena—and lost the bout, too.

Young had more to lose this time. The original Honky Tonk buildings, constructed in 1899, had escaped the fire of 1904, only to burn to the ground the following year from a faulty stove.[31] Now a bigger and better one stood near its ruins to rake in the railroaders' dough.

Shortly before the election the city council repealed the ordinance requiring voter registration. This rule previously helped to prevent election fraud and had helped keep Newman in office.

Newman, a Democrat, ran on the "Good Government" ticket, proclaiming himself to be an independent. Meanwhile, the Democrats were still deciding on a candidate after H. Earl Clack's nomination of Newman had been rejected. They finally drafted Ed Burke, a longtime Havre railroad engineer, after E. C. Carruth nominated him. Burke was unaware he was in a mayoral race until he returned from a train run. The Republicans were not in evidence unless they were unofficially behind Newman.

In April of 1908 the surprised Burke defeated Newman, 239 to 215. Newman tried again in 1910, but he received an even worse defeat at the hands of Dr. Duncan MacKenzie, 301 to 180.

Newman, while no longer mayor, served as president of the Sherbourne Dam project committee. Authorized under the 1902 Newlands National Reclamation Act, the irrigation project was to benefit the entire Milk River Country. Along with committee Secretary G. "Pop" Bennum of Harlem and Treasurer R. Trafton of Malta, it included representatives W. B. Sands of Chinook, J. L. Truscott of Glasgow, Andrew Nelson of Vandalia, and B. D. Phillips of Malta. The group went to Washington, D.C., in 1908 to confer with President Theodore Roosevelt over finalizing the undertaking in Glacier Park to stabilize the Milk River's water supply. Finally Roosevelt entered the stalled U.S.-Canadian negotiations and reportedly "persuaded" the Canadian government to sign an equal-use treaty by vowing to divert the entire Glacier Park water drainage system that flows north into Canada.

Newman's efforts to bring a vice-free climate to Havre, however, didn't go unrewarded. Hill gave the former mayor the lunch counter and newspaper railroad concessions for the entire Butte division. Newman moved to Great Falls to manage his businesses. There he was elected mayor and served in the legislature. "The Little Giant" had done well.

And Shorty Young and his fellow saloon owners enjoyed freely the prosperity gained from the G.N.R.'s $60,000-a-month payroll in Havre, the third largest on the entire line.

Surely this didn't go unheeded by George Francis. These reform efforts—although stalled temporarily—plus an expanded railroad presence, signaled the advance of civilization in the area. That in turn meant more land promotional programs, bringing more farmers and crowded, fenced prairies. Now was the time to establish his ranch, before it was too late.

The Ranch

THE PLACE FRANCIS PICKED for his half-section ranch[32] was about 10 miles west of town on bottom land just north of the Milk River and further north of the G.N.R. tracks between the Burnham and Fresno rail sidings. From Havre, one had to either take the north Milk River trail past other ranches, including the Thackerays—there since 1900—or take the south wagon road that paralleled the railroad and then go north across the river by boat.

The ranch house was built around a dugout that Francis may have originally used for several years on his horse-hunting trips. Unknown to Francis, buried on the hill above his dugout were the fossil remains of a dinosaur—perhaps an allosaurus or trachodon—measuring about 30 feet in length. These, along with other prehistoric remnants, were discovered some twenty-five years later during the Fresno Dam construction. He reportedly had a similar dugout in the Sweetgrass Hills. To the immediate south of Francis across the river were the Crosson brothers, Abe and Sam. They were in the sheep business until 1910. Perhaps this is what kept Francis from settling in the area earlier.

To the brick-front dugout, he added a red painted wood-frame house. The dugout portion then became the kitchen and his saddle room, where he also did his iron work, horsehair ropemaking, silversmithing on bits, bridles, saddles and spurs, and other handiwork. The cabin had only one window, facing to the south with a view of the river some 200 feet away. Surrounding the cabin some 50 feet distant were bullberry, cottonwood, and willow trees. To the southwest was a spacious barn, and beyond a large corral[33] of heavy poles with a branding chute and several connecting smaller holding pens. The hitching post had a capacity for ten or more horses.

Francis initially had cattle and horses on the surrounding open range and military reservation with his new brand, the Flying V or Pot Hook, but the large homesteader influx apparently stopped that practice. He kept some of his stock on the home ranch and the remainder on friends' ranches from then on. Horses were his main moneymaker, and he continued to range long distances to secure wild ones. Once driven back to the ranch, they were halter and saddle broken to sell as buggy, plow, or riding horses. He also bought some animals for training and resale from other cowboys, ranchers, and Indians, including Rocky Sprague and the Sailor brothers of Gildford. Long George was making quite a name for himself as a horse trainer, besides becoming known as a rustler of almost legendary proportion.

The tall cowboy couldn't have waited much longer to settle on any land, although he didn't legally file on his ranch holdings until 1916. But what homesteader would have argued with him anyway?

Congress had doubled the amount of land originally available under the 1862 Homestead Act in 1909 and, in 1912, reduced the prove-up time to three years, allowing the settler a five-month absence per year. This, combined with Hill's railroads[34] beginning a third major drive to bring settlers to northern Montana, finally eliminated any free range. Many came in 1910, but the lack of moisture again discouraged any mass migration until about 1912 when the rains returned. "The Empire Builder" had three separate railroad car exhibitions touring the eastern United States, proclaiming the virtues and profits of small-family farming, not mentioning that over 1,200 acres were necessary in order to have a profitable farm. Huge billboards appeared along the right-of-ways declaring that millions of acres of fertile, virgin land were available for the taking. Even pamphlets and books were written ballyhooing the new "Garden of the World."

Yes, northern Montana was proclaimed a poorman's paradise where a fortune could be made with little effort. Posters showed farmers plowing across the fields, turning over a furrow of gold coins. Who could resist? The propaganda worked: A steady stream of families came West with their dreams, worldly goods, and the family cow, in a boxcar or with a covered wagon.

In 1911 Havre had increased its population lead on Fort Benton, the county seat, by 3,878 to 1,143. Between 1909 and 1918, an estimated

75,000 people settled in northern Montana, and in 1910, the G.N.R. moved in 1,000 immigrant cars. In one day alone 250 homesteaders arrived in Havre; in 1913 the city had 1,600 homestead claims in one month, and between July of 1913 and the beginning of 1917, over 5,000 people settled in the new Hill County. With good grain prices, abundant rain, and the high soil fertility, the prospect of wealth looked endless, just as the railroad had promised. Thirty-five to forty-five bushels of wheat per acre were common. By 1912 farms had taken up forty-two percent of Montana's prairies.

The predictions Jim Hill made during a speech in Great Falls in 1902 were obviously coming true. He said, "Churches and schools will be erected where herds of cattle and bands of sheep are now, but farms are better."

Locally even more money became available with the closing of Fort Assinniboine and the opening of the military reservation to settlers. Neither the military nor the state's politicians could any longer justify the fort's existence, since none of northern Montana's Indians had scheduled any future wars with the local populace. The final blow to the fort came with the fiery destruction of its recently built waterworks. An ample and steady source of water had always been a problem. Consequently, in the spring of 1911, the last of the Second Infantry Regiment left for Wyoming, and the following December the post was turned over to the U.S. Department of the Interior.

Now the political interplay began over what the land should be used for besides homesteads. Such ideas as a permanent home for the landless Indians of Montana, a school for Indian children, a state insane asylum, an agricultural college, and a national park were presented.

Battles of a more physical nature happened, too. The fort's caretaker became so frustrated with the cattlemen-sheepmen clashes that he took sides and burned some of the sheepherders' wagons, which supposedly belonged to the Sprinkles. These battles weren't just confined to the fort's land, however. In the latter part of 1911, several clashes occurred between sheepmen and homesteaders in the area. The sheepmen also commenced to mix it up with the cattlemen, resulting in a gunfight at the P-Cross cattle camp on Box Elder Creek on December 28.

These violent struggles continued for the next few years among the remaining large cattle companies, the small sheep and cattle ranchers, and even farmers against farmers, as each scrambled for a piece of the range. These forays resulted in many fences being cut, livestock disappearing, and grainfields and gardens being trampled.

By 1916, all lands of the newly created Blaine and Hill counties were occupied by families living typically in two- or three-room cottonwood log houses chinked with mud and covered by a dirt or sod roof. A rare few could afford to order a house kit from the Sears, Roebuck catalogue. Others lived in sod and stone houses or clapboard and tarpaper shacks.

As the homesteaders moved in and broke up the grasslands, small towns and villages began to spring up, particularly along the train tracks where stations, water tanks, and section houses were located. Here, seemingly endless streams of wagons filled with wheat rolled into the newly built grain elevators. The G.N.R. "Skidoo," with just coach and baggage car, shuffled between the Hi-Line towns carrying freight, mail, and passengers.

According to local accounts "Paradise" began to disappear about 1914. The close living quarters—with two families to a section of land—resulted in neighborhood cliques and feuds. The unaccustomed hard work from clearing rocks and more rocks, sagebrush, and weeds, planting, and pushing a heavy plow also fueled the flames—and the constant wind and harsh living conditions added to the irritation.

And among these settlers were cattle and horse thieves. They improved their financial lot by slapping their brand on any loose stock they encountered. The winter was open season on the ranchers because the few remaining cowboys were at their busiest just trying to keep the herds alive and well.

By 1901 the various cattle roundup associations' range detectives had broken up, killed, or driven off the majority of the large gangs. But the new thieves were just several one- to six-man operations, and most of the large roundup associations no longer existed to curb them after 1907. Even the state brand book ceased publication in 1913. Of course some cowboys who were now out of work also helped fill the demands of a new population with stolen beef and horses.

In some cases the stolen cattle were taken to a ranch or a town shop, butchered, and the hides shipped out of town for sale where no one was finicky about the brands stamped on the skins. Other rustled animals were driven across the state and Canadian borders, and outside stolen stock brought back. Frank Lavigne became the chief officer for the Montana Board of Stock Commissioners, commanding a small force of state inspectors and detectives to combat the widespread thievery.

At the height of the homesteader influx and its accompanying problems, James J. Hill retired as the chairman of the board of the G. N. R.

and its subsidiaries, succeeded by son Louis. The elder Hill had recently seen his town of Havre become the county seat of the newly created county named Hill; a name perhaps not as popular as Bear Paw, but one more politically desirable. And too, his dream of freight cars bulging with cargo and immigrants had come true. His freight offices couldn't contend with the volume generated—and full cars of wheat and other farm commodities now moved eastward. "Most men who have really lived," he said, "have had, in some shape, their great adventure. This railroad is mine."

George Francis's view of the same years was quite different. In June of 1912 he wrote home expressing disbelief that it had been eighteen years since he had been there, and he planned to visit in the fall. He never did. (Since the arrest warrant was now history, perhaps he just couldn't face his mother because of the wrong things he had done.) He told of the homesteaders coming to the country and nearly driving the stockman out and that the large influx had dropped wages from $60 to $20 a month for stock work. According to Francis, about half of these settlers were previously accountants, school teachers, or occupations other than farming.

He wrote that he planned to explore land in British Columbia, Canada, in the fall. His interest there may have been because former P-Cross foreman, Tom Conant, operated a livery barn at Vernon, B.C., and had perhaps written "the boys" of the virtues of the mostly uninhabited mountainous province.

"I could never content myself on any dryland farm in this country," he swore. He ended the letter on a pleasant note, asking about different family members.

In another letter, written to a friend, he said of the homesteaders: "Their idea was that the Government had given them the country, and they began building shacks all over the prairie on the cattle and horse range, shooting and poisoning range stock as if they were that many coyotes. Such people have proven themselves to be a treacherous enemy to every old timer on the range."

There was also something else he could blame them for: In about 1905 they brought the Russian thistle with them in the grain seeds, probably the "Turkey Red" variety. It sprouted along the tracks, and soon tumbleweeds were piling up against straining fences and growing in the pastures and grain fields, even though the local papers prophesied that it was a short-lived phenomenon.

Francis probably had no interest in having a county seat any closer, either. It meant more people and a closer law force that he and his friends didn't want breathing down their necks.

The fight for carving out new Hill and Blaine Counties from Chouteau County was a definite adventure in itself. Fort Benton, Havre, and Chinook battled in the state legislature over county dimensions.

An editorial in the *Havre Plaindealer* poked fun at its rivals, saying:

Havre has received a black eye from the people of Chinook and (Fort) Benton who desire county division, and poor old Havre is in the condition of the man who was damned if he did and damned if he didn't. . . . Both the people of Benton and Chinook insist that they don't want Havre in their county, maintaining that she is a constant source of expense. If Havre is furnishing all the criminals for Chouteau County, as the people of these cities claim, and the county is rivaling Silver Bow (county residents) in the state pen, then why not make Havre the county seat and reduce expenses by sending criminals directly to the county seat. . . .[35]

The dilemma over who would occupy the former 179,200-acre military reservation was finally resolved, too. First, 2,000 acres, including the fort's buildings, was designated in 1913 to be the site of a state agricultural and manual training school, the "Assinniboine School," and an agricultural experiment station. During the great depression, some of its buildings were used as a W.P.A. transient work camp. Today, about fifteen of the original 104 buildings remain. Once a college was established in Havre on donated land with volunteer labor in 1929, there was no further use for most of the buildings, and they were torn down. Some of the brick was used to build Pershing Hall at Northern Montana College and various structures around town and the county.

Also in 1916 Congress set aside a strip of land 1 mile wide and 15 miles long, encompassing Beaver Creek as a playground, originally called (though it did not become) Assinniboine National Park. The city of Havre was made custodian of the land in 1917. It is a popular belief that local businessman E. C. Carruth, E. T. Broadwater, L. K. Devlin, and J. G. Holland, Sr., staked mining claims on this strip to prevent homesteaders from settling along the creek when the former military reservation was opened. Thanks to efforts spearheaded by Hill County Commissioner Ray Sands, it became a county park in 1947—in fact the largest in the U.S.

Although the Chippewa and Cree Indians under chiefs Rocky Boy (actually Stone Child) and Little Bear were allowed to unofficially settle on the military land in 1912, it wasn't until 1916 that an approximate 56,000-acre section was officially set aside for "Rocky Boy's Band of Chippewa and other homeless Indians in Montana." Initially only about 450 Indians found a home on the new reservation. It was considered better than the colony proposed for them 100 miles east of Edmonton, Alberta; better than sharing the Flathead and Blackfeet reservations; and superior to several other schemes that had been put forth. The bill was introduced by Montana U.S. Senator Henry Myers after much persuasion from *Great Falls Leader* editor William Boles (the only apparent major paper to show support), town founder Paris Gibson, his son Theodore, and Charlie Russell of the same city.

Little Bear realistically had accepted that the white leadership would reject him as the displaced Indian leader because of his participation and leadership in the killings at Frog Lake, Canada, during the Northwest Rebellion of 1885; hence he joined forces under Chippewa Chief Rocky Boy (Stone Child). Not only was Little Bear's principal wife a sister of Rocky Boy, but one of Rocky Boy's wives was said to have been a distant cousin of Little Bear's father, Big Bear. Rocky Boy's peaceful Chippewas originally came from Red Lake, Minnesota, and traveled across Canada and down to Montana. The tribes had intermarried too, but still attempted to keep their separate identities, although the Cree culture was dominant.

Another who played a key role in the creation of the Rocky Boy Reservation was Frank Bird Linderman, prominent author of several books portraying an authentic picture of Indian life and legend in Montana. Linderman was then a Helena merchant, although in the past he had been a trapper and woodsman, state legislator, assayer, newspaperman, and insurance salesman. He spent several weeks at his own expense in Washington, D.C., lobbying Congress on their behalf. At one point Linderman was able to get them emergency food rations from the Taft Administration and had it distributed from Helena's Fort Harrison; also he persuaded then Secretary of the Interior, Franklin Lane, to meet with Little Bear to personally hear of the hunger and wandering, the plight of camping near slaughterhouses and garbage dumps, knowing no homes but their ragged, dirty tents.

Through these combined efforts, the heavy lobbying against the land acquisition from Havre and Helena sources failed; and G.N.R. officials wanting the land opened to settlement were defeated.

Long George's future nemesis, H. Earl Clack, also profited from the homestead era, which was radically changing the face of the Milk River Country. Along with his drayline, Clack operated a coal mine to feed the dryland farmers' stoves. In 1908 he erected an office and warehouse and became the local agent for the Continental Oil Company. P. H. Brader became his rival with the Mutual Oil Company. Along with livestock feed he handled crop seed and built his first grain elevator in Havre to buy the wheat raised from the seed he sold. He shortly added grain elevators in the local communities of Burnham, Big Sandy, Kremlin, and Laredo and soon built a three-story brick building at Fourth Avenue and Second Street, housing a farm implement, auto parts, and hardware store. Above were apartments. If that wasn't enough, the Clack Company offered residential lots in "Clack Heights" just south of town and later built apartment houses in Great Falls and Missoula.

To further George's unhappiness, Ed Redwing continued to prosper; now a school board and bank board member, he bought the YT Ranch adjacent to his own in 1911. A family had to be forcibly ejected from the house and land. They had tried to buy from the YT owners, but had fallen behind in their payments and Jim McCoy had to evict them. Some of their belongings stayed for years in a small concrete house where the evictors had placed them. A year later, Redwing added John Kinsella's Saw Mill Gulch ranch to his holdings, making about 5,000 acres he now owned, and he rented two townships in Canada for grazing purposes. The Beaver Creek Valley rancher was desperately trying to acquire and keep rangeland for his stock as the homesteaders moved in and fenced around him.

Sometime in this period, Francis and Redwing had a short and violent confrontation. According to popular folklore, the conflict was caused by Redwing reneging on a promise to give a young neighbor boy a certain horse in the spring if he would help keep ice off some watering holes over winter. As the story goes, the boy approached Redwing at the rodeo grounds to ask for the horse in fulfillment of the bargain, and he refused— even denying such a bargain had been made. The dejected boy then happened to run into George Francis and ended up telling him the story. The horse he wanted happened to be in a nearby corral, so Francis roped it and gave it to the boy. Next he went looking for Redwing.

In another version, given by Jean Carruth, daughter of E. C. Carruth, Francis went to confront Redwing at the stockyards or holding area by the Pioneer Market's slaughterhouse and holding pen (at the present-day MSU-Northern campus), because Francis had heard that Redwing was shipping some cattle belonging to him. The argument turned violent when Francis knocked him down and tried to kick him. His boot spur rowel ended up in Redwing's mouth, and, with a few jerks, had his mouth bleeding badly. In both versions, he had several teeth broken or knocked out. Francis then went over to his horse and got his quirt, beating Redwing with it while he struggled to get on his horse and flee.

Did this make Francis happier? Probably not in the long run. And making a greater enemy of Redwing had been a mistake. Especially because in the near future when the storm clouds would hover over him, he would need all the friends—or at least neutral parties—he could get. But Francis wasn't done with the Redwing family yet.

Though Hilda seemed quite content in her larger ranch surrounding, she did tire of being housebound and wanted to spend more time outdoors. About 1910, Ed hired some household help, and Hilda returned to the cattle range. She rode a tall, black, bald-faced horse called "Neg" that her father had given her. She was well qualified because she knew the country, could handle the stock, and recognized brands easily. Hilda participated in roundups and, wearing her black union suit under her riding clothes, rode as far west as Lothair, a Hi-Line town some 75 miles distant, to retrieve strayed stock. She and Neg spent hard, long days together, gathering animals and enduring many winter days of sub-zero weather. Not stopping for meals, she lived on raw potatoes and canned tomatoes. One can only speculate whether she ever ran into George Francis in her travels.

On the local law enforcement side of the cattle business, George Herron replaced Harry Green as local stock inspector. Green was previously a Chouteau County deputy sheriff stationed in the Big Sandy area, and he had a ranch east of town near Big Sandy Creek along the Fort Assinniboine military reservation, later the Rocky Boy Reservation.

Green came to Big Sandy from the family home at Lewistown. He first worked at the post office and a butcher shop. His other brothers followed: Bob, a farmer; Mick, a drayline operator; and Lawrence, a cowboy. Long George knew the Greens well, perhaps through George Fleming, who was a Big Sandy-area rancher and former sidekick of Francis and the Aldoes boys. Harry and Lawrence were also getting quite a reputation for being top bronc riders at the local rodeos during Fourth of July celebrations. Perhaps Francis also rode in the events.

Harry, in particular, raised and trained race horses. He probably helped found the Big Sandy race track and rodeo grounds. Francis liked one particular horse in the Green corral; it was a big, strong, and high-spirited bay horse that kicked and bit and had a large star on his forehead and a black mane and tail. Francis decided he wanted the animal, and Green gave it to him. He named it Tony, perhaps after cowboy silent screen star Tom Mix's horse.

George and Tony soon formed a real friendship. How could it miss when they both loved sweets? With George's expert horse know-how, patience, and gentleness, the horse was trained, and the magnificent animal was said to have been one of the finest roping horses in the American and Canadian West. Some of the horse's other talents included opening a cookie jar and taking candy from George's pocket.

The tricks that the many hours of training at his ranch produced were soon to be used in rodeos. After Francis roped a calf or threw a steer and hogtied it, Tony would keep the rope taut until George raised his hands for the timer; then Tony would slack the rope and walk over to the captured beast. Putting his hoof on the ribs, he would shake his head up and down while George, hat in hand, bowed from the waist to acknowledge the applause from the grandstand. Another thing Tony would do when George sat on the ground was to come from behind and place a hoof on his knee. Or, Francis would lie down and pretend to be asleep, while Tony nudged and pawed at him until "awakened." Other horses in his personal stable were Flaxey, Medicine Man, Big Red, and Little Red.

Francis spent little time at the ranch after the rodeo years began, except to bring supplies from town in a Hupmobile or in the summer doing the rounding up and breaking of horses. He kept Tony at the ranch in the winter and at a livery barn in town the rest of the year.

He wasn't a working cowboy, leaving the ranch to neighbor "Black" Bill Acison to handle. In his thirties, Acison was a stocky 5 feet 9 inches, was dark complected, and had black hair and beard; he spoke in a low kind of voice. Little is known of him except that he had a tougher reputation than Francis and hailed originally from Fulton, Missouri. At one time he is believed to have had a blacksmith shop in Havre. No "non-club members" were allowed on the ranch without advance permission, and Acison and the boys saw that it was enforced.

Besides at the ranch, Francis broke stock in a corral near the Clyde Livery Barn on the west end of town. Then they were driven out to grazing land, usually by Francis and Ray and Nell Ellis, along with several cowboys who either worked for him or spent the winters on his place. These included George Aldoes, Andy Avery, Clayton Jolley, Frank Keple, Jack Mabee, Jim Massey, Orin "Shorty" Selby, Ed Timmons, and others. In 1915 his neighbors, the Crossen brothers, moved to town, so Francis took over their larger house across the river, giving his friends the use of the old ranch house.

Although he resented their presence, Francis did a lucrative business selling the dryland farmers horses and some calves. In one case, he traded some horses in exchange for ranch work to be done by Charles Clark's son Wade. Clark said that Francis took good care of his horses, bringing out feed, but he neglected the cattle. They had to forage for themselves, unless Black Bill and Wade could obtain straw after neighboring farmers had cut their wheat. The Clark boy drove the wagon with greys Pete and Jake while Blackie operated the hayrake. They drove the cattle to the river for water. Francis gave Wade a saddle from Texas as an extra bonus.

The general consensus of victimized settlers seemed to be that their stolen stock ended up at the Francis place or the (Big) Sandy Creek ranch, and some of it did. However, very few were willing to venture onto either place to find out. It was said that even Andy Avery received a bullet wound for nosing around on Black Bill's homestead.

The Sandy Creek ranch was the most ideal for thieving and disposing of stolen stock because it was near the main hard limestone crossing of the Milk River, which followed the old Fort Benton-to-Fort Walsh wagon road to Canada. Called Cypress Crossing, it had been the site of the area's first town, although vice-oriented. The ranch was owned by dairy farmer Albert "Ole" Oleson, who lived south of there. Various cowboys rented the place, possibly even Francis, for their mainly nighttime activities.

The Redwings did find cattle and horses of theirs within the close proximity of the Francis place, but they were always unattended. Many more probably ended up at the towns and ranches around the Cypress Hills of Alberta and Saskatchewan provinces. It was said that George's neighbors knew he had stock originally belonging to Redwing and others, but, as true westerners, they minded their own business. Besides, Francis didn't bother them.

F. M. Wilson, a rancher just east of Gildford, lost ten assorted horses during the night of July 31, 1912. Wilson suspected George Francis and associates, of course. When nothing came of the sheriff's investigation, he distributed a printed circular offering the thenlarge amount of $1,000 for their return. The circular gave detailed descriptions, and soon after, the animals were found, abandoned near Pacific junction where the railroad tracks separated to the west and south.

One Gildford area farmer, Thaddius Swinney, nearly always got his stock back. He would write Francis a letter, telling him about his stolen animals. He would receive a reply, telling him when he and his boy Lester could come to the ranch for a meal. Once there, Francis told him where his stock could be found. No further questions asked.

Some other one-time visitors in about 1916 were three young boys from the Gildford area: Ted Burfield, Jim Phelphs, and Walt Stuart.

The boys rode their ponies all about the countryside and decided one day to visit the Francis ranch. But they started too late in the day, plus got lost. Fortunately they met a stranger who sent them in the right direction.

Upon arrival, Francis saw that they were fed and put up for the night. The boys were rudely awakened, though, in the middle of the night by the whoops of cowboys and the pounding of hooves of about 50 horses being driven into the corral.

Unable to sleep further and fearing the animals were stolen, the boys snuck out at dawn, noticing the horses were gone.

The Sprinkle brothers owned grazing land nearby for their flocks of sheep; and when ready for market, they were driven through the bordering farms and ranches to reach the railroad loading pens at Gildford. This was a problem Francis and his neighbors shared and one that certainly helped feed their contempt for sheep. In their vendetta against them, they either shot wandering woolies or clubbed them, throwing the carcasses into the gullies. They also put up barricades, making the herders take detours, even though the Sprinkles offered them money for passage. Another agitation with the Sprinkles was the overgrazing of lands around the Chain of Lakes—the small, three to four shallow bodies of water to the southwest of the Milk River. The sheep grazed the grass short in the summer, leaving next-to-nothing for winter cattle grazing.

Francis hated sheepmen, but his feeling towards the dryland farmers was more ambivalent. There were instances of him calling upon some, bringing a side of beef or some watermelon or other food—and his friendship. The

Johnson family on the Wild Horse Trail and the Frazier family north of Havre were just two examples. And too, there was his Robin Hood image: stealing or helping others who were poor and hungry steal livestock and playing judge and jury over people, a law unto himself.

Those he didn't like or respect would find that the horses they had turned out in the fall had disappeared, and the "Francis Gang" would offer to find them for a fee. Since they, themselves, had secreted them, it was an easy and profitable chore.

Supposedly, Francis also sold some unbranded weaner calves to some larcenous nesters for cash; no questions asked. Only about a week later, the calves disappeared in the night, just as they had arrived, and were branded and placed in the Francis herd. With no bill of sale, they couldn't say anything publicly. What Francis gave with one hand, he could take away with the other. Reportedly Francis bragged openly about it later in a Havre saloon or pool hall without naming those who had been deceived: "Them fellers shore broke that scissorbill from suckin' aigs," said a grinning Francis. For it was always the ones he considered to be crooked who were fair game.

In another allegedly true story, Francis laughingly showed his pool hall buddies a supposedly confidential letter revealing that a stock inspector from Helena was going to pay the Havre area a surprise visit. It was said that no one lost any livestock for quite awhile until after two strangers had left town!

As the thievery increased, Francis was blamed for more of it, along with an interesting character named Howard "Humpie" Kidman. One anonymous friend said Francis didn't steal half of what he was blamed for—whatever that amounted to. Some of his friends and acquaintances who stayed at the old ranch did steal from his neighbors, and he ordered them off, since he considered the area around the ranch to be a safe zone.

Several horse thieves and cattle rustlers did operate in the area who had no direct association with Francis, although he was aware of them. Some operated from Canada, from several nearby communities like Cottonwood and Simpson, and from Beaver Creek Valley. Earlier, Francis was apparently involved in one "beef factory" located between Beaver Creek and the town of Laredo and run by a brother of a good friend. For reasons unknown, they had a falling out, causing them to become bitter enemies.

One rancher friend who lived about 4 miles east of the Francis place could vouch for the fact that Francis didn't bother his neighbors' herds. He said that Francis helped others with livestock bogged on the river bottom, rowed stranded people across in his boat, and acted as a pilot to guide stock safely through the abundant quicksand in the waterway. The rancher's wife, on the other hand, believed the range gossip that Francis was the ringleader of a large gang of livestock thieves, wasn't any Robin Hood, and stole from all classes of people. She saw times when Francis suddenly had large amounts of animals that couldn't be legitimately accounted for.

The Charles and Lillian Graham family didn't think Francis was the nice-guy type either. They lived on the south side of the Milk River between the Francis spread and Havre. Francis sometimes slept at their ranch when traveling back and forth to town. He came late at night and rolled up in their bearskin rug on the living room floor. One night he woke them up and startled the family when he tripped over the coal pail. He always stayed for breakfast and spoke little, leaving the family to believe that he was conceited and unfriendly, but they still extended him western hospitality—perhaps out of fear.

When George lived in town, the Clyde livery barn was one of his favorite haunts, and he kept Tony there at times. Vina Harvey married Bruce Clyde in 1914 and worked at the stables. She said that Francis was always very courteous to her, tipping his hat and greeting her with, "Good morning, Mrs. Clyde." He made a strongly favorable impression on her, because he was polite and neither drank nor swore in public. Like Charlie Russell during his earlier Chinook days, Francis and children got along well, mutually enjoying the sweets he bought and rides he gave on Tony. This didn't mean, however, that he had any less interest in a good game of pool, a game of chance, or his cigarettes, cigars, and pipe.

Francis somewhat fit what the Butch Cassidy gang called a "Gentleman Outlaw." He never drank to excess, was always courteous to women, was generous when he could afford to be to the poor, needy, and deserving, and was intensely loyal to friends. He didn't really like the drudgery of farming and ranching, but loved the wild range life and horses. His ranch was used partially as a front for rustling activities. Thus he seemed like a good bad-man, gaining popularity and public protection from nosey lawmen.

While living in town, he usually played pool and lounged in the Havre Hotel visiting with people, besides probably pursuing the fairer sex and buying and selling horses. Every so often he disappeared for a week or so. Was he at the ranch? On legitimate horse-hunting trips? Or was he out gathering up other peoples' previously scouted livestock and driving them out of the country? Surely his friends knew, while those in town could only speculate.

R. X. Lewis, the editor of the *Havre Plaindealer* until 1913 and a 1916 Stampede Rodeo director, had definite views on the subject: He said that Francis's gang was terrorizing the stockmen north to Saskatchewan and west to the Sweetgrass Hills and that the law was looking the other way. And unless he (Lewis) minded his own business, Francis had threatened to lasso him and drag his carcass as far as the Bear Paws and leave it to rot.

Good friend and neighbor Marie Gibson gave another view of his avocational activities. One winter's day towards evening she was returning home from town with a wagonload of furniture. It was well below freezing and snowing heavily. She decided to stop at the Sandy Creek ranch because the team was played out, and she was exhausted from walking along beside the wagon through the snowdrifts. At the north turnoff she saw the glow of a cigarette and heard the whinny of a horse. Once closer, she saw it was Francis. It turned out he was on guard duty. Francis asked Marie to please tell anyone who inquired of his whereabouts that he was sick and had been staying at her cabin for a week. George said that there were some cattle in the barn which they had planned to move across the river, but it got "too hot" for them. With that, he left.

She went to the door of the ranch house where she was met by "a little sawed-off man with a brown mustache." This was Orin "Shorty" Selby. Selby said she could stay the night and that he would put the cattle out in the corral and her team in the barn. She went back outside and brought the horses a bale of hay, while Selby stoked the fire, made some coffee, and fixed her bacon and eggs. Marie noticed that he was nervous and paced the floor, and several times she heard noises upstairs, but Selby said it was just the cat. Finally she got up her courage to ask who was upstairs; Selby replied that he didn't know. When she said that she would check, Shorty volunteered to go. Once he was upstairs, she heard a hushed conversation. Finally Selby came back down with another man who was carrying a bridle and silver-mounted spurs. The new face said he had to go for a ride along the river, and he'd stop and warm up at the Gibson place. She didn't identify him, yet it was obvious they knew each other. Most likely it was Jim Massey.

Shorty admitted to her that the cattle were stolen from a homesteader living near Fort Assinniboine. They had tried covering the animals' tracks with a few of his horses trailing behind for a short distance, yet the farmer had been able to follow his livestocks' trail to the Sandy Creek barn; then went for the sheriff after a brief, fruitless discussion with Selby. Shorty told the drylander that he had gone trapping and knew nothing about any livestock. Five men were originally hiding upstairs until the angry farmer left.

The next morning while Shorty was fixing breakfast, Marie harnessed her team, letting the stolen cattle out of the pen per her last night instructions. Shorty decided to accompany her home and trap around there for a week or so, since he didn't want to face the law and cattle owner alone. While he was making preparations to leave, the sheriff appeared—on foot. His car was stuck in a snowdrift by the main gate. They helped him dig out the car, and all the while, the sheriff gave Marie strange looks as if to say: "What are you doing here?" Shorty volunteered that he was going to Marie's to trap for a few days. No further conversation was recorded by the embarrassed Marie, nor did she say whether they were questioned about the cattle. The sheriff made no attempt to enter the ranch grounds, either.[36]

Two days later, Marie had two more visitors at her homestead. One was the undersheriff and the other a stock inspector. They had left their car on the road and walked down the hill to her homestead near the river. The officers asked her about how far it was to the George Francis ranch. She told them it was about 1½ miles further west. Next they asked if he was home and who else was there, and as previously instructed, she said yes, that he had been sick the last week with the flu. She didn't know how many of the boys were with him though. The lawmen then had breakfast and casually questioned her about the episode two days earlier. She told them why she had stayed the night; and yes, there were cattle in the barn; and that she only saw Shorty Selby, who had just returned from trapping. They left, leaving a silver dollar for the breakfast. (It is doubtful they went on to the Francis place.)

The little drama continued about one week later. This time, the two lawmen were accompanied by an officer from the Helena office of the Montana State Board of Livestock Commissioners, possibly Chief Detective Frank Lavigne or his assistant, Leslie McCann. He asked the same questions, only he wanted to know how many cattle she had seen and what brand they carried. In response, she judged there were about thirty, and she hadn't noticed their brand markings. He asked their color; she said they were white-faced Herefords. The unidentified lawman continued to hammer away at her about what brand was on the animals. Becoming angry,

Marie told him she didn't know anything further and wouldn't testify. That concluded that!

Later in town an unidentified individual approached her and offered to split $1,000 if she would identify George Francis as the leader of the cattle thieves. Apparently some of the boys were in jail, suspected of cattle thievery, but none would talk. "I had considered asking Francis for hush money," he said, "but I was afraid my carcass might end in the Milk River under the ice." Marie terminated the conversation by threatening him if he should cause Francis or her any trouble. Surely he didn't fear her threats, yet he knew she could tell people who could do him harm.

Contrary to some reports and in agreement with others, Marie said that Francis did have a legitimate herd of cattle, helping to supply Havre with beef.

Possessing other people's livestock, as Francis did at times, was only a misdemeanor if by "accident." Even branding someone else's stock wasn't serious if you didn't try to sell it. When the law did find illegally branded stock on a man's ranch, the first defense was to scream frame-up. If that didn't work, the rustler paid a fine of $50 or so. Of course the thief's neighbors looked the other way because they were more or less "tarred with the same brush."

In January of 1914 Redwing found himself on the end of such a brush: He was charged with one count of altering the brand of a Conrad Brothers Circle C steer to his own Lazy PN brand. Involved in the investigation were stock inspectors George and Charles Herron, Jim McCoy, and soon-to-be stock inspector, Harry Green, plus several P-Cross hands as state witnesses.

The trial was short, and Redwing was convicted of having altered brands, requiring the payment of a fine of $500. The penalty could have been more severe, it was said, if the state's main witness, Frank Hundley, had not left the country. Hundley was a neighbor of Redwing's and was accused of doing the actual branding. Redwing was suspected of paying Hundley $3,500 to leave before the trial and hiding him on the Coburn Brother's ranch near Globe, Arizona. Bob and Will Coburn formerly had a ranch in the Little Rockies with their father, Robert. Another supposed state's witness, George "Shorty" Card of the P-Cross, was reportedly beaten badly and had to be taken to the veterans hospital at Fort Harrison, Montana. Later he was transferred to the Warm Springs hospital, where he died from the apparent effects of chronic alcoholism. Of course the boys would have said he died from the lack of booze, not too much.

This is only one of several similar charges filed against Redwing by several ranchers in this general period of time, but his only conviction. George Francis was the complainant in one case.

Redwing's apparent unofficial defense in all these cases was that this was retaliation by the cattle thieves for his help in the removal of a crooked stock inspector.

An adjacent northerly neighbor of Redwing, Charles "Slick" Wilson, contended that Redwing approached Wilson after the trial and offered a large sum of money to rid him of Francis once and for all. Instead, Wilson told Francis, and from then on, Francis referred to Ed as "Go Shoot."

Wilson had once been a Diamond R wagonmaster, along with Simon Pepin and a former cattle ranching partner of Will Broadwater, the first mayor of Havre and manager of the Broadwater-Pepin-Broadwater trading post at Browning on the Blackfeet Reservation. Broadwater had had a ranch by Pacific junction just previous to his return to the family home at Memphis, Missouri.

Francis felt cheated that Redwing didn't go to prison, and Redwing felt frustration because Francis was still alive to go on tormenting him. Francis continued the "campaign" by writing letters to the Redwing and Ryan families through 1915.

In one addressed to Delia Ryan, Hilda's mother, he said: "Go Shoot" was a cattle thief and Hilda had married him for money; and furthermore, Redwing had to pay his neighbor to leave the country. He asked her: "Would you accept me as your son-in-law if I could get your present one up in the pen for a few years?"

The following month, Hilda Redwing received a rambling letter addressed to "Madam Go Shoot." Francis wrote of their former relationship and breakup ten years ago and how they hadn't gotten along since. (Even though several untrue rumors had been circulated that they were having an affair.) He indicated that Ed was guilty of stealing cattle and that Hilda had lied on the witness stand (in the Conrad Circle C case) to protect him from a prison sentence. He further asserted that her husband was a coward and picked on young boys.[37] He bragged of beating Redwing and making him run, expressed the desire to be friends again, and wanted her to stop telling lies about him, claiming that she kept telling everyone he was still stuck on her and wrote her letters. His bad reputation, he claimed, resulted from his earlier association with Redwing, also that a certain individual was running a butcher shop, using stolen stock and blaming Francis as a cover.[38] Lastly he suggested that she had even made eyes at him in the courtroom.

Hilda wrote a reply, although it's not clear whether she mailed it or not, according to daughter Rose (who has since died). She began by thanking George for his "gracious letter." She mentioned that, since they had said good-bye ten years ago at Barney Casey's dance, Francis had been telling lies about her and Ed, accusing her of having had a sexual relationship with Ed before they were married, which she denied vehemently. She also denied either spreading untrue stories about him or making eyes at him during Ed's trial.

She disavowed that they had stolen any cattle or that Ed had paid Hundley to leave the country. Taking the offensive, Hilda reminded Francis that he had sent them word of his having shot two of their saddle horses and used them for coyote bait and that he and his partners had stolen horses in Idaho and sold them in Sheridan, Wyoming. Moreover, that Ed had gotten him out of trouble when Francis had stolen a horse from the Sprinkles and shot a colt belonging to Diamond Bar ranch owner, Walter Brown. And lastly, that they had found several of their cattle at his Milk River ranch with altered brands.

She concluded, "I never flirted with anyone when I was a girl nor would I now. I got mad when you made silly gestures at me when going from the courtroom to the hotel. A woman is entitled to the last word. I don't think it will be necessary for me to write to you again. Send no more letters and I don't know why you are so mean—I never gave you any reason for doing it."

Ed Redwing also received a letter during the trial. It was posted from Great Falls, supposedly from a J. W. Peacock of Raymond, Alberta. The letter's writer expressed that he knew Redwing was innocent and was being framed. The writer further advised him to get a good attorney and that (defense) witnesses were available for hire, etc.

Delia Ryan received a second letter, this time from "Hugh B. Fallguy, Secretary of the Havre Gang." It glowingly expressed how wonderful Ed Redwing was, how he deserved the hearty approval of the public.

These antics hardly erased or soothed George's hate for Redwing, but maybe it did finally put to rest the vain hope he had carried regarding Hilda over the years even though he exhibited more hate than love towards her. Perhaps now he could allow himself to enter another serious relationship.

Yet, for years, those who had known them best speculated on what a fine couple they would have made, what a fine ranch they would have had, and how grand they would have looked riding together across the range. And no doubt it would have influenced Francis's decisions about which fork in the road he would have taken and saved him much grief.

But, in the interim, he still had much to do, which included finding a new love and acquiring a business partner.

The Pardner

THERE WERE CERTAINLY CONTRASTING ATTITUDES about George Francis. He was shy, he was arrogant; he was friendly, he was standoffish; he was an intellectual, he was simple-minded; he loved horses, he killed rustled horses when the law got too close or for revenge; he was a good man and a respectable rancher; he was king of the rustlers and public enemy number one.

Among his friends, however, there was one rule that had only one interpretation: the frontier code of loyalty dictating that neither was a friend ever betrayed nor a promise broken, even when it was to a person's best advantage, and once a favor was done it was never forgotten. If the above was to be revoked, then the "rattlesnake code" of warning before striking was invoked. Some of the major quarrels in the West were between men who had been friends/partners. It's true he had many friends among the cowboys, ranchers, and townspeople, plus some settlers. But perhaps the friend who most significantly changed the course of his life was Jack Mabee.

John C. "Jack" Mabee, Jr., was, in some ways, the antithesis of Francis: he was handsome, very sociable, outgoing, and well proportioned at 6 feet 1 inches, 190 pounds. If not on the range, he could be found in saloons and fraternal clubs such as the Eagles, Elks, and Moose, enjoying drinks with friends and playing high-stakes poker. His major flaw was his quick temper and his propensity to fight. Pound for pound, he was probably as tough as they came, too.

Mabee was originally from western Oklahoma, then called the Indian Territory. He made his entrance into the Milk River Country when he bought the Gildford (Montana) Buffet from Ed Pearl and then sheriff of Hill County, "Hank" Loranger. Pearl also owned the Gold Bug Saloon in Havre. The newly named "John C. Mabee Saloon, Wine, Liquors and Cigars" was located on the southeast corner of a main intersection; the street on the north paralleled the east-west railroad tracks. Directly north across the tracks was the train depot, and next door to his business was the Farmers State Bank. The street to the immediate west was the main business thoroughfare, connecting the Hi-Line wagon road north to the Canadian line. The newcomer probably first met George Francis in Gildford, either at his saloon or while Francis was driving horses or cattle through town. Since Francis knew most of the locals, they probably developed mutual friends, too.

The town of Gildford, in the "Big Sage Country," was originally the Dayton Railroad siding, which developed as a trading point for ranchers and cowboys. At the Sage Creek crossing, the Schwartz family operated a general store and post office. The pioneer ranchers included Byron and Henry Schwartz, H. C. Sprague, M. T. "Slim" Sprague, Clinton and Howard Sailor, Henry Brough, and the MacKenzies. Here problem-plagued cowboy Bert Davey, some twenty years previous, had walked to the depot minus his clothes and horse.

As the homesteaders began arriving in numbers in 1910, the community was moved about 1 mile east along the creek. Soon the fledgling town contained 300 people and thirteen businesses, including a newspaper, two banks, seven lumberyards, a school, a grain elevator, an Episcopal church, and Mundy's flour mill—the first in Hill County.

Before coming to Gildford, Mabee had worked for the Conrad Brothers cattle ranch on the Marias River with range located between Fort Benton on the south and Chester on the north. Loranger had operated a hotel-bar in Chester before moving to Havre, and perhaps this was how Mabee learned of the impending sale of the Gildford bar. Previously, the Oklahoma cowboy worked at the McNamara and Marlow ranch near Big Sandy, but reportedly he couldn't get along with the foreman.

Mabee came by his cowboy ways honestly. His parents, John, Sr., and Emma (Williams) from St. Louis, had owned a cattle ranch near Sweetwater, Texas. Sweetwater, the Nolan County seat, stands on the old Western or Dodge City trails where lanky and wild Longhorn cattle were driven north through the Indian Territory to Kansas and beyond to Nebraska, Wyoming, and Montana.

Bad times occurred during "The Big Die-ups" of 1886-87, when the combination of overcrowded ranges, long, dry summers, and severe winters resulted in the death of millions of cattle (and sheep) throughout the western prairies.[39] The magpies, buzzards, coyotes, and wolves had never had such a feast since the wanton slaughter of the buffalo.

The Mabee family suffered, too, and moved to the probably greener pastures of Greer County, which was then part of Texas and still on the main northern cattle trails. Its county seat of Magnum was established in 1881 by a number of ex-Confederate soldiers given the land by the state of Texas. In 1896 the U.S. Supreme Court ruled that the lower main stream of the Red River was the Texas-Oklahoma border, and Greer County became part of Oklahoma. So while Jack always liked to say he was born in the Indian Territory, he was really just a Texan in disguise!

At first operating from a combination dugout and shack, Jack and Emma, with two-year-old son Roy, began a new ranch with their few remaining animals. With a creek flowing through their new land, crops could also be raised and they could swim in the hot summer months.

Adjacent to them was the Indian Territory, consisting of the Five Civilized Nations plus Cheyenne, Arapaho, Commanche, Kiowa, and Apache lands, so it wasn't unusual for the Mabee family to have Native American visitors. Once a small group walked in and inspected Emma's kitchen, opening her woodstove to see what was cooking . . . and then left without incident.

The family grew with the births of Jack in 1888 and George in 1891.

Sometime in this period of expansion a new house was built. When Emma was pregnant with Jack, it was arranged that she would be taken to a neighbor who was a midwife for help with the birth. Jack put her on a mattress in the wagon with the onset of labor pains. Birth was imminent when they arrived at the woman's house, and the unnerved Jack hurried the midwife and her husband back to the wagon, where they lowered the mattress to the ground. There Jack, Jr., was born, receiving against his mother's wishes the nickname of "Prairie-dog John"; hence Jack always said that he was a man born not only of the prairie, but on the prairie too.

Misfortune again crossed the Mabee family's path during the winter of 1895. John, Sr., contracted pneumonia and died from a damaged heart, leaving Emma with a ranch to handle and three boys to raise: ages four, six, and eight. So the sons became cowhands at an early age. The labor was made a bit easier, though, as they also availed themselves of the creek for skinny-dipping. Ray and Jack hung their clothes on a tree limb, but young George seemed either to have memory problems about where he left his clothes, or his brothers hid them, and often he returned home nude.

Emma did remarry, but it was a brief and unhappy union. In 1898, she married James Brown, a schoolteacher and later Greer County clerk. To this joining was born Fred, Frank, and Florence. Later James and Emma entered the mortgage abstract business with a partner named Blalock.

Roy, the eldest Mabee boy, bought some land from Brown and grew dryland crops that possibly included wheat, pecans, potatoes, and soybeans. He had to haul water from a distant spring for the stock animals and household use. Jack wasn't interested in farming life, leaving in his teens to work on a cattle ranch in an unknown part of the Southwest and later going to Wyoming on a cattle drive. Along the way he is believed to have viewed Wild West shows and participated in fair contests and rodeos. He then reportedly worked on a ranch near Miles City, Montana, before he eventually ended up in Great Falls, 330 miles to the northwest. Many herds came through Miles City to northern Montana; consequently he was only following the flow westward to the last of the open range and free grasslands.

The Mabee-Brown families believed the young cowboy owned a cattle ranch (won in a card game?) and wholesale meat business near the Electric City. He did work for such a Great Falls enterprise, since he was visited there by family members, perhaps when the twenty-year-old Mabee married a small, attractive woman, twenty-two-year-old Clara Coit, in 1908. The wedding, performed by the Reverend E. P. Giboney and witnessed by Clara's sister Edith, was held at the Frank and Madge Coit family home at 411 5th Avenue South. Mr. Coit worked at the Anaconda Copper Company smelter and later for the G.N.R. as a brakeman and conductor.

Jack apparently worked briefly for the railroad out of Great Falls, but didn't like the hard work any more than farming. The bar he and Clara later bought in Gildford brought them more ease, except this didn't completely satisfy his ambition either, and he sold it to rival saloon owner J. B. Moore. Moving on to the bigger boom town of Havre, they lived in veritable luxury at the Havre Hotel. Jack co-leased the notorious rustlers' ranch on Big Sandy Creek, 6 miles west of town. His partner was Frank "Ikkie" Keple, a business associate of C. W. "Shorty" Young.

Besides helping breed horses at the Francis Milk River ranch and buying animals for the Sandy Creek ranch, Mabee sometimes bartended at the

Havre Hotel bar. Later he may have also been in the automobile business with former sheriff Hank Loranger, selling Hudsons and Essexes.

He enjoyed participating in the "snipe hunting and badger-fighting season," when not working. Those initiates into the sports were usually eastern dudes, traveling salesmen, or newly arrived businessmen who had registered at the Havre Hotel. Hotel manager E. C. Carruth usually steered them into one of the events. The only prerequisite was an ignorance of the games and the wherewithal to buy drinks afterwards for the participants and audience.

In one such badger-fighting contest held at the Buffalo Saloon, recently arrived attorney Ben Hur Moore was the honored referee for the bout between Pete Barrett's ferocious canine, which was "just meaner than hell," and Jack Mabee's powerfully jawed badger with slashing claws, giving it the reputation as a savage fighter. A neutral party had to be used, it was explained, because the rest of the crowd had bets on the animals. In the pre-fight rhetoric, Mabee's camp said that Barrett's dog couldn't lick his own feet, while Barrett's backers responded that Mabee's badger had lost its dentures.

The barroom floor was cleared for the fight with the crowd situated in elevated positions on chairs, table tops, or even a grandstand of sorts. The badger's barrel was on one side of the room with a burlap bag fastened over the front to give the nocturnal animal privacy and darkness. Trailing from the barrel was a rope attached to the badger's neck. When pulled, the knot was supposed to release once the animal was free of the barrel . . . if it was tied properly. Moore was to perform this feat from the relative security of the bar top.

The crowd became tense and hushed with Barrett and his dog in the ready position; the moment of truth had arrived. Phil Clack witnessed it and handed the tale down to his grandson, David. Here is that description:

> Ben, the man of the hour, was kneeling on the bar top, cigar firmly clamped in his teeth, the rope in hand ready for the big moment. He gave a tentative tug on the rope, but met some resistance. There seemed to be a little movement, and someone thought they heard a growl. Ben got a better grip on the rope and this time gave it a good jerk. Out popped—not a badger—but a very heavy and ornate chamber pot! It was noted by one reporter that the cigar Ben had in his mouth fell to the floor, bitten in two.

The thunderstruck and no doubt red-faced Moore had received his initiation into the proper social circles of Havre; once he bought drinks for all, that is. At the moment, the "dignity" of the ceremony was probably lost in the hearty laughter and knee-slapping that the crowd had been holding back. What Clack failed to mention was, usually the pot contained beer, sausages, and toilet paper. The same trick was played over and over again with the victims becoming the eager tricksters.

Some gullible pilgrims also received invitations to go on snipe hunts. The newcomer was told how wonderfully delicious the bird tasted and how hard the wild fowl was to catch. That night the entertainment committee took the unsuspecting hunter a good distance from town, usually to an insect-infested swamp tract. He was given a brief description—probably not coinciding with that of the true sandpiper-like bird—a lantern, and a gunny sack. "Just squat down and hold the bag open," they told him, "the light will attract them. We'll move your horse off so the snipes won't be scared off." Eventually the victim realized there were no birds and, to his dismay, found his supposed co-hunters had vanished with his horse. The next morning one conspirator came back with his horse, and he returned bravely to town for his round of ridicule and salve to soothe all the bug bites, while they explained that in reality snipes were neither a delicacy nor native to Montana.

Being a woman, Antoinette Marie (Massoz) Dumont missed all this fun, but she would soon gain more positive recognition for her riding skills. She became a close friend and neighbor of George Francis. At 5 feet 4 inches, 135 pounds, the brown-haired and blue-eyed girl of European heritage showed she was as tough as the next guy, only better to look at.

Her parents migrated from Belgium and lived at Holland, Manitoba, Canada, where she was born on August 18, 1894, about the same year Francis came to northern Montana. When she was five, the Massoz family moved to a farm at Langdon, North Dakota, sharing a partnership in a restaurant. When times got tough and crops failed, they returned to Belgium, where Marie received her introduction to the French language and customs. They returned to Canada just after her older sister died in the province of Manitoba and settled near the new farming community of de Bellevue, Saskatchewan.

With her older brother working on the railroad, Marie had to help her father plow and plant crops. Since childhood, she had displayed an affinity for handling, riding, and training horses. Her father, Joseph, was proud of Marie's ability and called her "his right hand man." She had a black pony and helped ride herd on the cattle. The abiding love she developed for animals and the great outdoors, coupled with early responsibilities and an independent spirit, would be a major influence on her future.

Bravery was another necessary trait she developed at a tender age. Each day was a new adventure, riding 8 miles each way to school through wilderness. Because it was necessary to leave quite early in the morning, her father provided escort the first few miles and used the trip back for hunting of the plentiful game.

Among the wildlife seen daily were packs of coyotes. She carried a club her father had fashioned to keep them at a respectable distance. But one rather large "coyote" was undaunted and kept a close, regular vigil despite constant shouting and club-waving motions. Marie later recalled: "I wanted to be brave, but my head grew cold when the coyotes followed me." Making the situation even worse, the family didn't believe any coyote could be as large as Marie described. The matter was settled one Sunday afternoon when the predator followed the family wagon from church, while Joseph was out tracking the very same animal on another trail. No one doubted her again. A few days later, Mr. Massoz cornered and killed the animal in its den. The "coyote" was a good-sized wolf! From then on, her father insisted Marie carry an old muzzle-loading shotgun to school; she was quite proud to be the only student carrying a firearm.

In her spare time, Marie shared a twenty-five-unit trapline with her dad; in addition she had traps of her own in the surrounding woods. They collected 25 cents for a muskrat skin and from 50 cents to a dollar for a badger skin. Barely a teenager, she had already accomplished more and experienced more adventure than many adults.

After three years at de Bellevue, the family moved on to the small railroad community of Duck Lake, where Mr. Massoz operated a livery barn. Marie, of course, spent the weekends in the thick of the activities. She developed a new interest in watching brothers Alex and George halterbreaking horses. Mainly Marie rode already gentled horses, but soon she became interested in the challenge of riding the unbroken ones and even managed to stay on sometimes. She did team-break horses, besides helping brother Alex in the plowing of the fields at their farm, and helped mother

Marie in the more traditionally feminine task of running the boarding house. Father had a fierce pride in his daughter's skills with animals, although mother worried she would be a tomboy for life since she could see the boys were uneasy with Marie's strongly competitive spirit.

It was no surprise to anyone when she helped brothers John and Bernard drive a herd of cattle north 100 miles to market at Prince Albert. At night each took a two-hour run guarding the cattle. A near tragedy occurred when an old bull charged and knocked Bernard off his horse, and John had to dispatch the beast with an axe. From then on Marie had a healthier respect for the handling of cattle.

Last, and perhaps most important, she rounded out her education by helping to train race horses for Duck Lake's annual fair. Marie had by then sampled most of the aspects of handling horses and cattle.

Once school was completed at Duck Lake, she began nurses training at St. Paul's Hospital in Saskatoon, but she returned after one year. Perhaps her mother felt more satisfied that one last try had been made at erasing the tomboy in her.

About this time, the Massoz family decided to move to "Hill's paradise" in Montana, near Burnham, west of Havre. Marie stayed in Canada and married a neighbor boy, Joseph Dumont, whom she had only known for a short time. He spoke to her of many dreams that never reached fulfillment. The young couple lived for three years in a small shack with very little food or money. During this time, Marie gave birth to three children, the youngest of which died at three months of age. It isn't clear what her husband did for a living—perhaps he farmed—but Marie had to work part-time to help support the family. Finally it was decided, probably at her insistence, to follow her parents to the Havre area as their personal struggles worsened.

So, in August of 1914, with their two children, Lucien and Lucy, they left Wakaw, Saskatchewan. Marie, needless to say, was very happy to be reunited with her parents, brother Alex, and sister Bertha. They established a homestead and built a log house on it about 1 mile east and across the river from the Francis place. Her parents' farm was between the two, but on the north side of the river. Joe went to work in a coal mine with her dad and brother, and Marie cooked for the miners. Soon Joe decided to seek work elsewhere and found employment on a ranch near Cascade, between Great Falls and Helena. Marie's parents also left to work on a ranch near Great Falls where their son was foreman.

Consequently the again-pregnant Marie faced the winter alone with two children, working hard and surviving on the few chickens, geese, and turkeys they had brought from Canada. Times were tough enough for Marie: She couldn't afford getting sick, too. Her mother then returned and stayed for five months until Andrew "Buster" was born on July 4, 1915, and then left for Havre to nurse daughter Bertha back to health. Marie telegraphed Joe to come home and take care of his family. Joe returned briefly, but then decided to return to Canada permanently. She wasn't left alone long because mom and dad returned to their farm in the fall.

The following year Marie began working at either a restaurant or hotel in Havre. Her parents took care of the children. She only saw the kids on the weekend, but she took the summers off to farm and garden and spend time with them. Perhaps as either therapy or curiosity, Marie bought a saddle horse, spending as much time as she could learning the lay of the land of the Milk River Country. It wasn't long before she discovered George's ranch, watching him, Andy Avery, "Black Bill," Ray Ellis, Clayton Jolley, Jack Mabee, Jim Massey, Shorty Selby, Ed Timmons, et al., breaking wild horses to use for saddle and team animals. She quickly developed a comradeship with them and soon was riding bucking broncos with their encouragement and assistance.

Ray Ellis was probably the most experienced race horseman and early championship rodeo performer among the group, although Jim Massey had won the bareback bronc-riding championship at the 1912 Calgary (Alberta) Stampede. Ellis hailed from Amarillo, Texas, and was born there in 1889. The 5 feet 8 inches light-brown-haired and blue-eyed cowboy grew up on a Texas cattle ranch and moved with his parents to a farm near Provost, Alberta, in about 1907. Until arriving in Havre about 1912, he competed in rodeos and fair-riding contests throughout the American and Canadian West, winning his share of awards. Reportedly he introduced the local cowboys to bulldogging, otherwise known as steer wrestling. On the social front, he married Nell Hauser, daughter of Havre barber, Reuben Hauser. After a short stay in Canada near his parents' home, they returned to Havre when his mother died and abandoned their yet undeveloped homestead. Ray continued to work for the Francis ranch, and Nell and Emma (Mrs. Jack) Mabee cooked for the boys at the old Francis ranch house while they rounded up and broke horses. Later the couple served as caretakers for the ranch owned by Shorty and Lillian Young until the Youngs' divorce and its subsequent sale.

Of Francis's close friends ever-smiling Clayton Jolley lived the longest, dying in 1969 at eighty-one. The tall, wiry, sandy-haired cowhand came to Montana in about 1910, homesteading northwest of Gildford near Sage Creek. He lived in Seattle, Washington, and worked on farms on the outskirts of town and the railroad before coming to the Big Sky Country.

Jolley spent three years working for the large Wallace cattle ranch of Saskatchewan and western Alberta, whose brand was a big cowboy hat. He competed in many rodeos and county fairs in the bucking horse contests and later as a rodeo clown and trick charioteer. One unconfirmed story circulated the range that he had once been a clown with the Ringling Brothers Circus. In western Canada, he gained fame for riding two infamous outlaw horses: "Elkwater" and "Barrelhead." It is believed he competed in the 1912 Calgary Stampede along with Jim Massey. Once settled in the Milk River Country, he managed Joe Moore's Gildford saloon when the owner moved to Havre, promoted rodeos, and in later years worked as a desk clerk at the Grand Hotel on Havre's west First Street.

An acquaintance and probable visitor to the Francis ranch was the distinctive-looking Howard "Humpie" or "Humpback" Kidman. Kidman was tall, wiry, and stooped with a prominent hump on his back. His clean-shaven, weather-beaten, and hawk-like face sprouted a big Roman nose. He dressed in old work clothes, and he wore a small Stetson hat. He rode what was described as a splendid black stallion, possibly called "Grey Eagle," wearing his V-D brand. It was named for a bird and obviously not its color.

Kidman came from Beadle County, South Dakota. It was rumored he was once a school teacher, but as with so many others, in truth he was just an uneducated farm boy. He had a 320-acre homestead north of Rudyard, which was about 26 miles northwest of the Francis ranch.

Another colorful and false tale circulated as to how he came to have the humped back: that he was caught in bed with another settler's wife, and the irate husband grabbed a large object such as a skillet or a smoked ham shank and struck him on the back. Nor was it a war wound as some wondered, but most likely a birth defect. He was drafted in World War 1, completing basic training at Fort Lewis, Washington, and tending horses until discharged because of the "physical handicap."

Kidman's notoriety stemmed from having been the reputed one working horse thief of the area, although he did have one young cowboy help him. It was said he was not a good rider, and yet he could rope, throw, and

104

brand any horse. He worked mainly at night, branding any and all animals he found with a converted cinch ring. Many of the better animals were sold to buyers out of state, and the poorer ones sold to the canning factory. Kidman owned as many as 1,200 horses at one time, it was said, yet he had little to show for it. Perhaps he sent money home. There were other horse thieves who found it easier to steal from Kidman because of the size of his herds. Besides, how could he complain?

The phantom thief ate little while working; he survived on dried apricots and prunes, but he would catch up with the hunger at the Thackerays' Milk River ranch or the Clydes' Beaver Creek Valley ranch, among others. Like Francis, he loved sweets and could devour one of Mrs. Clyde's pies at one sitting. "The cutting spoils the pie," he always said. Kidman spent his leisure hours at the Will Thackeray ranch. There he had his own place to lay his head and smoke his pipe.

Even though a known horse thief, he was generally well-liked and welcome at certain ranchers' homes, as long as he was "on the square" with them. He was quiet, close-mouthed, avoided trouble, and generally stayed out of the saloons. He was believed to have been proficient with his revolver if he did encounter problems. However, he didn't always escape trouble: Once he was found unconscious after being struck with a fence post. Perhaps this was someone's "subtle" way of telling him to leave his horses (or wife) alone. Another time Will Thackeray went looking for his absent visitor, finding him lying ill on his shack floor covered with only newspapers. Thackeray put him on a horse and brought him back home for care. He probably saved his life. In another serious situation, Kidman's horse became very ill, and the lone cowboy had to shoot off the lock of the Rudyard general store in the middle of the night to obtain carbolic salve for an infected wound. A man came to investigate, and Kidman asked him to guard the store until morning and said that he would pay for the medicine and damage later.

Kidman, per the local rumor mill, joined with Francis as supposedly being the "only" major livestock thieves in the Milk River Country. This tickled pink the dozens of other resident rustlers.

Nevertheless, Francis was soon to gain a more positive image as a rodeo star and promoter. The coming of the drylanders brought good as well as bad results for a few like Francis: While they took up the last of the green grass, they also liked cowboys dressed in fancy outfits and ten gallon hats performing on wild horses and steers in an arena.

Cowboy contests of skill evolved naturally from the day-to-day cowhand duties. During the spring and fall roundups when all the area ranches got together, it was characteristic for the cowboys to argue about who was the best rider, the fastest roper, or who could stay on a certain good bucking horse the longest. Inevitably riding and roping contests were held at the end of roundups and bets placed on their favorites. These Sunday afternoon contests on the range were eventually moved to town and formalized as county fair contests or rodeos, a word adapted from the Spanish *rodear*— meaning the roundup of cattle.

The forerunners of rodeos were the Wild West shows of Buffalo Bill and Pawnee Bill and the Miller Brothers 101 Ranch show. They featured perhaps 250 riders—black, Indian, Mexican, and white—who were salaried like circus performers, doing feats of riding, shooting, re-enacting stagecoach robberies, Indian-Army battles, etc., representing life as it was on the plains.

Soon the more organized exhibitions and professional contests of skill followed, beginning as early as 1846 in Santa Fe, New Mexico Territory, and 1869 at Deer Trail, Colorado Territory. These contests blossomed in the 1880s with the first commercial rodeo held at Prescott, Arizona Territory, in 1888. Others followed at Albuquerque, New Mexico; Miles City and Wibaux, Montana; and Dublin, Fort Worth, Pecos, and San Angelo, Texas, until it was rare that any western town or county seat didn't have rodeos on the Fourth of July or at the annual fair.

The Cheyenne Frontier Days rodeo in 1897 brought the first big money prizes, totaling $4,000 with the 1912 Calgary Stampede rodeo hitting the $20,000 mark.

In the Milk River Country, racing horses and foot races were the first local competitions during the Fourth of July picnics and other gatherings. The earliest rudimentary race track may have been laid out on the John "Bear Paw" Griffin homestead. A former Diamond R freighter and P-Cross cowhand, Diamond Bar rancher Griffin was reputedly the first settler on the Clear Creek drainage of the Bear's Paw Mountains. He was said to have owned some of the finest racehorses in the Territory, like "Sorrel Stallion" and "Blair Athill," and trotting horses, such as "Victor Ennis." Merritt Flannagan of Ada, and George Herron of the Fort Assinniboine civilian settlement and later Havre, were also foremost race horse breeders.

Havre's unofficial race course extended from Tenth Street on Third Avenue to Auld's Livery Barn on Second Street. When held on the Fourth of July, the day's events were concluded with a fireworks display. Some of these programs were participated in by Fort Assinniboine personnel—featuring not only horse, pony, and harness races, but baseball games, military band concerts, a parade, and even automobile races.

A city race track came into being about 1909 and was located about 1 mile west of town; it was organized under the auspices of the Havre Racing and Fair Association, and presided over by J. C. Bailey and J. S. Carnel.

Newly founded Hill County formed its own fair and racing association in 1912. The group acquired forty acres from one of the town fathers, Joe Demars. The land was situated on the east end of town just south of the railroad tracks and the main east-west road. With James J. Hill's $1,500 contribution, the fair association hired Frank Reichel as foreman and a crew to build a grandstand and exhibition buildings, plus the laying out of the racetrack. A sign inscribed "J. J. Hill County Fair" stood over the entrance gate.

The first three-day fair in October of 1912 commenced with a speech by Louis W. Hill, son of James J. and newly made chairman of the railroad's board of directors. He was introduced by local Episcopal minister, Louis J. Christler, who was dubbed "Bishop of all Outdoors" and proclaimed to be a nationally known "golden-tongued orator."

Christler started his Havre-area ministry in 1907, arriving from Auburn, New York, where he was a curate for seven years. He was sent here as a missionary to cover an area extending north to the Canadian line, south to the Missouri River, west to Glacier Park, and east to the North Dakota border. He was a large, tall, and very handsome and well-proportioned man. He had a thick mane of black hair that tossed frequently from the many body motions he made while preaching or lecturing to overflowing crowds at the various meeting halls, civic centers, and fraternal lodges. He could keep an audience spellbound (in the days of no microphone) with his talks on the merits of Montana patriotism, succeeding in life, etc. As one rider put it, "Few men have become so thoroughly identified with Montana." It was an impressive way to begin the fair.

Along with the display of prize-winning vegetables, grains, flowers, plants, and livestock, there were two daily biplane exhibition flights by Montana aviator T. T. Moroney, five horse races, and one harness race every afternoon. In addition there were motorcycle races, open-air athletic events, and Indian and cowboy horse races. A total of $41,000 in prizes was awarded for all the fair events and exhibits, mainly provided by the G.N.R.

An added attraction was an exhibition of cowboy skills. George Francis won the steer roping contest with a time of one minute, forty-five seconds. Jack Moody was second at two minutes, thirty seconds. No results were given for the bucking horse contests or other events. These times weren't bad in comparison to Tom Horn's[40] championship time of 49.5 set at the Territorial Fair at Phoenix, Arizona, in 1891, or the earlier record of one minute, 17 seconds set by a Mexican vaquero in 1864.

These rather crude rodeo shows were difficult to stage without the use of chutes, corrals, or fences. Wild horses and steers had to be contained before, during, and after the saddle and bareback wild bronc riding, bull-riding, and calf- and steer-roping events. The wild horses were blindfolded and "snubbed"—tied to a tame horse until ridden. There was no time limit on the bulls and horse-riding events, and the judges fired a pistol when satisfied or the animal became riderless.

The September 1913 fair was an even more elaborate affair. Barnstormer Moroney returned with his biplane, and the ever-popular harness and horse races were held again. One new addition was a ferris wheel, on loan from the mile-high copper city of Butte's Columbia Gardens Amusement Park. Another was the debut of the Great Falls band in concert. And the cowboy contests were now officially called "The Wild West Show," under the management of "Long George" Francis.

The second fair paid tribute to its guest of honor, James J. Hill. Added to the fair entrance placard was his portrait and the words, "Empire Builder." Christler again acted as master of ceremonies to introduce the senior Hill and his family.

At the podium Hill reminisced about his first trip to Montana and how he had selected Bull Hook (as western divisional headquarters) because of its excellent water. The rest of his speech was devoted to describing the development of the new farming era. He said that at seventy-five he was happy to see Montana take its place as an agricultural state.[41] He concluded his talk saying: "Be good neighbors, work for each other and you will always have an old man who will wish you Godspeed!"

The local papers' description of the fair included copies of Christler's and Hill's speeches, a description of the farm exhibits, and praises for the band of cowboys under "Long George" Francis "for keeping the crowds thrilled every minute during the bucking and riding contests, showing many stunts never seen before." No contestant winners were listed; however it is known that Francis won the steer-roping contest over Matt Morgan from Stanford, Montana, and an unnamed Canadian rider won the bronc-riding contest.

The 1912 Calgary, Alberta, Stampede added to the prestige of the already existent North American rodeo circuit. Promoted by Guy "Cheyenne" Weadick and backed by George Lane and three other wealthy Alberta ranchers, its $20,000 purse was the largest ever offered. And its popularity certainly didn't hamper the efforts of Francis to develop a major rodeo in Havre.

Francis, along with Jack Mabee and Ray Ellis, put on a rodeo in Gildford in 1913. Probably because of Francis's notoriety and increased celebrity status, a large crowd was attracted from all over the Hi-Line. The G.N.R.'s local passenger train, "the Skiddo," put on extra cars to accommodate the heavier traffic. The Havre infantry unit of the state militia kicked off the show by marching and then firing their weapons as a finale. One member, George W. "Brownie" Brown, remained a lifelong fan of George Francis. His father was a partner in the pioneer Meat Market, and Brownie worked for both the F. A. Buttrey and the H. Earl Clack companies.

Apparently it wasn't customary yet to record local rodeo results, but it is known that Matt Morgan won the bronc-riding contest, and it is believed that Francis won both the steer-roping and bulldogging events. In fact Clint Sailor bet Francis that every horse Francis and Ellis brought could be ridden; then he sent for Morgan, who did ride them all. Another rodeo was held at nearby Hingham, and they went to stage a rodeo west across the Rocky Mountains at Kalispell, providing Mexican Longhorn cattle and bucking horses. At the latter, Mabee is supposed to have won the steer roping while Francis won at bulldogging. Either Francis alone or the same bunch staged a rodeo at Medicine Hat, Alberta, and later at Minot, North Dakota, under the Flying V banner. It was reported that he competed in the Dakota contest and won several prizes.

The increasing prosperity of Hill County and northern Montana and the residents' eagerness for entertainment certainly helped the financial success of the show. The 4,986-square-mile[42] Hill County, with its some 30,000 residents, contained several incorporated cities, forty-one churches, a commercial college in Havre, a high school, 121 grade schools and 144 teachers, a hospital, twelve newspapers, fourteen banks, two breweries, and five manufacturing concerns.

The discovery of three natural gas wells just east of Havre led to the renaming of the "Sunburst City of the New West" as "The Gas City" (and not the spicy food that James "Hot Tamale Jim" Shawlee sold from his lunch wagon). Meanwhile, Great Falls, with its hydroelectric dams on the Missouri River, first became known as "The Power City" and was later renamed the enduring title of "The Electric City." Eventually Havre lost its new moniker, which the present-day restaurant owners probably appreciate. The replacement nickname, "The Hub (Oil) City," never caught on since, like gold, a major strike never materialized.

The city and county were prospering, but the fair wasn't; it had lost money since its inception. Finally the G.N.R. officials took a five-year lease on the site, which temporarily relieved some of the county's financial burden.

In turn, the Great Northern Montana Stampede Association Inc. was formed to succeed and assume the debts of the Hill County Fair Association. If it prospered, the new corporation would receive title to the fairgrounds' property. The agreement stipulated that three-fourths of the profits would go to improve the grounds: double the grandstand capacity, further level the grounds, and install gas fixtures to illuminate the fairgrounds for night shows. The railroad pledged to actively help promote the fair events.

The new Stampede Association's officers were George Francis, president; Jack Mabee, vice president; and F. P. Gable, secretary; and other organizers were Jack Edwards, A. L. Britton, T. E. McCroskey and H. G. Stevens. The directors were J. J. Blair, who was Farmers State Bank president and Chamber of Commerce president; C. W. Young, saloon(s) owner; Sid Hirschberg, theater owner; Bert Gourley, bakery owner; R. X. Lewis, former *Havre Plaindealer* owner; and Frank Keple, rancher-C. W. Young associate. Though not named, E. C. Carruth had to be credited with helping put the deal together. The first rodeo under the new organization was held in 1916.

Francis appeared to be riding near the high point of his life with the budding of his rodeo career. A somewhat unclear newspaper article said of him: "George Francis winning laurels of the West—putting this city on the map in the great Frontier Days, roundups and (rodeo) days being given by some of the western cities in which early life in the country is being reproduced for the movies of the country and the gala day for cities staging these affairs. The city of Walla Walla (Washington) is the most recent to have such a celebration."

The new celebrity was listed as having finished second in the steer-roping contest in the previously mentioned 1915 Walla Walla rodeo. Other rodeos in which he is said to have placed in the money since 1912 included Fort Benton; Pendleton, Oregon; Spokane, Washington; Belle Fourche, South Dakota; and various other towns in the western U.S. and Canada, but apparently none in Idaho and Wyoming. From the Spokane contest it is believed that he won a beaver stetson hat, which he gave to a friend, Mrs. Clyde Roper (Eglantine). They owned a farm north of town and both had Havre businesses.

If Francis had stuck to the rodeo and kept his stock business honest, he would have lived down the whispers that he sometimes rode the wrong trail, as many originally did in those days. However, George just seemed naturally to be drawn to disputes, and he found himself embroiled in one over land along with Mary Martin and Margaret and H. Earl Clack, for which he would pay dearly.

The Land Feuds

THE YEAR 1913 HAD BROUGHT GEORGE FRANCIS mixed blessings: On the up side, he was fast becoming a rising star on the rodeo circuit as both a participant and a promoter, and he had finally established a ranch. On the down side was the vast influx of settlers who were closing off the rangeland and water holes to the rancher's herds.

Perhaps because of H. Earl Clack's agricultural business interests and perhaps because Clack already had large land holdings in the area, either personally or through family members, Francis decided to make him the scapegoat for his intense frustration and sometimes hatred towards the interlopers. And too, there was the grudge Francis carried for the near-fatal beating Clack gave Phil Brader, and lastly there was the dam incident on Beaver Creek about ten years earlier involving his friends, the Herrons. Whatever his main motivation, he was foolish to put himself in unnecessary trouble with someone as powerful as Clack, who was also aligned with the growing reform movement—especially considering his extra-curricular nighttime activities.

During the earlier years of tending livestock, Francis had crossed much of the property owned by the Clack families, which was situated northeast of Fort Assinniboine near Squaw Butte and the Cement Hills, about 2½ miles southwest of Havre. Included in these various properties was a piece of land filed on in 1909 under the Desert Land Act of 1877 by Margaret Clack, wife of H. Earl.

Under their final prove-up application dated October 18, 1913, they claimed the 307.6 acres[43] had been continuously irrigated since 1910, and at least 170 acres were in cereal grains. The water source was partially from the Havre Irrigation Company ditch from Beaver Creek, which provided the water for all the Clacks, Sands, Timmons, and other investors' properties. And part of the water came from dams built on Morris and Sanders coulees with two connecting lateral ditches 3 feet wide, 2 feet deep, and ¼ mile long.

Francis contested their ownership, making the allegation that the claimant had not irrigated the required one-eighth of the property and in fact had wholly failed to irrigate any portion of it. He also claimed that running water only stood in the irrigation ditches for one or two hours a day during the growing season, which wasn't sufficient to overflow and be distributed on the land. A hearing was then held at the Havre branch of the United States Land office, Department of the Interior, on August 19, 1914. It was opened in 1910 because the Great Falls and Glasgow offices were overwhelmed with homestead applications. Unfortunately the impersonal hearing transcript could not convey the color, conflict, and tension the resulting testimonies must have produced.

The first witness for George Francis was H. D. Halverson, a Havre civil engineer. Francis had hired him to examine the irrigation and pumping system and draw a survey map, except Halverson could shed little light on the controversy because the ditches were very dry at the time of his inspection. He said that the land looked capable of being irrigated from what he observed, but couldn't tell from his cursory examination whether these ditches had previously contained water. Lastly he said that good-looking crops were growing on the land.

Future Hill County sheriff Roscoe "Doc" Timmons then testified. The previous year he had been appointed deputy state veterinarian. His family lived on a ranch about ½ mile distant from the Clack clan, and his sister, Cornelia, was married to Phil Clack. His parents' farm was irrigated by the same canal. He attested that he had never seen any water on the land or anyone irrigating it, while visiting his parents. His brother George, on the other hand, said that some of the land had been watered.

Andy Avery of the Havre-Kremlin area was the next witness. At that time he did work for George Francis. Avery said in his testimony that the main irrigation and the coulee dams sometimes contained water, only he never saw water in the ditches on the disputed land.

Others who gave similar testimony were John Buskey, George Aldoes, William Sanno, and A. W. Morrell. Francis gave the concluding testimony.

Francis stated that he was well acquainted with the property in question and had been for several years prior to their 1909 claim, having worked across the property at least three or four times per year since about 1910. He had examined it recently along with Halverson, Avery, Ed Sartain, and one other person whose name he could not recall. He swore that he saw no indications of irrigating water and, furthermore, that some of the ditches on the property didn't even connect to the main ditch or water supply, In fact, he said, some of the property on the south was too far from any water supply to be served by irrigation. And the dam on Morris Coulee was of recent origin; it had not been built at the time the property was first acquired. He based his irrigation expertise on the fact that he was raised on an irrigated farm (in Idaho), making him familiar with this process. He conceded the land was not desert in nature, meaning crops could be raised without water, and at times the coulees contained water that the crops didn't need.

Now the Clacks had their turn. The witnesses were H. Earl's half-brother, Weaver Clack; former employee John W. Reed; Havre photographer P. A. Brainard; H. Earl, himself; civil engineer John F. Daoust; brother-in-law Ray Sands; and Margaret Clack appearing briefly as a rebuttal witness. Written final prove-up depositions came from Margaret Clack, Phil Clack, and farm foreman Stephen Cromwell.

The several testimonies basically said that the dam on Morris Coulee was built in 1910 and did irrigate the land in question from 1911 through 1914. The ditches provided were adequate to do the job, irrigating at least one hundred acres from Morris Coulee, sixty acres from a Havre Irrigation Company pumping station, and twenty-five acres from Sanders Coulee. Extensive testimony was given and a survey map presented as to how much water was available, the dam's capacity, and the size and power of the pump.

Further evidence was offered as to what farming was accomplished. About 215 acres were cleared of rocks and plowed, and some winter wheat, oats, barley, rye, and flax raised. H. Earl showed photographs to portray their efforts and told how much money was spent.

In rebuttal Halverson, two of the Timmons brothers, Joe Demars, and photographer C. A. Bell presented testimony. Halverson contended the water storage wasn't sufficient to irrigate the land. It was brought out that water was only available in the early spring and the coulees were dry by early summer. Then Timmons and Demars testified it wasn't a good practice to irrigate before the crops were planted. Bell verified the pictures he had taken for Francis that had been presented into evidence. Further testimony from Francis then followed in which he explained the pictures and the condition of the ditches shown, plus further unrecorded testimony to back up his contentions.

Next it was up to the federal officials to make a decision by studying the transcript. They felt that Halverson had not made a complete inspection of the land, relying too much on information given by Avery and Francis. They further believed that the Timmons brothers had not been around the property enough to make good witnesses. Also the testimony presented by Francis's group, denying the presence of any water in the ditches, was not accepted because of the preponderance of the Clack witnesses' testimony and evidence that water had in fact flowed on the land.

And lastly, they felt George Francis's testimony could not hold up against that of such witnesses as Weaver Clack, who lived near the property and assisted in the development of it, laborer John Reed, and of H. Earl Clack, who had charge of the property for his wife. The officials weren't impressed with Francis's argument that Margaret Clack hadn't owned 761 shares in the Havre Irrigation Company before October 13, 1913, although she appeared to claim that she did—when final proof was submitted with payment of $307.06; therefore, the property was actually owned by her husband.

In conclusion they felt the Francis side had too much of the indefinite and "I don't know" variety of testimony. Such issues as whether crops were raised, how much money was spent on the land, and whether the land was desert or non-desert in character were not at issue. The only legal point to be considered was whether the land had been irrigated or not. This, they ruled, the Clack group's testimony proved. Therefore, Francis's challenge was dismissed.

Actually, compared to the fraud practiced by many western ranchers to acquire public grazing lands, this was a serious attempt at meeting the proof-up requirements of the Desert Land Act. One of the illicit practices of the dishonest was to pour a cup of water on the ground every day to satisfy the irrigation requirements. Again, why Francis and company specifically engaged in this fruitless and unwise battle, whether for old grudges or new, is lost in history.

This wasn't the last land dispute Francis was a party to. The next conflict involved a woman who was determined to hold on to some land that

H. Earl Clack wanted badly. Francis stepped in the middle, and like Don Quixote de la Mancha, he became the errant knight, charging to the rescue of the maiden, Mary Martin. While Clack wasn't disguised as a windmill, he eventually unseated Francis. Though in the end, Quixote decided knighthood-in-flower and its accompanying chivalry were dead, we don't know if Francis likewise came to any such conclusions over his actions. He probably didn't.

This land dispute began in 1916, the same year the Redwings began construction of their new home. Ed had only planned to refloor the old house, but Hilda said she would have none of that since he had bought a new Oakland touring car the previous year. The Redwings were now probably one of the top three independent area ranchers along with Robert Felton and Thomas Connelly. They had also been recently blessed with a third daughter, Margaret Mary, born October 31, 1915, who joined Delia Meryl and Edna Rose.

A crew of carpenters under contractor Charles Harper built the house on the old Y-T ranch land while the family lived in the old Y-T ranch house. Hilda cooked for the whole crew as they built the ten-room, two-story house, with indoor plumbing and battery-operated lights. T. S. Elwell did the masonry work. Once finished, the vacated Y-T ranch house became a school. The previous year the ranch's haystacks and sheds had burned during a larger fire that had burned as far east as the Clear Creek road. The fires were attributed to George Francis, of course.

If Francis did commit arson, it may have been done in frustration at his failure to put Ed Redwing behind bars for cattle rustling, the beating of prosecution witness George Card, and the alleged offer by Redwing to pay "Slick" Wilson to murder Francis. If he was also guilty of setting the fires near the sheep ranches of Sprinkle and Blackwood, he could have been motivated by the summer grazing of sheep on the Chain of Lakes near his ranch where the sheep cropped the grass, leaving nothing for the winter grazing of cattle. Finally the frustrated ranchers and homesteaders began blocking the trails when the sheep approached.

The fires occurred in the early morning on Saturday, October 30, the day before the Redwings' youngest daughter was born. That Friday evening, an all-night dance and supper was being held at the Ada school on the George Ramburg ranch, 17 miles southwest of Chinook on the Clear Creek road. A strong wind was blowing, yet the gathering was in full swing until Ramburg announced that a prairie fire was burning furiously outside.

Apparently one of Blackwood's ranch hands who was just coming to the dance had seen some riders starting the blaze in a big coulee southeast of Ada. The other fire was in the haystacks of the old Y-T ranch near the barn, corrals, and sheds in the overgrown grass and weeds. Also Redwing's haystacks were set afire at the former Kinsella ranch on Sawmill Gulch 12 miles to the south.

A prairie fire was a threat to them all, and the dancing party turned out to fight the fire. Riders on horses dragged cowhides, gunnysacks, and whatever else they could find over the burning range to smother the flames. The fire, however, didn't result in the arsonists' desired effect: The wind turned the flames so instead of going northeast to the sheep ranches, the flames whipped southwest towards Little Box Elder Creek, where cattle ranches were located. Eventually the combined efforts of all the local inhabitants stopped the blazes before any great harm was done.

One of the few amusing incidents of the night occurred when Ole Ehlang stopped for a moment to get his breath. He saw the face of Lawrence "Pat" Patrick, the black servant of the Blackwoods, who had driven the children to the dance. Not realizing who he was and wondering how close to the fire he had gotten, he shouted: "Lord God Almighty, man, and how did you get so black?"

The Redwings had nothing to laugh about, though. They lost over 200 tons of bluejoint hay needed for winter cattle feed. The big barn was saved, but the cattle sheds and bunkhouses burned.

The major consensus was that George Francis was involved in some way in starting the fires, especially at the Redwing places. The devices used to ignite the blazes were wooden boxes about eight inches square with a tin top. On the base were driven three shingle nails that held a small candle upright among them. The bottom was filled with kerosene, so when the candle burned down, it ignited the fuel. Thus the arsonist(s) could have been far away, establishing an alibi. Some that failed to ignite were found at one scene. Francis was certainly capable of devising such a gadget.

Francis was seen in the general fire area early that day by a respected, reliable witness; also a sweaty horse was supposedly found on Beaver Creek by Fort Assinniboine that belonged to an unnamed Francis employee who was said to be a convicted horse thief. He had supposedly lit the devices that Francis had earlier planted, then turned the horse loose and took the train to Fort Benton. Since no one came forward as a witness to these events, neither Francis nor anyone else was prosecuted.

There were two other unlikely versions: one, that two hard-ridden horses carrying Shorty Young's brand were found the next morning at ex-wife Lillian's homestead, located further north and west, with fresh auto tire tracks leading off to town from there. This ranch house was perfect for such a story since it was the reputed cache place for stolen goods. And the other story went that arsonists had been hired to frame Francis because he had been stealing so much livestock. But one could ask: Would anyone risk burning his own ranch down to get even—unless he lived a safe distance? One such man with several motives was mentioned by friends of Francis. He lived several miles to the northwest and knew and sometimes employed two brothers who they felt were capable of such acts. One person who didn't believe Francis had done it was W. C. Blackwood. Although at odds over sheep grazing, they had a respect for each other that rivaled opposing generals in a war.

While Redwing lost the hay and ranch outbuildings, the only other major damage was the further tarnishing of George Francis's reputation, and the following year of 1916 would add even more conflict to his life. But it would add laurels, too.

Trouble began brewing when the remaining unreserved portions of the old military reservation were opened to settlers by lottery. Participating in the drawing was the Martin family, originally from Quebec and then Chicago, who had come to Havre in 1900. Peter and Cecelia lived on a homestead north of the Milk River. He worked as a machinist at the G.N.R. shops. Their older children, Mary, Tom, and William, applied for the lottery-awarded land. Mary was employed at the post office and earlier clerked at Stringfellow's Havre Commercial Company store; she could have met Francis at either one or both.

The land of Mary's choice was situated near several Clack properties, including the one parcel Francis had disputed recently. Mary was successful at the land drawing, winning a 189-acre parcel against eight other contestants. But H. Earl Clack challenged her right to the property. Actually the Clack squatters' claim covered part of another separate unit awarded through the lottery to Hugh Elliot.[44]

In this instance at least Clack and Martin were represented by attorneys: the former by W. B. Sands and L. E. Choquette, and the latter by Eglantine (Mr. Clyde) Roper. All legal papers that had to be served on Clack were said to have been done gleefully by George Francis.

The initial hearing was conducted in Havre on April 25, 1917. It involved many of those who had previously testified in the Clack-Francis land dispute and several more. The proceedings were even more heated. Outside the hearing room the action went beyond words by both sides.

Clack claimed prior right to the property because he had occupied the land first in December of 1911 under the authority of an 1896 law that read: "All lands which have been or may hereafter be excluded from the limits of the Fort Assinniboine Military Reservation in the state of Montana, shall be open to the operations of the law regulating homestead entry." Consequently he moved on to the property after the official abandonment in November of 1911 and placed a shack upon it and dwelled in it per the Homestead Act requirements.

It was described as a one-story, one-room, 16- by 20-foot wood-frame building put up in January of 1912 for $400. In March of 1915 it was replaced with a $1,200 wood-frame bungalow having four rooms. A three-wire fence was placed around the property, shade trees and crops planted, and irrigation ditches dug. A half-mile road was graded to the property and a telephone line brought in. A garage, outhouse, and barn were added, besides a swimming pool, swing set, etc.

As with the prior land dispute hearing, conflicting testimony—although more extreme—came from both sides. The first witness called for Clack was John Doust, a Great Falls civil engineer and surveyor. Doust explained he had been hired by Clack, L. K. Devlin, and E. C. Carruth to survey and locate claims into half-mile squares on the military reservation in December of 1911. He said he returned in 1914 to stake out the H. Earl Clack homestead entry in question.

The next witness was Ed Sartain, former trapper, wolfer, cowhand, and now rancher. Sartain had been on Francis's side during the first land dispute, and he had been on friendly basis with Francis for at least thirteen years. He testified that he personally knew of the existence of a Clack cabin on the property in 1912. In addition, he claimed he had seen the Clack family on the property several times during 1914; furthermore, that it had the appearance of being occupied. Additional testimony came from John Harris, Arthur Sanders, John Reed, and A. H. Schmidt. Harris and Sanders lived near the contested property; Reed worked there and had his own homestead north of Havre; and Schmidt was the caretaker for the fort from 1912 through 1914.

Harris said the house was occupied by someone in 1912 because an automobile was on the premises, fences were built, dikes constructed, and lights were on in the cabin.

Sanders further corroborated Clack's assertion that a cabin was on the property in February of 1912 and that he observed Clack on the land about once a week, although he had never seen any lights on. In 1915 he witnessed the construction of a new house and the family moving in. From then on he noticed the house lights were on.

Reed, from Moose Jaw, Saskatchewan, testified that he resided on the property from 1912 to 1914. He moved a cabin onto the land in 1912, put up the fence, and dug the irrigation ditches. Reed said Clack was in residence there in 1912, and he saw him frequently during that year, 1913, and 1914. In addition, Reed planted a small crop in both 1915 and 1916. He also affirmed that a new house was built in 1915 and the Clacks moved in.

And lastly Schmidt told the hearing board that he tried repeatedly to get Clack to vacate the property because he had been instructed to keep people off the military reservation, but Clack refused, saying he had squatter's rights on the land. Schmidt then wrote for further instruction from the special agent of the General Land Office, Department of the Interior, and received a reply to leave Clack alone. After telling him of this, Clack then put up a house and made improvements to the land. The former caretaker further stated he saw both Clack and his family on the estate several times before the new house was built in 1915.

Mary Martin's witnesses were W. J. Hughson, a Mrs. Ovnard, George Francis, William Olsen, John Wallace, Charles Herron, Thomas McDevitt, John Devine, and Ray Ellis.

Hughson, a cowhand for George Francis, explained that he was in the vicinity of the property from 1912 to 1914. He first saw the cabin on the acreage in 1912, but at no time was there any furniture inside. He indicated that in a year's time the door was falling off its hinges and the floor was collapsing from cattle occupying it; in addition the lower half of the windows were broken. He believed that no one had lived in the shack, nor had he seen anyone around it. Besides the shack being built, the only sign of activity he noticed was some fence building in 1914.

Mrs. Ovnard, a local domestic, had worked at the Clack home in Havre during 1914 and 1915 (320 First Street—"The Stone House"). She held that the family—including H. Earl—lived there all the time, and they had only been gone a few evenings. When she stopped working there, the family was preparing for their first visit to the homestead, according to her testimony.

Next came George Francis. He gave his background as having lived in and around Havre since 1894; he had been familiar with the land in question and had traveled on it once or twice a month since 1912, and he had known H. Earl for 15 years or more. He first noticed the shack in 1912 while looking for cattle during the spring roundup. Though not going inside, he had observed there were broken windows and it looked unoccupied. The same was true throughout 1913, except the door hung open and it looked empty. He went inside the shack in 1914 and found it empty and the floor broken from the past presence of livestock. He saw an irrigation ditch, with no bridge crossing it to allow an automobile to reach the cabin.

Next to take the stand was another rancher, William Olsen, who lived six miles west of Havre. Olsen grazed cattle in the area of dispute during the years in question, and he had used the shack for summer shade and winter shelter several times. He affirmed that he saw no signs of habitation. P-Cross cowboy John Wallace gave similar testimony, as did rancher Charles Herron, pioneer Havre businessman Thomas McDevitt, and cowboy Ray Ellis.

John Devine, Hill County Clerk and Recorder, testified that H. Earl Clack was a registered voter in precinct No. 18, giving his residence as 320 First Avenue in Havre. He didn't change precincts to embrace the disputed land until September 30, 1916.

Mary Martin's testimony was not recorded because it "covers a period of time not with the issues. . . ." Attorney Eglantine Roper testified briefly to correct an error in an affidavit where "peaceful" was used instead of "physical."

The last witness was Orris Bennett, Special Agent of the General Land Office. His presentation involved inconsistent testimony of H. Earl Clack and John Reed[45] from the files of the previous August 1914 contest between Francis and Margaret Clack. The record showed that Clack gave the Havre address as his residence, not the homestead southwest of Havre. Reed gave his residence as 34 miles northeast of Havre near the Canadian line. He testified that, except for the year 1913, he spent the winters on his own homestead and part of the summers working for Clack. This prior testimony conflicted with their current attestations.

Next came Clack's rebuttal testimony, probably on the following day. The witnesses were E. C. Carruth, a business associate of Clack's Havre lawyer; Mr. Choquette; George Bourne, a principal stockholder in the H. Earl Clack Company; Paul Timmons, a young neighbor of the Clacks; Steven Cornwell, a current farmhand; and former laborer, John Reed. What their extensive testimony boiled down to was that Clack did have a frame building on the place, that it was furnished, that the family lived there prior to 1914, and that the vandalism which happened in 1913 and/or 1914 was repaired quickly. Lastly Clack, himself, took the stand. He repeated the assertions that the shack and its furniture were placed on the property in 1912, that the vandalism occurred in 1913, that he had lived in it, etc.

Clack's claim to the property was rejected on October 25. The hearing officers agreed with Mary Martin's contention that no prior settlement was allowable under the Congressional Act of February 11, 1915, or the President's Proclamation of October 2, 1916. Therefore Clack, like all the other entrants, had to make application for the lottery, paying all the necessary fees, which he had not done. Since he had not applied correctly, his request had been rejected by the local office and not placed in the drawing. Whether he had met the homestead law requirements or not was considered irrelevant.

This was far from the end of the legal battle, however. Clack in turn appealed two days later, and the decision was reversed on August 14, 1917, accepting his prior claim under the Homestead Act of 1862 as valid. The litigation of the case continued from the local U.S. Land Office, to the Register and Receiver's Office, to the General Land Office Commissioner's headquarters in Washington, D.C., to the Division H Contest branch, to the Secretary of the Interior, and ultimately to the Supreme Court. Finally in 1929, the homestead was awarded to Mary Martin, who had since married John Lumpkin. Clack and Bourne even tried to bring pressure to bear on the government land officers in 1918 through Montana U.S. Senators Henry Meyers and Thomas Walsh, but their efforts produced nothing.

Several additional reasons were given why Clack's claim was not valid in the final analysis. First, if an exception had been made in his case, then the entire land drawing system was invalid. Second, they said Clack had tried to take advantage of others and circumvent the system. Even his mother had filed upon a piece of adjacent land and won, yet he was unwilling to take the same chance and comply with the same requirements as the other contestants. And lastly, Clack already owned a homestead, and it came to light that he had transferred it to his wife prior to making the present claim.

The transfer to his wife, Margaret, was ruled not in good faith because of a secret deed kept in a box under the bed, yet he had publicly led his creditors to believe he still owned the land.

So, in the end, the testimony of George Francis and his friends really wasn't the deciding factor, although they did take an active role in protecting Mary's interest. Clack thought too much, it appears. He filed a petition on November 1, 1917, in Havre District Court to prevent Martin from occupying the land since a shack had been moved onto the property. He complained he was being threatened by a large group of men (led by Francis) who had broken down his fences (to move the shack in), running autos and horses over the land (in towing the shack) and ruining his crops and hay. Apparently nothing came of his complaint because no legal action resulted.

Of course the situation may have been affected by the fact that Victor Griggs, associate of Shorty Young and friend of George Francis, was county attorney; and since a reform-minded state government led by state Attorney General Sam Ford was trying to close down Havre's red-light district and Clack was a member of the reform movement, Griggs wasn't going to listen to his complaints anyway. Besides, Martin had a legal right at that point to put the shack built by her father on the property.

Clack responded by moving the Martin cabin off the land with his delivery wagon teams, but Bruce Clyde and Ed Roper used their dray teams to move the cabin back. This happened several times.

The battle challenged Mary. She was an early "women's libber" with strong religious and moral values, believing in equal rights and having as much grit as anyone. She continued to work at the post office by day and lived on the homestead at night. Some evenings on coming home, she found beer bottles, cigarette butts, and such garbage; in the wee hours she heard people prowling around outside and possible gunshots or firecrackers fired or thrown from passing cars. She had different family members stay with her, and perhaps members of "the Francis gang" checked on her. She said it was spooky at night when car lights turned onto their property off the county road, since she didn't know whether it was friend or foe.

Clack finally gained temporary title for all but a single north lot in October of 1923. The following year saw Mary joined by her new husband, John Lumpkin, as the battle continued. Lumpkin had been employed by the railroad since 1912 and was at present a locomotive engineer. He came from Arkansas, having spent his youth in Hood River, Oregon. He served in World War I with the Army Engineer Corps of the Fourth Division.

Sometime during this period of turmoil, Mary's original cabin was either burned to the ground or was dismantled completely by "persons unknown." So John and some of his railroad friends built a new one, towed it out there at night, and then hired the Skinner family to be caretakers. The family had a picture taken by Mary of Clack pulling up her rose bushes. Mary also had a confrontation with him in which he slapped her face. John was afraid to take any action against him because he was so powerful.

On the adjoining property was the Weaver Clack family. The Lumpkins thought well of H. Earl's half brother and had no problems with them. One of Weaver's four sons, Louis, and his wife Elinor, now occupy the farm.

In town the Lumpkins lived at 537 Fourth Street, diagonally across from St. Jude Catholic Church. Sometimes on Saturday night, beer and whiskey bottles were thrown on their lawn so the parish members would see them. No further destruction occurred at either place, though.

On the day the U.S. Supreme Court reaffirmed the final decision, giving the property to Mary Martin-Lumpkin, John received word from their caretaker that Clack was destroying everything he had built or added to the property. When Lumpkin arrived, Clack's crew was removing everything: the house, the shrubs and flowers—even the water well casing. He went so far as to dump manure down the well so it would be unusable. John tried to reason with Clack, offering to buy all the improvements on the land, but Clack refused his offer, allegedly threatening him with bodily harm if he didn't leave. Lumpkin gave up and, backing away, returned to town.

Today the Lumpkins' second cabin still remains, and wheat is grown on the flat level ground. Both John and Mary are dead, but the family plans to keep the land after all their parents went through to obtain it. Regrettably George Francis never lived to see the final results of their combined efforts.

George apparently never felt any personal fear from his actions opposing Clack, any more than he did against the sheepmen or Ed Redwing. He even seemed to "favor" Clack and Sands' horses with his brand. He acted as if he were untouchable, and maybe he was, with such allies as Shorty Young and associates.

Perhaps he put this out of his mind, along with any contemplation of future action against or from Clack, as he now geared up for the first Great Northern Montana Stampede of 1916. It was to be the pinnacle of his rodeo career.

The Stampede Rodeos

THE DATE WAS JULY 4, 1916, AND the first four-day Great Northern Montana Stampede rodeo had begun. The rodeo grounds were located on the east end of town, just south of the main east-west Hi-Line Roosevelt Trail. The grandstand was packed with thousands of boisterous people, sweltering in the hot afternoon sun. The dusty grounds in front of them was boarded off into stalls and chutes for the rodeo stock. The entry fees, varying from $5.00 to $20.00 per person, had been paid, and all afternoon and into the evening the 101 men and women contestants made the earth shake as they rode bucking broncs, gave stunt-riding exhibitions, roped buffalo and big steers, wrestled wild Mexican Longhorn steers to the ground, milked wild cows, raced wild horses, and more. All told, there were sixteen prize events and $16,000 in prizes with numerous riding exhibitions. The first big rodeo staged in northern Montana generated interest and enthusiasm comparable to a major present-day sports event.

The star attraction was contestant No. 68, Long George Francis; not only was he a genuine cowboy, but the tall, slender, and fancily dressed rider had all the charisma a showman needed. He had some help from a beautiful big bay horse with a black mane and tail and a white star on his forehead: his trick horse Tony. He was considered to be one of the finest cow-cutting horses ever seen on the western rodeo circuit, and the two of them could give an audience—whether cowboy or pilgrim—the thrill of their lifetime. The cowboy felt something more than the casual observer:

an inner pride to see his profession brought to such a high art. If anything could bring a tear to his eye, besides remembering his mother, this was it.

The applause began as the crowd recognized Francis and Tony at the starting line ready for bulldogging, and it swelled as the steer left its chute and Francis urged Tony after the steer once it had crossed the 30-foot taped starting line. With the hazer riding abreast to the right to keep the long-horned brute from veering off, Francis urged Tony into a rib-to-rib position with the steer. He leaped off and wrapped his right arm over the animal's neck and gripped the base of the right horn (or anything else handy) with his right hand, his left hand grabbed the tip of the left horn, and he threw his weight onto the steer's neck, twisting the head up. His long legs kicked outward to avoid the maddened critter's hooves until the beast was forced to the ground. Francis now lunged forward and downward against his own left elbow, twisting the animal's neck while he dug his heels into the ground as brake, resulting in the steer losing balance and falling onto the ground on his side. When he gripped the steer's lips with his teeth and his hands were up in the air, the timer's watch stopped. When he released his hold, the hazer helped directly or stood by with his rope in case the animal tried to gore Francis when released. This all happened in a maximum allowed time of two minutes.

Francis also demonstrated his winning form in the steer roping contest. A steer was again released from the chute and given a 30-foot start. Tony turned without a touch of the reins, often anticipating the steer's turns and making a shorter cut. On the run, Francis played out six or seven feet of rope, anchored to the saddle horn, swinging it in an oval above his head while twisting his right shoulder backward and forcing his right hand further to the rear. When close enough, he twirled faster and his hand shot forward—swish!—releasing the noose and encircling the steer's horns. He yanked tight while Tony changed directions, obliquely away from the ensnared animal. Twang! went the tightening rope, yanking the steer off its feet and flipping it onto its side by its own momentum to crash solidly onto the arena's hard, dusty ground.

With Tony keeping the rope taut, even if the animal moved, Francis rolled out of the saddle, going down the rope and pulling the short piece of rope off his belt to lash the stunned steer's hind feet and one forefoot together. Francis then stood erect with both arms in the air for his time and then returned to Tony while the rope tying was inspected by the judge.

But wait, the show wasn't over. At Francis's command, Tony trotted up to his master and planted a hoof on the downed steer's ribs, simultaneously shaking his head up and down while Francis bowed stiffly from the waist to the roaring crowd with his ten-gallon hat in hand.

It was said Francis could also duplicate the exhibition feat of Texan Bill "The Dusty Demon" Pickett, who originated bulldogging.[46] In this version, once the rider grabbed the horns and twisted the head, he clamped his teeth on the steer's upper lip and threw his hands up, jerking himself backward. He was dragged along until the animal went down.

Yes, the rodeo brought a lot of excitement to the Havre area; and to make it all possible, Francis, Mabee, and the other Stampede officers and directors received support from both the railroad and the city. James J. Hill gave $1,500 to build the grandstand and exhibition hall beneath. The city merchants raised an additional $3,700. Probably through stock solicitation and a bank loan, the Stampede organization raised another $2,300.

The rodeo's theme was "The West As It Was," and its motto was: "Let 'Em Ramble." Over 10,000 people paid 50 cents a head per day to view the events. The railroad publicized the rodeo, giving reduced rates to those riding the coaches to Havre. When a special passenger train arrived, it was met by all the cowboy and cowgirl rodeo contestants, led by Long George. Local businesses sent out sale circulars with Stampede advertising on the reverse and had giveaway promotions.

The advertisements for the Stampede proclaimed that world champion riders would be coming from all over the western U.S. to participate, including 1912 Calgary Stampede champions Tom Threeperson and Jim Massey. James J. Hill had been originally scheduled to officially open the festivities, but he had passed away at his St. Paul home the previous May.

The official Stampede program boasted that the rodeo was being held in the heart of the last and best of the great West. "Here," it read, "will be assembled upon the week of July Fourth the greatest aggregation of plainsmen ever congregated in the northwest." Perhaps the cowboys scoffed at that, but the pronouncements surely thrilled the homesteaders.

The program prologue went on to say that Havre was a growing and prosperous city of 6,000 with excellent schools, six churches, the most extensive railroad machine shops and roundhouse in the state, three banks, the largest department stores in northern Montana (Buttrey's and Havre Commercial), a fine county seat building, pure city water from the mountains, and abundant, cheap natural gas. It is interesting to note that two of the major advertisements were for Phil Clack's ice business and H. Earl's General Store and five grain elevators.

The Longhorn cattle used in the rodeo were near extinction, having been replaced by meatier, but less sturdy English, Pacific Northwest-raised Shorthorns (Durham strain) and Herefords. However, Francis, at much expense, was able to find some Longhorns in Mexico and had them shipped to his Milk River ranch where they were kept in pens. Once, unknown to Francis or his cowboys, the steers broke loose and drifted northward into his neighbor's vegetable garden. Owner, Stephen "Dutchie" Kiehn, frowned upon this and shot several of the browsing bovines.

When Francis made his weekend trip to the ranch, he was informed immediately of the incident, and in a fury, he rode for Kiehn's homestead. He spotted Kiehn riding his horsedrawn hayraking machine, and Francis came at him from the rear with his pistol cocked and struck him with the barrel on the back of the head, firing simultaneously in the air. Kiehn thought he had been shot as he fell to the ground. Kiehn reportedly begged for his life—possibly promising to pay for the dead animals—while Francis pointed the again-cocked Peacemaker at him, promising to really shoot him if he bothered his stock again. And admittedly Kiehn could have saved much aggravation by telling Francis's men the cattle were in his garden. The cattle could have been retrieved, and no doubt he would have received compensation for the damaged garden.

Later Kiehn took a load of vegetables to town, and celebrated the sale with a drink at a Havre First Street saloon.[47] Pushing his luck, he complained to the barkeep of his rude treatment by George Francis. Unknown to him, Jack Mabee was standing nearby, and Mabee, exploding over the slight to his friend's name, tore into the hapless Kiehn with both fists.[48] Kiehn went flying, and so did his profits—coins spilled every which way from his pockets. The bystanders scrambled for the money, ignoring the fight. Kiehn's reckless act had now cost him money and several lumps.

A few Longhorns short, the Stampede rodeo of 1916 began with opening speeches by Montana Governor Sam Stewart, Havre Mayor Thomas MacKenzie, and the Reverend L. J. Christier. The crowds were so unexpectedly large that the hotels were filled and overnight accommodations had to be made in schools, public buildings, and 200 private homes. Christler's Episcopal Church members provided meals in the Agricultural building on the rodeo grounds with 35-cent breakfasts and 50-cent lunches and suppers. The Stampede organization also had a food-serving operation, with breakfast items including ground Montana corn mush, flapjacks, Shot-Gun Jones ranch sausage, sowbelly, and eggs.

The dinner menu featured Let 'Em Ramble soup, native Montana Jack fish, squaw mulligan stew, maverick and coyote stews, sage hen, Powder River-style beef ribs, roast leg of porkey pine, and Governor Stewart roast, Virginia City-style. The most expensive meal was 60 cents. George Francis was pictured on the menu and listed as chef and Jack Mabee was named second cook. At the bottom of the menu, below the desserts of Milk River pudding and cowboy's delight, was the admonition: "During the Stampede while we have company, all Cowpunchers will be expected to eat with their fork."

But table manners were not a requirement to be a winner during the many hours of grueling competition. Francis continued to show his championship form, winning the bulldogging contest with an overall time for three steers of four minutes, twenty-three seconds; Mabee was second at four minutes, twenty-eight seconds; and Massey, third at about five minutes. This gave Francis, $350 and a bridle; Mabee, $175 and a pair of gloves; and Massey, $75.

Francis also won the steer roping contest with a cumulative time for three steers at two minutes, forty-two seconds, to win $300 and a fountain pen. Ira Triplett was second at three minutes, forty-six seconds, winning $175 and a box of cigars, and Mabee was third at about four minutes, taking $75. In addition, Francis won $250 for bulldogging from a loose horse and another $250 and $10 in clothes for bulldogging from a motorcycle and $75 for best-dressed cowboy and roping outfits. Mrs. Frank Gable won the same for best-dressed cowgirl, although her champion bulldogger husband couldn't beat the local boys.

Other winners included Lillian (Mrs. Shorty) Young in the cowgirls race; Jim Massey, best bareback bull rider; Wilkens Williams, best bareback horse rider; "Powder River Billy" in the horse-bucking contest; Charles White in the amateur roping contest; Frank Gable for trick riding and fancy roping; Charles Powell in the stagecoach race; Charles Powell again and Steve Adams for the wild-horse relay race; and Clayton Jolley in the cowboy standing-horse race. Jolley had no luck in the horse bucking contests, being thrown off the same horse twice.

Other locals, such as George Hockett, E. J. Sartain, Ed Timmons, and Howard Sailor, didn't fare as well; however, local public stenographer Marie Cyre finished second to Lillian Young in the cowgirls race.

Each day of the rodeo, a parade was held with all the participants and led by "Captain" Jack Edwards. The silver-adorned Francis and Tony were at the front, carrying the American flag. A less precise mounted drilling unit was the Havre Rangers, a newly formed volunteer cavalry troop. Formed in connection with the rodeo was the Havre Cowboy Band, or more properly the Montana Marching Club, apparently getting its nucleus from the old Havre city band formed in 1900. Its thirty-five sometime members with Francis as bandmaster participated in parades and other rodeo events. Francis liked to throw dimes to the children along the parade routes. Trombone player, Ed Timmons, rode a bull and wore Francis's fancy clothes since they were the same size. In 1916 they performed at the St. Paul Winter Outdoor Sports Carnival and returned in 1917 wearing heavy black-striped wool coats with some 100 Havre citizens marching behind.

The rodeo was a big success and a personal triumph for Francis and his associates. And though he should have come away with over $1,200 in cash and prizes, he probably never saw any of it because rumors circulated that the man entrusted with the rodeo receipts took off for parts unknown. This theft was apparently neither publicized nor the money recovered. The Stampede organization did have to borrow from the bank to cover expenses and pay prize winners.

On a last ill-fated note, once the rodeo was over, one of the buffalo wandered off the grounds and "politely" passed away. The other was released on the Rocky Boy Reservation where it soon disappeared.

Francis was a successful rodeo champion, yet at nearly forty-two, he was statistically too old to be a rodeo performer on the "suicide circuit" or "athlete's crap game." He bruised and sprained easier, hurt worse, and mended more slowly than his younger competitors. At least he had sense enough to stay away from the bucking contests that could break up a man's insides after too many years. He did take some bad spills during bulldogging. In one case, John Lumpkin and the rest of the horrified audience witnessed him take a hard dive to the ground, temporarily losing consciousness. Tony must have sensed something amiss because he trotted back and stood over him until he got up. Steer wrestlers also sustained much damage to their knees from meeting the ground feet first at over 20 miles per hour. And ropers could lose or maim fingers, besides other injuries from spills.

After the rodeo, Francis wrote home, telling them he had suffered some injuries (including a stomach wound), but they were almost mended (as of the July 16). He also enclosed several picture postcards of his triumphs.

The same year, a Fourth of July celebration occurred at Harlem, Montana, 42 miles east of Havre on the main railroad line. Here Jimmy Moran, who was recently from Minot, North Dakota, and currently a farmer-rancher near Cleveland and sometime Matador cowhand, won a twelve-round lightweight boxing match against George Lutton of Alberta. Moran had once been a world-class lightweight contender when living in New York state. This was his last boxing bout, however, before he moved on to Havre, later becoming police chief. His and George Francis's paths would cross in curious ways.

Another eventful happening of 1916 was the beginning of the anti-liquor campaign by the Anti-Saloon League and the W.C.T.U. The Reverend P. H. Case led the local battle to add Montana to the growing list of adjacent dry states.

And lastly, while not as earth-shaking as banning the bottle, noted Western author Zane Grey came through Havre in October of 1916 to gather information for a new book, perhaps *Wildfire* or *The U.P. Trail*. There were certainly lots of horses and trains around Havre, and perhaps he had even heard of George Francis's horse, Tony.

The following year the Stampede was even bigger and better. The rodeo received good coverage in the *Great Falls Tribune* since the Electric City had no fair or rodeo of its own. Their efforts were concentrated on the state fair at Helena. Advance publicity naturally centered on Francis and Tony. The show ran from July 4 through July 7. The Havre Stampede Association corporation directors expanded their budget by increasing by $20,000 the stock issued.

While the rodeo featured $16,000 in prizes and attracted champions from as far away as California and Texas, people weren't feeling quite as festive. The show's publicity shared the headlines with the war raging in Europe. The U. S. had entered the conflict in April and began raising "an immense army" via a lottery draft system. By June, many Montana boys were training in England or France.

Yet Francis and Mabee tried even harder to make the rodeo better. The arena was enlarged, bleachers added, and the grandstand roofed, adding $1.50 reserved seats in the resulting shade. A famous clown act, Se Perkings and wife from Kansas, headlined the festivities. An added attraction was a replica frontier town to be called Cypress—in honor of the old tough camp catering to soldiers once located on Big Sandy Creek at the Milk River in the 1880s. The "town" was populated with cowboys, Indians, Chinese, and counterfeit gunfighters, bullwhackers, gamblers, and outlaws and was situated south of First Street on Sixth Avenue, just east of the midway. The midway featured the ferris wheel from Butte's Columbia Gardens. Again T. T. Moroney brought his biplane for exhibition flights and rides.

Cypress, with a saloon, dance hall, and gambling hall, was also a pint-sized Wild West show: "A dollar show for 50 cents." The crowds watched gunfights, Indian attacks, lynchings, stagecoach arrivals, horses square dancing, precision horse riding by Fannie Sperry-Steele, cowboy band concerts, and other theatrics from a 3,000-seat grandstand. To really liven things up, a bull named "Johnny Pleasant" was turned loose in Cypress every night. The animal was apparently named in honor of Ma Plaz's son.

Along with the advance publicity centering on Francis, other major rodeo talent being promoted was Nat Aspinwall, Frank Gable, Fanny Sperry-Steele, Jack Hastings, Rufus Rollen, and Nez Perce Indian Jackson Sundown, current Pendleton Roundup champion. Unfortunately missing from this lineup was the *Police Gazette* all-round cowboy champion, Enos "Yakima" Canutt from Colfax, Washington. Francis would be up against such tough bulldoggers as J. O. Banks, "Dutch" Seidell, Jim Massey, "Iron" Mike Hastings,[49] and Jack and Roy Mabee. This was indeed a rodeo featuring the best.

The show had become too large for the management staff to handle at the First Street and Fourth Avenue office and required an additional person to be hired as a bookkeeper and office assistant. A train carload of bulls arrived from Texas (these didn't escape to eat Kiehn's garden), and the bucking broncos were secured from Marias River rancher John Brinkman,[50] who was also a prominent rodeo-event judge and friend of George Francis. One of the horses was named "Go Shoot," in honor of Ed Redwing, presumably. Browning (Montana) rancher and contestant Charlie Powell also furnished animals.

The feverish behind-the-scenes activities of getting advance men, ticket sellers and takers, ushers, livestock tenders, starters, timers, judges, pickup and flag men, etc., were completed, and it was time to "Let 'Em Loose" and "Let 'Em Ramble!"

For four hours, people filed through the grandstand gates. Every reserve seat was sold by noon. And the capacity crowds more than got their money's worth in thrills and spills. A crowd estimated at 7,000 attended the first day's events, not including those watching from surrounding hills and the tops of boxcars. The highlight of the day came when Fanny Sperry-

Steele and Fox Hastings performed trick riding on "Dismal Dick" and "Timberline," respectively. This was the last major rodeo appearance by Steele, the world's lady bucking horse champion, before she retired to her ranch in the Helena area's Prickly Pear Valley. She had been a champion rider since 1907.

Twelve cowboys competed for a $600 purse in the bucking-horse contest. Championship rider Frank Seeley met his match when he came roaring out of the chute on a horse called "High Tower," which sent him hurtling through the air and crashing onto the hard ground. When things went right, the rider stayed on for about forty seconds, controlling the horse with one rein, 6 inches from the horse's neck with either hand holding, and the other pointed high in the air. Both feet were solidly in the stirrups, as the cowboy raked the animal's sides with his spurs from neck to hindquarter.

Francis and Mabee initially gave bulldogging exhibitions only, to give others a chance at winning. Francis caught the horns of his first bull well, but was thrown partly under the perimeter fence, forcing him to eat dirt. He recovered quickly, though, and brought his animal down and held up his hand for time. Mabee took his steer down quickly and may have equaled the then-current world's record, which was about twenty-three seconds. But it was only an exhibition, and official time keeping wasn't being done.

The excitement continued in the bull-riding exhibition. Tex Richardson dismounted before the protecting riders could reach him, and the bull charged, catching Richardson squarely between its horns and tossing him in the air. The cowboy was pulled out from beneath the bull's feet as it attempted to gore him again. Richardson received much applause when he was able to stand at last.

That evening at the Cypress replica frontier town site, Mexican bull-fighter Joe Perez gave an exhibition of his talents—or lack of luck. He slipped and fell, and the bull charged, but it was diverted when a quick-thinking member of the audience threw his seat cushion, hitting the animal. It was followed by more cushions, till the befuddled bull forgot about his intended victim and the matador was carried off.

The following day at the arena, Francis suffered injuries during bull-dogging. When grabbing the steer's horns, he was slammed to the ground and lost consciousness. He was moved by ambulance to the Sacred Heart Hospital, and when he returned later, he was given a standing ovation. In yet another accident on the following day, he received a 4-inch-deep wound when a steer's horn pierced his stomach. Away he went again in the ambulance. He took his licks in the steer-roping contest also, when a steer hit the end of the rope with so much force that it rolled horse and rider twice and broke the lariat. Neither suffered any serious injury.

Mabee had his troubles, too. Although he made a good leap and had a solid hold on the animal's horns, they both went down and turned complete somersaults with Mabee fortunately coming out on top. In a different try, Mabee's horse fell from under him, wrenching his knee so badly that any attempt to remove his boot resulted in pain, so he wore them through the night.

On a lighter note Francis wagered with Jim Massey that he would bulldog the "slickhorn red steer" and throw him directly in front of the grandstand. This steer got away from Massey the day before, having only been conquered once, by Francis, at the previous Stampede. The papers didn't mention whether the tall cowboy accomplished his boast or not.

Now that the fun was over, both Francis and Mabee rode for money the final day of the events. Francis placed first in the bulldogging and Mabee came in second; their times were between forty-five and fifty seconds. Mabee won the steer-roping contest with his brother Roy, from Anaheim, California, taking second and Francis taking third.

Marie Dumont entered her first event: the cowgirl's race. She placed third behind Marie Cyre and Vern McGinnis. Perhaps just as important, she met her future husband, Englishman Tom Gibson of Red Deer, Alberta. He was a Canadian champion. Best cowboy and cowgirl outfit prizes were again awarded to Francis and Mrs. Frank Gable. The best roping horse award went to Jack Mabee's "Red Horse." Other first-place overall winners were Tex Crockett, "Powder River" Billy, Steve Adams, H. E. Bertrand, Charles Powell, Rufus Rollen, Ed Sartain, Art Staton, and Ben Burnett. George's friends, Ed Timmons and Jim Massey, finished second in the wild-horse race and second in bareback riding, respectively.

Evidently the top money winners were Hi-Line men: Jack Mabee, Steve Adams, George Francis, and Charles Powell. For Francis this was against much stiffer and younger competition. They announced afterwards that next year's Stampede would be even bigger. The nightlife program of the frontier town would be expanded and the seating capacity increased.

The first three days of the rodeo drew a total of about 16,000 fans. The final and fourth day, 4,000 were around to watch a grand parade through downtown Havre and out to the fairgrounds. Lillian Young fell from her horse during the parade, but wasn't injured and remounted unassisted.

Mention was made that the events were all captured on film, perhaps by local boy, Art Staton, who dabbled in the film business. Charlie Russell attended the show and made two pen sketches of Francis. One showed him bulldogging a steer with it veering off to one side, and the other pictured him towering head and shoulders above two other cowboy contestants.

As author Walt Coburn put it: "Truly Francis had the world by the tail." The dream of having a class A rodeo equal to the Cheyenne Frontier Days, Pendleton Round-Up, or Calgary Stampede was coming true. Having been vaulted to celebrity status, George found kids in great numbers following at his boot heels. The young ladies adored him, and other cowboys admired him or felt jealousy. Mabee apparently accepted his status as second banana gracefully, happy to share in the glory.

Francis wrote home soon after the program, as he had the year before, telling them a party offered $1,000 for Tony and his silver-mounted saddle and accessories. He said that the rodeo was a big success in every way and he had earned $900 in the competition, beating out eight of the best bull-doggers in the world. The show, he noted, grossed $51,000 and netted $13,000 after expenses. He added that he had promised a friend (whom he didn't name) he would quit performing in rodeos. (After all, rodeo performing was a young man's game.) He admonished his family for not writing, although he had never kept his promise to visit them. But neither had any family members come to visit him.

Another rodeo where Francis reportedly did well was the Pendleton (Oregon) Round-Up. He performed there possibly as early as 1913 and definitely as late as 1915. The Round-Up activities probably gave him some of the ideas for the upcoming Stampede rodeos: the horseback-mounted cowboy band, a frontier town replica built of rough, weather-beaten lumber called "Happy Valley," and bullfight exhibitions. The spectators bought play money at the bank to gamble and drink. Entertainment included an opium den with real celestials (Chinese) and a bank robbery. The first-class rodeo had been held since 1910, adjacent to the city in Round-Up Park, paralleling the Umatilla River. Their theme, "Let 'Er Buck," and Walla Walla's Frontier Days, "Let 'Er Kick," obviously influenced the Stampede's future theme of "Let 'Em Ramble."

Francis came in a respectable overall third in the bulldogging contest in the 1914 Round-Up. His single best time was twenty-eight and one-fifth seconds. The winner was Sam Garrett of Munhall, Oklahoma, the "World Champion All-Around Cowboy" and Police Gazette gold and silver belt holder. His best individual time was twenty-five and two-fifths seconds. In comparison, Francis looked pretty good. No other Havre-area cowboy finished in the money.

For the 1915 Oregon contest, Francis and Mabee rated individual attention in the pre-publicity. So did Jim Massey of Snyder, Texas. This time Francis only managed an overall fourth in the bulldogging, although he had a good single time in the steer roping. Both Massey and Mabee had poor days. However, Mabee gained praise for sticking with a bull that had dragged him across the grandstand. Neither Francis nor Mabee entered the Round-Up again. Massey, at that time, must have accompanied the boys back to Havre to reside on the Francis ranch for about two years. Perhaps lack of money was his prime motivation, or he just did it on a lark.

During one of those rodeos, he was accompanied by Mabee, Andy Avery, Claydon Jolley, and Harry and Larry Green. Jolley had a brush with the law when he was mistaken for a wanted cattle rustler who resembled him and happened to be participating in the same rodeo. Jolley was finally able to convince the lawman—probably Umatilla County Sheriff and Round-Up president Tillman D. Taylor—of his true identity, but not until the true culprit got away. This probably amused his friends to no end as he reputedly swung a wide loop himself.

Jolley got revenge, though, since he knew the fugitive had a place of business in Great Falls, where he butchered stolen beef and burned the hides. So the group stopped off on their way home and appropriated all his meat-cutting equipment.

Francis's private life was taking a definite turn for the better, along with his prospering public life. He met and fell for a woman named Amanda Spears. Her sister, Louise Arno (or Peters), and her son, Alvern, accompanied by Amanda, had just arrived from Minnesota. Spears was a well-educated person, graduating from Mankato (Minnesota) State Teachers College in about 1908. She financed her college education by working in her spare hours as a maid at the home of a wealthy grocery-chain owner. She was born near the Twin Cities at St. Paul Park and resided at Farmington before coming west on her great adventure. Amanda, blue-eyed, dark-haired, and taller than the average woman in her day at 5 feet 7 inches, came from tough German farm stock and was a robust, hearty woman who loved the outdoors.

The Minnesota party had to wait for the rodeo to end before a land locator could take them to their new homesteads, both about 48 miles northwest of Havre and lying between the tiny farm communities of Simpson[51] and

Fairchild. Amanda's homestead was the farthest north, near where the Lost River flows into the Milk, a stream originating at Lake Pokowski in Alberta. It is believed George and Amanda met somehow that day and became fast friends. Perhaps Francis even helped build her wooden shack, which was covered with old flattened-out condensed milk cans.

Sister Louise became chummy with John "P-Bell" Koltveit, who was foreman of the Barney Simpson ranch located near the Canadian border, Wild Horse Lake, and the Oldham general store and post office. Brother Ernie Simpson's main ranch was just southeast of Louise's. John and Louise soon married. Meanwhile Amanda began teaching at the Spring Coulee School just east of Simpson in the fall of 1917. The school board provided living quarters just north of the building.

Amanda became a good friend of the Simpson brothers and the large Charles Smith family whose homestead was near B. Simpson's ranch and Shorty Young's summer place. She was able to see Young's temporary Border Saloon business, which operated from a converted ranch house to cater to the prohibition-dry Canadians, local residents, and those city dwellers who came because much of his Havre operation had been shut down by the state attorney general's office.

Amanda reportedly became a heroine, sucking the venom from Ernie Simpson's leg after a snake bite and administering first aid. Barney Simpson went to Alberta when the hordes of homesteaders arrived, and brother Ernie moved on to Great Falls in about 1919. Louise died about a year earlier, leaving Amanda's life emptier. She took on the task of raising her nephew, and no doubt her romance with Francis helped fill the void.

Marie Gibson would soon have her own budding romance. After the 1917 Stampede, the 5 feet 4 inches, 135-pound, dark-haired beauty with a French accent began her rodeo career in earnest. About this time, she earned a nickname she never accepted or appreciated: "Buckskin Mary." Marie acquired this moniker when a livery barn owner observed her quickly regain control over a skittish and troublesome buckskin-colored horse that was loaned by Francis for her trip to town. Only a few close friends dared call her that, since she considered it no honor. It was never part of her rodeo billing as Marie Dumont or later Gibson, and those today who call her by that name are not showing her the respect that they intend. Actually she was known as "Ma" on the rodeo circuit.

After the 1917 Havre Stampede, she next entered the Medicine Hat, Alberta, rodeo. There, for the first time, she rode bucking broncos in public.

Her first horse stumbled just out of the chute and went down with Marie on his neck. The rodeo manager remarked jokingly that she had bronc-riding confused with bulldogging! This didn't faze her, however, and by the third day she was performing well. She continued on the Canadian circuit to Moose Jaw and Battleford, joining up with a small Wild West show. At times she had to contend with the ridicule of other, more experienced women riders, when her riding efforts were not the best. Marie told one such agitator: "When I have ridden as much as you have, I'll do better. Besides, I have three children to support, and $25 a horse looks good with winter near and money hard to get."

She dropped out of the show after the Winnipeg, Manitoba, performance and visited with various family members in the area, then returned to her old home town of de Bellevue, Saskatchewan, for a week. Her husband still lived there with his parents. She talked with him, imploring him to come back for the sake of the children, if nothing else. He promised he would soon follow, telling her to go home.

She returned to their Milk River homestead and spent the winter acquiring lumber for them to build a barn and fix up the cabin. She left the children with her parents because the cabin wasn't warm enough. Thus, besides taking care of the livestock, her daily routine included visiting her parents and children.

Winter came and went, yet there was no sign of Joe. In need of money she left the children still in her parents' care and again returned to Saskatchewan. Marie again saw Joe while she was working at a tailor shop in Moose Jaw. He asked her for money to get home—120 miles to the north—promising again he would return to their Montana home, but she no longer believed him.

She again went to Medicine Hat and rejoined the Wild West show, putting her old life behind her. She improved steadily, gaining more respect as she rode increasingly tougher horses and consequently earning more money—$125 a month and expenses. One of her specialties was to ride any horse that no one else had been able to stay on during the show. She passed a hat around the crowd and usually collected around $100, since there was no prize money offered for the extra feat. She worked hard at trick riding too. Across-the-street neighbor Mrs. Bruce Cuinal Clyde remembered seeing her practice long hours between rodeo tours on West Second Street at Thomas's Livery barn corral,[52] which was next door to Marie's soon-to-be home.

At a Stettler, Alberta, performance, she once more met Tom Gibson. The transplanted clean-shaven Englishman stood a slender 6 feet 4 inches, with brown hair and blue eyes. She joined him in the company's performances throughout Alberta and British Columbia until closing down at Nelson, B. C. Thereafter, Gibson found work at a ranch breaking horses, whereas Marie helped in the ranch kitchen and with the horses in her spare time. She wrote several letters to Joe, hoping to settle their relationship one way or another. She received no reply and returned to de Bellevue to obtain a divorce. She never saw Joe again, and she and Tom married the following summer.

Marie was definitely on her way to a happier life, but her friend George Francis's newly found hopes and dreams were being threatened. On November 3, 1917, he was charged with allegedly stealing a small bay Belgian mare from Phil Clack. These charges came only a few months after Francis had testified for Mary Martin and only one month since he helped put her homestead shack on the property disputed with H. Earl Clack. Of course, neither George nor his friends believed this timing was coincidental.

Clack said the mare had been missing since March 1, 1915. The first action was cancelled by State Attorney General Sam Ford on December 14, 1917, because two key witnesses, Jim Massey and Clyde Welch, had left town. This action was reinstated on January 30, 1918, and a trial was held in February. The district court jury declared him guilty. He was to be sentenced by judge W. B. Rhoades on March 4, but he never showed. Francis became a fugitive.

Naturally, this temporarily stopped his successful rodeo career and prevented him from seeing Amanda. If he returned, he faced a prison term. Consequently, he had to stay in hiding when Mabee put on the third Stampede alone. Francis must have felt a deep frustration at how things had turned sour again. At least he had Amanda and many good friends . . . Thank God for these blessings.

The 1918 Great Northern Stampede rodeo was only a one-day event, held on July 4, before just 3,000 fans. It was certainly no reflection on Jack Mabee's talents, but some of the magic was gone without Francis's involvement. And too, the war in Europe now embraced the U. S. Montana accidentally sent twice its allotment of soldiers overseas, meaning many young men had disappeared from the local scene. As described by Janet Allison in *Trial and Triumph*, "For the grownups in the Milk River country, it was not a happy time. Young men were off to war from every town and community, and people were dreadfully worried."

Along with wartime rationing, the ranchers suffered a shortage of rail-road cars to ship cattle to the Chicago auctions. The farmers endured too: The previous spring was one of the driest and coldest ever recorded. This was no doubt an influence in turning their frustrations against Americans of German descent. As described by Dan Cushman in *Plenty of Room and Air*,[53] the people's wrath—formalized with the Montana Council of Defense and its county chapters—turned against anyone with a German or even German-sounding name; for Germans had suddenly become the cruelest, most bloodthirsty inhuman animals in the world. Didn't their soldiers bay-onet babies and cut off the hands of Allied Force's nurses? In retaliation, locals and neighbors were beaten, made to kiss the flag on their knees, and buy extra war bonds.

Rumors flew of German spies landing everywhere to sabotage factories and of "moles" being sent to America years before to spring out when the German plan to conquer the world was finally put in motion.

Perhaps they might even be a neighbor. As if this hysteria wasn't enough, further stories circulated of impending invasion, bombings, and landing of spy planes or dirigibles.

The Stampede went on in spite of all these carryings-on. Before the show, the audience heard a recorded four-minute Fourth of July speech by U.S. President Woodrow Wilson. Then a few patriotic speeches followed, given by local dignitaries. Finally the rodeo began with a cowboy's horse race, fol-lowed by an exhibition of bareback riding on wild horses. The crowd did some extra cheering when Clayton Jolley, dressed as a rodeo clown, jumped on a riderless horse that had bucked off its rider and stayed with it. Next came a trick-riding exhibition by Johnny Mullen of Eagle, New Mexico.

The bucking-bronco contest was won by Ed Timmons in one of his best performances, followed by Jolley on his "official" ride. Mullen won the steer roping with a time of fifty seconds, in comparison to Francis's 1915 second-place finish in the Walla Walla rodeo of forty-one and one-half seconds.

Two events later came the bulldogging competition; first out was Jack Mabee. He jumped from his horse and threw the steer directly in front of the grandstand. Both Mabee and the big animal turned a full somersault; his winning time: twenty-seven seconds. The final event of the day was the wild-horse race won by Gildford's Howard Sailor. The show concluded with the frenzied riding of several wild bucking horses, all riders mounting simul-taneously.

The fourth and final Stampede, held July 3-5 of 1919, had new conflicting forces to contend with. While the war had officially ended with the
Treaty of Versailles in June of 1918, many people had sour faces because
Montana had become a "dry" state. The large numbers of homesteaders
with families demanded a change in the cowboy-prostitute-saloon-and-
gambling-hall town environment. What had gone on fifty years before in
the Kansas cowtowns of Abilene and Dodge City was now commonplace—
minus the gunfire—in Havre.

In combination with a local reform job led by the Reverend E. J. Huston and attorney C. R. Stranahan, State Attorney General Sam Ford continued to wage war against prostitution and big-time gambling in Havre
and other Montana communities. Now state prohibition had been added to
his enforcement duties. Even the weather had become oppressive: The rain
clouds were being chased away by warm dry winds, bringing the driest year
on record.

The Stampede returned despite these depressing conditions. It was called
a "Victory Celebration" because World War I had ended. A new feature to
enliven the festivities was a former Canadian Air Force Curtiss light biplane
that Mabee is believed to have won in an obviously high-stakes card game.
The plane had a 43 feet 7 inch wing span and measured 39 feet in length. A
publicity campaign for the coming rodeo was to be conducted by staging
flights between Havre and other north-central Montana communities.

There was speculation that Mabee had a second purpose in acquiring
the aircraft: to transport alcohol from "wet " Alberta and Saskatchewan. It
was said the plane could carry one hundred or more cases of whiskey—
bought at $10 per gallon and sold in Montana for $40-$60 a gallon—
resulting in a profit of about $3,500 per trip. The plane apparently was
never reliable enough for such large-scale endeavors, however.

Even though in hiding, Long George hadn't been forgotten: The ads
for the Stampede in different Montana newspapers displayed prominently
a picture of Francis, Tony, and a bulldogged steer.

The rodeo wasn't the only main event staged by Mabee. The northern
Montana "Bear Cats" engaged the Great Falls Smelter "Ingots" in a series
of baseball games. The combination of the expanded rodeo, the ball
games, and the aerial stunt work by a former combat pilot by the name of
C. R. Ennis, believed to have been local, perhaps produced the best Stampede of all, maybe making up for the thirsty fans' loss at the confiscation

of bootleg beer from the basement boiler room of the nearly new Liberty Hotel on Havre's First Street.

Unfortunately, no results were printed in the *Havre Plaindealer*, and no copy of the *Promoter* can be found for that date. Ed Timmons and the Mabee brothers evidently won their share of prizes. Mabee enhanced his rodeo appearances by arriving on the field in the biplane, and departing in it afterwards. The aircraft was sponsored by Clack Oil Company, probably much to George Francis's chagrin. The businessman provided the fuel to promote his new Hi-Power gasoline brought in from the Oklahoma oil fields. How Mabee felt towards Clack isn't clear, but he had to face the reality of needed financial backing. He sold the Gildford bar that year, possibly to help finance the rodeo.

The announcement came the week after the Stampede that Ed Timmons, Havre cowboy and rodeo performer, had accepted a movie offer and would be moving to southern California the following week. At the previous year's Havre rodeo, Timmons had been the star of a documentary film taken by both the state of Montana and Arthur Staton of the Western Film Corporation. Staton, a local boy whose family had a large boarding house in Havre, raised race horses, operated a coal mine south of town, and had been engaged in film work in California the last three years, according to the news story. Reportedly, Staton made a Western movie in the Glacier Park-Flathead Lake area, which is thought to have been called "Where the Rivers Rise." He also participated in the Stampedes.

One wonders whether Francis would have gone instead of Timmons if he had been able to avoid trouble with the law, although he would have wished his friend well. While Francis's fame on the rodeo circuit remained, little else of his life stayed intact. His ranch was gone, reclaimed by the bank, and he had a prison term hanging over his head—along with mounting legal bills. He really had nothing much to offer Amanda for their future together. Perhaps a lesser man might have run off to California with Timmons. Many wanted men did just that, becoming Western movie actors and extras. However, this was not for Francis; he was determined to beat the charge. In fact he turned himself in that same week.

Life was also becoming rough for his oldest rival, Ed Redwing. True, he had a nice ranch and holdings and three wonderful daughters; but because of harsh winters and dry springs and summers, he had no hay crop and cattle feed was scarce with the cattle losses heavy. Redwing was forced to mortgage his town property to buy oil cake at $85 a ton and poor hay full of cattails and weeds for $60 a ton from Minnesota. Added to this was the collapse of beef prices after the war.

He bought replacement cattle—reportedly financed by the Portland Loan Company—and, with Hilda's help, trailed them to 2,000 leased acres near Two Medicine Creek on the Blackfeet Indian Reservation. In 1919, with the whole family's help, he moved the new cattle and the Beaver Creek Valley herd across the border to leased pasture on the Ross and Wallace ranch. Before this move, it is believed he sold some mature animals for slaughter and bought calves from a Salt Lake City company.

During June of 1919, when Ed was at Browning with the cattle, Hilda decided to visit her Havre friend, Bess Bond. Bess was to come out to the ranch for Sunday dinner, but neither Hilda nor any of their three hands could drive the Model T touring car. Not being afraid of new challenges, she had them crank up the engine, and off she drove. Sort of. She crashed into a formation of sloping red rocks just below the house, and the car overturned, putting Hilda in the hospital for two weeks, minus part of one upper ear. At least Hilda's friend could now visit her more conveniently.

H. Earl Clack had things much better. He opened a chain of service stations beginning in Havre, Great Falls, and Kalispell. They carried his Hi-Power gasoline, Hi-Lite kerosene, and Heccoline oils and greases. He built a warehouse on east First Street along the G.N.R. right-of-way for the storage of oils and the compounding of greases.

Francis probably felt it was no victory that Redwing's ranch was failing, since all the ranchers were in the same predicament. That Clack was prospering was most likely a very bitter pill, especially since Francis was fighting a desperate action to avoid prison.

The Trial

THERE WERE CERTAINLY CONFLICTING GOOD-BAD LABELS given to the character of George Francis, as previously mentioned. Either he was a good man and a respectable rancher, or he was king of the rustlers and public enemy number one.

Perhaps the only outsider who really knew the extent of his criminal activities was Rose Vosen-Cady. She homesteaded seven miles south of Kremlin near her parents and brothers. Her shack was made of railroad ties and finished with lumber scraps. She was well known as a nurse, having received training in Wisconsin; her most famous patient was George Francis.

When seriously ill, perhaps with the killer Spanish flu or typhoid fever, he was brought to her place. The bed was too short so a chair was placed at the end for his feet. He was delirious most of the time and is said to have revealed many secrets. Once coherent and learning of his babbling, he swore her to secrecy. The most she would ever say was what a gentleman he was, and not the bad man that some people thought.

It is true he had many friends among the cowboys, ranchers, and townspeople, plus some settlers and even clergymen. With them all he had one rule: the frontier code of loyalty which dictated that a friend or partner was never betrayed nor a promise broken—even if it was to a person's best advantage. Once a favor was done, it was never forgotten. A version of the old cowboy code of conduct still exists, especially among the professional rodeo people of today, who are generally tight-bonded, generous, and a courageous breed of cat.

Nevertheless he was gradually acquiring enemies other than Ed Redwing, H. Earl Clack, and their friends and associates. The theft of cattle and horses from targeted ranchers and drylanders didn't enhance his reputation, never mind the stock he didn't steal but received the blame for, anyway. He enjoyed some protection resulting from the old frontier custom of neighbors minding their own business and being responsible for only their own possessions and property as long as he didn't steal from them.

The ethics and customs of the free range were eroding, however, with the advent of the more conservative and religious business people and settlers with wives and children. They didn't look upon the turning of a card, the selling of sexual favors, or the dispensing of alcohol as legitimate professions. Men and women considered to be respectable lived normal, workaday lives, raising families and geraniums. They believed nights were for sleeping, and daylight was for hard, earnest labor.

The enforcement of law was also shifting: It was becoming the responsibility of law officers rather than individuals to protect family and property. It was becoming the neighbor's duty to report criminal activities, and no longer was a stranger to be welcomed who came from parts unknown "whippin' a mighty tired pony." Rugged individualism was gradually yielding to group conformity, both in work habits and morality.

Of course, in response, the native Westerners could reply: "If these new settlers are so high falutin', how come we have to put locks on our doors now?"—thus ending the Western hospitality custom of "the latch string is always on the outside of the door."

Conversely, as the local reform movement grew, so the reputation of the vice element declined. Shorty Young's once "good name" as the red-light district king now bordered on notoriety. Hence the protection once provided to Francis by Young's friendship would soon work against him. And with the 1918 county election won overwhelmingly by the reformers, Francis would have no friends left in office other than Deputy Sheriff George Herron.

Long George had other troubles brewing. Some of his friends were upset because he no longer allowed them to keep stolen stock on his ranch. He may have been attempting to go straight for Amanda's sake, or perhaps he was just being careful, either running stolen stock on the Sandy Creek ranch or moving them immediately out of the area. Whatever his reasons, some of his friends considered this to be disloyal. This may have precipitated the meeting that was held in a barn southwest of Havre by a group consisting of long-standing enemies and a few new faces: some former pals, upset for whatever reasons, who didn't mind taking some cash. Their intentions were to find avenues of getting him out of the way.

It is believed this meeting resulted in the legal problems that began for Francis on November 3, 1917, when a True Bill of Indictment was issued against Francis by the grand jury. The document charged him with the theft of a three-year-old Belgian bay mare named "Mandy's Baby," weighing about 1,200 pounds, having a white star on her forehead, and said to have been owned by Philip D. Clack. The brand had been allegedly changed from Clack's Seven-Bar Lazy B on the right thigh to the Francis Flying V or Pothook, and later traded to E. C. Carruth for a beaver coat. The animal was supposedly discovered missing about March 1, 1915, over two years earlier.

Francis entered a plea of not guilty five days later; bail of $1,500 was posted, and the trial was set for November 17. Several continuances were granted for both sides to procure more witnesses. Finally on December 14 State Attorney General Ford asked that the action against Francis be dismissed the day before the trial because two important witnesses subpoenaed by the state—Crossen brothers ranch hand Claude Welch and Francis ranch hand Jim Massey—were "not available." The defense was also having problems locating two crucial witnesses: local rancher Charles "Slick" Wilson and former Gildford butcher Sonny Walkup, but had fifteen other witnesses lined up.

The lack of two witnesses wasn't the entire reason for the state dropping its case, according to County Attorney Victor Griggs. He said the indictment was defective, and they had no case to begin with.

Francis went even further: He bought space in the *Havre Promoter* to air his grievances. He complained that his attorneys had made every effort to bring the case to trial so the horse could be produced in court. This, he asserted, was the only way he could prove the evidence against him was false and show the general public what a flimsy and malicious affair "they" had tried to perpetrate. Now, after much expense to himself and the county, the state dropped the case.

He placed the blame for the trumped-up charges against Ed Redwing, without directly naming him, only saying a "would-be cattle king." George said Redwing was seeking revenge because he had helped to convict him of grand larceny for cattle stealing at the request of the Montana Stock Association representatives. (They were his friends, including Harry Green and George Herron.) "At the time of my arrest," Francis continued, "the brave gentleman made the statement he had plenty of money to spend on such guys as Francis, and he could buy all them cheap Haverites for $1,000." Privately Francis and his friends believed that H. Earl Clack was the dominating force behind the indictment, not Redwing, but they were apparently afraid to attack the powerful foe publicly.

He next went after Phil Clack, again not naming names, only calling him "a certain gentleman with a flat wheel." (He had a deformed, shorter leg.) He claimed Phil Clack was taken by surprise when informed by both county and state officials that in order to prove a changed brand it would be necessary to skin the horse's brand area and look at the flesh side to determine which brand came first. He said the mare disappeared conveniently, so Clack would not have to defend his false accusations, and that he then spread the story that Francis had again stolen the mare. "All these blood thirsty tales were intended to create public resentment against me," Francis wrote.

It was true that Francis and several of his supporters, including Victor Griggs and former Warbonnet foreman and stock inspector Frank Anderson, had pushed for the skin removal to prove the Francis brand had been on first. Unfortunately for whomever, the mare was found shot and cut up in the Milk River near the Francis ranch; the brand was mutilated. It was claimed the mare was stolen the second time from the Clack barn while the family was away on a picnic.

Francis went on in the newspaper to say he felt vindicated because the lowest class of criminals and degenerates and their stool pigeons were unable to frame him, and his accusers should be shunned as if they were the plague. He closed by saying, "A county official with his family of deputies is now trying to convey the impression that they dropped this case against me because they had a better one coming up; this shows that he must have had a hot case as no one has ever heard of him dropping anything unless it was so hot that he could not carry it away."

Only on the last point Francis was wrong. A new action was filed against him on January 30, 1918. The following day District Judge W. B. Rhoades issued a bench warrant for his arrest. George Colter, Young's gambling games boss, and Jack Mabee provided a $2,000 bond for guaranteed appearance. Trial was set for Monday, February 25, 1918. Francis was represented by attorneys J. P. Donnelly and Frank Carleton.

Francis had obviously underestimated the state and local reform forces. He was also caught in a squeeze because his powerful enemies were aligned with them. They considered him part of Young's Honky Tonk retinue known as the "Havre Gang." Recent action by Assistant State Attorney General A. A. Grorud had closed seventeen residences and hotels that allowed prostitution and gambling. These included Young's Honky Tonk complex, consisting of The Montana Hotel and Grill, the Parlour House, and thirty-eight cribs. All the furniture was removed, and Young, manager William Murdock, and madam Florence Goodwin were arrested.

To add insult to injury, this happened just before the Stampede rodeo when business would have prospered.

Combined with this was Francis's reputation in some circles as being the ringleader of a gang of cattle rustlers and horse thieves that operated throughout northern Montana and the adjoining states and provinces. Francis received credit for the disappearance of almost every horse and cow; thus it would be tough to get a fair trial locally. Even so, he didn't try for a change of venue. Apparently Francis felt comfortable about the trial being conducted in Havre.

With all these forces at work, the trial began in the Hill County courthouse. The jury, made up mostly of hostile farmers (according to the Francis forces), were Thomas A. Abbott of Lothair, Tony J. Alex of Rudyard, Harry E. Denton of Goldstone, jury foreman Riley M. Hadlock of Joplin, Oscar L. Harvey of Kremlin, H. M. Reams of Box Elder, John Rudegard and E. J. Rice of Gildford, Otto Scharfe of Laredo, Carl Sorenson of Kremlin, and Marlow R. Wilson of Joplin. Perhaps the Francis defenders were right that the jury felt negative towards him, but it surely didn't help when threats were made against them by the "Havre Gang."

Actually these were neither the first men drafted for the trial nor were those chosen originally all farmers. Five were excused for cause, including Francis's former business partner, Frank Reichel, and former Havre educator and then insurance agent, Thomas Troy. Seven other prospective jurors were challenged successfully by both state and defense. The entire process took only four hours.

Prosecuting the case with Grorud was Great Falls attorney George Hurd, representing the Montana Stockgrowers Association. Chief defense attorney, Joseph P. Donnelly, was already a veteran at representing Shorty

Young and his associates through the anti-vice trials. Later in the year Donnelly faced old friend and Butte lawyer Burton Wheeler, who was hired to help prosecute the local prohibition cases. Wheeler had previously served as U.S attorney for Montana, and he would become a U.S. senator in 1922. It was said that Wheeler and Donnelly put on quite a show in the courtroom, shouting, snapping, and growling at each other while having lengthy, "wet" poker games nightly in the Donnelly home. George Francis also dropped in at the Donnelly's.

Donnelly was said to have been a brilliant criminal lawyer with perhaps his only limitation being a drinking problem—although some believed he had three strikes against him in Havre: He was a Democrat, a Catholic, and attorney for Young and Francis. Donnelly was raised on his Irish immigrant family's large Iowa farm, and in later years he received an extensive education at St. Mary's College of Kansas, Creighton University of Denver, and finally, Georgetown University of Washington, D.C. His law career took him and wife, Mary, of St. Louis to the Philippines, San Francisco, Butte, Helena, and finally in 1917, to Havre until they returned to San Francisco in about 1931. It's debatable whether his "status" in the community helped or harmed Francis's case.

At least twenty-one witnesses were sworn in for the defense. Francis testified on his own behalf. Other defense witnesses were W. C. Pedicord, A. W. Morrell, Ray Ellis, Floyd Modill, Roscoe "Doc" Timmons, J. H. Fenton, Jack Mabee, V. R. Johnson, Orin "Shorty" Selby, Edna Fenton, A. H. Thompson, E. L. Walker, Orville Marianda, Byron Schultz, Victor Griggs, and Claude Welch. Negative character witnesses against the Sartain brothers' testimony were cigar store and pool hall owner C. C. Brundage; Justice Court Judge W. B. Pyper; Havre Trading Company owner Harold Archibald, and Farmers Bank president and Stampede director J. J. Blair.

Several witnesses called by the defense for the cancelled first trial were not summoned for the second. These included Harry Green, C. Stacey, George Herron, Harry Broadwater, John Crites, Ted Huntley, and Clayton Jolley.

The chief witnesses for the state were Phillip D. Clack, Paul Entorf, A. R. "Porky" Sellars, John and Ed Sartain, E. C. Carruth, Andy Avery, Herman Timmons, E. B. Thomas, John Reed, and Frank Lavigne. "Black Bill" Acison, one of Francis's chief accusers, didn't testify, although he was subpoenaed for the first trial. Perhaps he had a change of heart, or his testimony wasn't considered necessary. P-Cross foreman Jack Edwards was also not summoned for the second trial.

Interestingly, Abe Crosson, who helped start the whole thing, was never called, either. At the time, he was chief Hill County commissioner. Jim Massey for the state and Sonny Walkup and Charles "Slick" Wilson for the defense were never located. Claude Welch returned from Pueblo, Colorado, but this time to testify for the defense.

The legal action had begun when Francis's former friends, Bill Acison and Andy Avery along with Claude Welch, had given damaging statements to District Stock Inspector Sellars regarding the finding of a bay mare and her colt. The animals, found by Welch, were stuck in the quicksands of the Milk River in the spring of 1915. It is not clear what Acison's role was in this incident. There the river bordered the Abe Crosson ranch where Welch worked. Acison's place was nearby, and Francis's ranch was directly north across the river.

Welch and the Crossons were unable to free the animals, so word was sent for Francis to help out. He and Ray Ellis responded, and the horses were rescued. Once freed, Crosson noticed that the mare had a suspicious fresh-looking Francis brand over an older one belonging to Phil Clack. This information was given (then or later) to officer Sellars, who took several affidavits. No action was taken on this until about two years later.

The next happening in the chain of events, according to the prosecutor's story, occurred when local homesteaders Harold and Paul Entorf, Sr., purchased from Francis a team of black work horses, which were on display at Bruce Clyde's livery barn. When the brothers returned ten days later to pick up the team, one was missing and had been sold again. Francis assured them he had a replacement horse at his ranch. They waited through a year's exchange of letters, and he still hadn't replaced the horse. Finally in April of 1916, Francis instructed the Entorfs to come out to his ranch where he gave them a stake horse (loaner) to use until he could find another matching black horse. This, by all appearances, was the same bay mare previously pulled out of the Milk River with her colt. The brothers broke and used the mare on the farm and for wagon trips back and forth to Havre.

The Entorfs said the mare had more than one brand on her, but the marks were blotched and, other than the Francis brand, could not be deciphered. They didn't worry about this since it was only borrowed. They said the horse also had a barbed wire scar three inches above the fetlock joint on the right hind leg. This scar was subsequently used to identify the mare's remains when later found in the Milk River.

On one trip to town, they were hailed by Francis and told to bring the mare to Ed Thomas's livery barn because he had traded her. They were given another horse, apparently from Mabee's and Keple's ranch. Then, in November of 1916, Francis traded the bay mare, valued at $225, and two other horses to E. C. Carruth as payment for a beaver coat with a price tag of $600. Francis had seen Carruth wearing the Alaska beaver coat at the Havre Hotel, which he managed. He wanted the coat in spite of it being too short; as tall as he was, he had to have another band of beaver added around the bottom. It was evidently not a satisfactory addition, being a different shade of fur that didn't blend well.

The bay mare was kept in Thomas's livery barn for a few months due to illness. It was delivered to the Carruth farm just west of Kremlin (a town Carruth founded) once it was fit, and subsequently it was identified and claimed by Phil Clack a few days later on January 19, 1917. Francis then had to make good on the loss to Carruth.

At the beginning of the trial, Donnelly had to leave town on a short business trip. The lawyer didn't expect the jury selection and trial to move along so quickly, and his partner Carleton was overwhelmed. It was said by pro-Francis people that some initially introduced state's evidence was obviously false, or misleading, yet went unchallenged by Carleton, damaging Francis's defense.

Hurd gave the opening statement, outlining the state's case. Next Phil Clack took the stand in the only testimony on Monday afternoon. Clack told the court that the mare was born on his ranch in the spring of 1912 to a mare named Mandy and was branded about ten months later with the Seven-Bar Lazy B brand on the right thigh. He kept her in the pasture during 1912, and in the spring of 1913, the mare was turned out on a public grazing land known as the Squaw Coulee range, located southwest of his ranch. After that, he saw the animal about every two weeks. He left the horse on the range that fall, not seeing her again until late in the season of 1914. Phil said that she was one of his best animals and he really appreciated her.

Clack continued his testimony, describing the mare, and told how he searched in the spring of 1915 on her accustomed range, finding no sign of her. He made several trips around the area looking for her, even inquiring of the local ranchers—including Francis and Mabee. It wasn't until January 19, 1917, that he saw the horse again when visiting Carruth's Kremlin ranch. He examined the mare and found Francis's Pothook brand covering his own.[54] Carruth allowed him to take her home.

Clack later saw Francis in the Havre post office and informed him that the mare was now back in his possession. Clack stated Francis wanted to see the animal. Francis didn't recognize the animal from Clack's description since he handled so many horses, but maintained his brand was on first.

Attorney Carleton then cross-examined Clack, trying to discredit his testimony. It was brought out that Clack had worked the mare before her colt was born, showing a lack of the affection Clack claimed. Clack didn't agree. Carleton also presented evidence that Clack told County Attorney Griggs he first lost the horse in 1916, later changing the date to 1915. Clack denied this.

They had several more unrecorded exchanges; however nothing was noticeably gained by Carleton except for entertaining the courtroom crowd. Judge Rhoades finally called for order, chiding them that they were not comedians and further telling Carleton to desist from aiding in the merrymaking. A *Havre Promoter* reporter described the conflicting testimony he witnessed: " . . . one side or the other will be proven to have a vivid imagination and a consistent bunch of fair story tellers by the time the trial is ended." As the testimony progressed, there appeared to be two separate mares with colts, one belonging to Clack, the other to Francis, both having identical barbed wire scratches.

The following day Clack resumed his testimony. He declared he had branded the mare himself, hence he knew no other brand was originally present. In addition, he described the star on Mandy's Baby as being about the size of a 25-cent piece. Carleton, in cross-examination, tried to show that Clack and Francis had not been on speaking terms for some time. This was denied by Clack, even though out of court he held Francis to be responsible for the theft of several stallions and causing trouble in the heated disputes over two plots of homestead land involving H. Earl and Margaret Clack, Mary Martin, and George himself.

E. C. Carruth testified next for the state. Carruth was a powerful man in his own right. Besides being managing partner of the Havre Hotel and having his ranch and real estate, insurance, and loan office, he was a prime mover in the development of Havre. He had a strong hand in the establishment of the Stampede and later the Havre fairgrounds and racetrack. Whether it was the establishment of Hill County, the Northern Montana Agricultural Experiment Station, a better town fire department, a flax factory, or better schools, Carruth's hand was in it. Politically he was very strong—the "Mr. Democrat of northern Montana." He knew several governors well and served in various fish and game positions.

Unlike the Clacks, however, he was not a reformer and had a close, perhaps low-profile association with Shorty Young and associates—and knew many cowboys and old-time ranchers. He was on friendly terms with Francis, although he had been a witness for H. Earl Clack in the homestead land disputes and was a business associate of Clack and his Havre lawyer, L. C. Choquette. There is no hard evidence he bore Francis any ill will, though.

Carruth testified he bought the mare in question from Francis in November of 1916, but she was ill and remained at the Thomas livery barn for about two months. It was a few days after the mare was brought to his ranch that Phil Clack came on a business errand and discovered his long-lost mare. Francis then replaced her with one belonging to Jack Mabee.

Next to appear was Andy Avery, a former friend and employee of Francis, who earlier had been an enthusiastic Francis supporter against H. Earl Clack in the homestead disputes. Avery now worked on the Carruth farm and also did handy work and may have been bartending at the Havre Hotel. Avery related he had worked at the Francis Milk River ranch for about one month in 1915, breaking horses and doing general ranch work. During that time, he claimed, he had personally seen a "certain mare" carrying the Seven Bar Lazy B brand of Phil Clack driven into the corral by Francis. Francis then had Avery saddle or harness train the animal. When he noticed the Clack brand on the animal, he asked Francis why he wanted to break it, and Francis replied that he guessed he knew what he was doing. The witness said he quit about ten days later.

He further testified he saw the mare again when she was at the Thomas livery stable in Havre, but he didn't pay any attention to the brand. When the mare arrived at Carruth's ranch, he thought this was the same one he had seen and handled at the Francis ranch, although now it didn't seem to have the Pothook brand, only an "uncertain brand," crudely done. He concluded with the recounting of his long experience as both a cowboy and bronc rider in Texas and Montana.

The defense, with Donnelly now present, tried to break Avery's story, asking him if in fact this wasn't a frame-up, and wasn't it true he had tried to get Ray Ellis to present false testimony, too? And further, that he and Black Bill (Acison) had been offered $1,000 each by Ed Redwing and a Sprinkle brother to frame Francis? Avery firmly denied it. (He wasn't asked if H. Earl Clack had offered it.) Donnelly next asked if Avery didn't first tell County Attorney Griggs he saw the mare at the Francis ranch in 1916 instead of 1915? Avery again answered in the negative. He did admit to Donnelly he didn't like Francis, but didn't say for what reason.[55] Avery did say that he didn't actually break the pregnant mare because it was too balky.

Next, Herman Timmons took the stand. He was the son of Joseph Timmons and the younger brother of Ed and Rosco "Doc" Timmons. The high school student lived at his parents' farm southwest of town. Timmons was a court veteran, having testified in the previous land disputes. He told the court he frequently rode the range herding cattle and was familiar with the different local brands. He said he rode to the Francis ranch in 1915 to pick up two horses and, while there, he saw three horses in the corral with the Seven-Bar Lazy B brand. One was the mare in question; she had a colt with her. Later he saw the same mare in town with both the Clack and Francis brands on her.

In cross-examination, the defense pointed out that the Timmons and Clack families were friendly, and that Phil Clack was married to Cornelia Timmons. The defense could have asked a most pertinent question: Why wasn't Phil Clack told sooner? If he was, why didn't he take action right away?

Following Timmons, Paul Entorf told his story of acquiring the mare from Francis to use on his and brother Harold's farm and the subsequent return of the animal to Francis at the Thomas livery barn. Afterwards, Ed Thomas corroborated Entorf's testimony that they brought a mare belonging to Francis to his livery barn, leaving her for a month until Carruth's foreman picked her up with two others. He added nothing in regards to the brand dispute.

A familiar figure, J. W. Reed, took the witness chair. Reed had testified for the H. Earl Clacks in the two earlier land disputes. He said he lived near Phil Clack's ranch (which was true, since he lived on H. Earl's nearby homestead from 1912 to 1914), although his own homestead was northeast of Havre. He stated he knew of Phil Clack's mare and that he had seen her on his ranch since 1914 and saw her again in front of H. Earl Clack's store with both the Phil Clack and Francis brand.

The last state's witnesses for Tuesday were F. C. Lavigne, chief stock inspector, and local stock inspector A. R. Sellars. Both felt the Francis brand was the most recent when the mare was inspected about February 5, 1917, after clipping the hair from around the brand, thus agreeing with

Phil Clack that it was originally his horse.[56] Sellars disavowed any past discussion with Francis in which Francis had denied branding the animal or wanted the mare's branded skin removed to prove it.

If Jim Massey had been found, he would supposedly have testified to seeing the mare on the Francis ranch, bearing the Clack brand alone, but he had no desire to attend the trial and was thought to be on sojourn in Mexico.

With the conclusion of the state's testimony for the day, Donnelly called for the case to be dismissed on the grounds that no evidence had been introduced to show the mare had either been stolen by Francis with a felonious intention or that the horse had even been in his possession. Judge Rhoades denied the request. Now Donnelly and Carleton had the challenge of determining how the mare, which bore no Clack brand before entering the Thomas livery barn—only the Francis brand, the barbed wire scar, and a brand which was "blotched and could not be deciphered"—came to bear the Clack brand.

Actually their solution was simple. On Tuesday, February 26th, attorney Carleton made a preliminary statement, saying something to the effect that the horse in dispute was originally Long George's and was in fact stolen from Francis by Clack.

The first defense witness called was A. H. "Al" Thompson. He co-owned two Box Elder livery stables and had a ranch in the area. He later worked for the Cowan and Son general store there. He said that, while helping Francis, he originally had branded the mare's new colt in 1912 and had placed him with his mother and the other Pothook-branded horses in Byron Schwartz's pasture. Schwartz and his brother Henry owned a ranch about 3 miles north of Gildford. Henry was a U.S. Deputy Commissioner and would serve one term as Hill County sheriff beginning in 1920. He built the first home and store in Gildford.

The prosecutor asked Thompson to describe the brand. It sounded considerably different from what the state's witnesses had described. E. T. Walker, a Gildford stockman, stated he had ridden with Thompson at the time in 1912 and backed up his story.

Orville Marianda also testified that in 1914 he had put the same horses with some of his own, including the mare and her now two-year-old colt, into Byron Schwartz's field near Gildford. (This and Thompson's testimony conflicted with Andy Avery's earlier statements that the mare was pregnant in 1915.) Marianda said he saw the same mare behind the Mint

Saloon in 1917, pulling Phil Clack's ice wagon. He was sure it was the same horse because it had a wire cut on the left hind leg received in Schwartz's pasture—only now the mare had a bar running across the Pothook brand. Again, his description of the brand, like those of other defense witnesses, differed from the state's witnesses.

Byron Schwartz was the next defense witness, perhaps the strongest and most creditable. He affirmed previous testimony that the described animals had been in his pasture since April of 1914, where they remained for about one-and-a-half years. The bay mare, he explained, had been wire-cut while in his pasture, and in 1917 he had also seen the mare attached to the ice wagon behind the Mint Saloon. Upon examination, he noticed the Pothook brand had been altered with a bar or scratch drawn through it. Lastly the details of the altered brand were discussed thoroughly.

Next to appear on the witness stand was County Attorney Victor Griggs. Perhaps his testimony on Francis's behalf wasn't as helpful because of his known friendship with Francis and some of the vice elements. Nevertheless, Griggs said he was approached by Phil Clack and O. R. Sellars about the stolen mare in the early part of 1917. He asserted that, at different meetings, Clack twice said the mare had disappeared sometime in the latter part of 1916. The mare was then in the possession of the Entorf brothers. In a later conversation he said Clack wanted to change the time to the spring of 1915, also that he refused to have the branded skin area removed. In his discussions with Andy Avery, he claimed the same date conflicts occurred. And finally, Griggs stated he viewed the mare behind Clack's store, and in his opinion, the brand was clearly the Pothook with no other brand on it. He said none of his conversations with either Clack or Sellars produced any evidence to refute Francis's ownership of the mare.

During cross-examination, Griggs claimed he had agreed to go with Sellars to gather affidavits, but instead Sellars went without him. With that action, "I refused to handle the case to suit Clack, and therefore advised him to take the case to the attorney general's office, which was done." Ford and Grorud were already prosecuting gambling and prostitution cases in Havre.

The last witness for day two of the trial was Claude Welch. Along with Bill Acison and Andy Avery, he had given the original statements to Sellars as to the appearance of the brands of the mare pulled from the Milk River. He was one of the prosecution witnesses who had been sought for the first trial which was cancelled. Welch repudiated his alleged, earlier written testimonial, claiming he had never signed any such statement presented to him by the brand inspector. He now claimed he had seen only the Pothook brand on the mud and sand-covered mare.

Neither Charles Wilson or Sunny Walkup were located to testify, nor were Andy Nordin or Ted Hundley to make an appearance. Reportedly Wilson would have sworn that Ed Redwing told him he would pay $5,000 to land Francis in the state penitentiary, and Nordin would have maintained that both Andy Avery and Bill Acison tried to convince him to go in on the frame of Francis. Hundley would have supposedly added that Avery and Acison were getting $ 1,000 each from Redwing to frame Francis.

The first two days of testimony were described as rather mild and monotonous in comparison to the sensational third day, when over 1,000 took turns watching the day and evening sessions. The first defense witness and star attraction of the day was George Francis.

On the stand he told of his limited knowledge of the mare in dispute. He remembered seeing the mare on his ranch twice during a one-week period in 1916, and he acknowledged he let the Entorf brothers have the animal to use on their farm in early April of 1916. The next he saw of her was in February of 1917 being used on an ice wagon of Phil Clack's. He had heard Phil was claiming ownership, so he went to Stock Inspector Sellars, asking him to go with him to see the horse. He requested of Clack that the portion of skin around the brand be removed to verify the original brand, but Clack refused because he said the horse was too valuable. (Sellars denied earlier that such a conversation had taken place.)

Since Sellars refused to go with him, he then requested of Byron Schwartz and Orville Marianda that they inspect the horse to see if they remembered it as his; and they did. He denied having any conversation at the ranch with Andy Avery in regards to refusing to break the mare or its belonging to Phil Clack. He also declared it untrue that Clack checked with him when on the alleged search for the mare. He vowed the Clack brand wasn't on the mare until later, when seen on Clack's ice wagon.

He gave his version of the conversation that occurred with Clack in the post office in January or February of 1917, according to his recollection. Recounting the conversation, he claimed he told Clack that he was doing him a wrong by accusing him of putting his brand on a Clack horse. He maintained Clack's only reply was that all he wanted to do was be peaceable about it and keep the horse.

Court was adjourned for the morning and resumed at 1:30, when Francis concluded his testimony. It was brought out in the afternoon questioning that since Francis was president and manager of the Stampede rodeo, he spent little time at the ranch anymore, the point being that many things could happen over which he had no control or knowledge. For instance—although it couldn't have been brought out—it was known that cowboys laid off from other ranches stayed there over winters, sometimes keeping stolen stock there. Looking back to then, Nell (Mrs. Ray) Ellis-Bickle said that Clack cowboys drove some of their horses into the Francis corrals during roundup, which they may or may not have picked up later. At the trial, Francis concluded his defense-directed remarks with the revelation that he had asked Griggs to prosecute him for the theft of the mare to prove rightful ownership, but he refused.

A *Havre Promoter* reporter wrote that Francis's testimony concluded "with a dramatic flourish aided by his counsel as the defense rested its case."

Attorney George Hurd began cross-examination by questioning whether Francis had seen the evidence and affidavits procured by Sellars. He replied he had. Next, would Francis explain his relationship with Griggs? He responded that Griggs handled his civil matters, such as suing the G.N.R. for running over his stock. He had also visited Griggs' office concerning Stampede rodeo matters. Had Francis seen the mare after Paul Entorf had returned it to the Thomas livery barn, and given her to Carruth? He replied no. Hurd wanted to know when or by whom the mare was gentled. Francis supposed she was either trained by the Entorf brothers when using her as a harnessed horse, or perhaps it was done by Avery in his work for Francis. Actually it was done by the Entorfs, as brought out by earlier prosecution testimony.

Next came questions about the brands on the mare. Francis used a blackboard to draw his brand and the Clack brand, claiming his brand was the original on the horse, and he believed skinning the animal was the only way of proving which of the two brands were put on first. Hurd tried to upset that argument, probably referring to Lavigne's and Sellar's previous testimony.

Francis went on to deny Hurd's accusations that he had either been to the Clack ranch in his Hupmobile on Sunday, November 4, 1917, or had taken the mare to his place, killed it, and thrown the carcass into the Milk River. Next he was asked if he had hauled the animal in his car with another person from the Clack ranch.[57] He again replied no. And finally, Hurd questioned whether Francis had been in Havre anytime Saturday so he would have known of the indictment, giving him a motive to steal and destroy the mare. Again, no. Francis was then dismissed, and Phil Clack was recalled to the stand.

In his rebuttal testimony, Clack attempted to clarify several points, claiming Claude Welch did sign an affidavit in his presence about the suspicious-looking brand on the mare he helped pull out of the Milk River. He further alleged he saw Francis on Sunday morning, November 4th, within 150 yards of his ranch house, and later that evening the mare was stolen from his barn while the family was on a picnic. Seemingly it was Clack's and Sellar's word against Welch's, with Acison abstaining, and without either side presenting evidence to the contrary, since apparently the affidavit wasn't presented in court or the signatures verified.

In addition Clack asserted he knew the unshod hoof prints of the mare from all others. Presumably late Sunday evening or Monday morning he followed them over plowed grounds and through a fence that had been cut. From the fence line, he claimed he followed the approximately 3-mile trail across the prairie, where it led him northeast past the corner of Shorty Young's ranch (now the Hill County fairgrounds), where he lost the tracks. He said at the time Sheriff George Bickle and an unidentified third party were with him.

At this point they went to town and picked up Ed and John Sartain, whom he considered experienced trackers. They helped pick up the trail leading west and turning north about 15 miles from Young's ranch to the Abe Crosson ranch, which was leased by Francis at the time.

In Donnelly's cross-examination of Clack, described by the *Havre Promoter* as a "severe grilling," the rancher said Francis had two other people in his car that morning. One, he subsequently identified as Orin "Shorty" Selby, and the other's identity he was unsure of—possibly a neighbor of Francis's. He had seen them both before and after that time with Francis. Donnelly hammered at Clack over the coincidental timing and suspicious circumstances in which the mare disappeared: the day after Francis was indicted. Clack conceded he had heard of Francis's indictment on Saturday, November 3. He worked the mare on the ice wagon that day and Sunday until noon; afterwards she was taken back to the ranch. Reiterating how he had reported the theft to Sheriff Bickle and took up the trail, he again emphasized the trail was easy to follow because the mare was unshod. The obvious point Donnelly was trying to make: Clack had to destroy the evidence of his over-branding of the Francis horse now that the case was going to trial, and especially since Francis was demanding the brand area be skinned.

The next testimony, given by the Sartain brothers, was considered the most memorable and gave fuel for conversations of experienced cowboys and ranch owners, including some who were not particularly Francis supporters. Not only did they consider it incredible, but laughable. But apparently the jury didn't see it that way. The *Havre Promoter* called their testimony "the highlight of the trial."

John and Ed Sartain were rugged 6-footers who came from the wheat-fields of Kansas and later made their home in Illinois. They had a spacious two-and-a-half-story house at the southwest corner of Fifth Avenue and Tenth Street in Havre, and adjoining homesteads about 5 miles southeast of Havre on Clear Creek Road, where they raised, raced, bought, and sold horses. They were said to have made good money selling horses to the Canadian and British armies during World War I. In their early years they had a large pack of Russian wolfhounds that were used in hunting wolves and coyotes for bounty. They worked the area north of Havre to Medicine Hat, Alberta, besides working various other jobs as cowhands, teamsters, etc. Around Havre they once were employed by Pepin's P-Cross and reportedly worked at times for both Ed Redwing and H. Earl Clack. John was also an auctioneer.

John was the first to testify. He recalled being summoned to Phil Clack's ranch and being shown a certain trail to be followed. It led northwest from Clack's pasture by Fort Assinniboine (by Shorty Young's ranch) to Pacific junction on the G.N.R., then west beside the railroad tracks, across Big Sandy Creek, and through Jack Mabee's ranch. Next the trail went further northwest through Burnham, across fields where they found two cut fences, and finally ended within half a mile of the Milk River near the rented Francis place, a distance of about 15 miles.

Judge Rhoades threatened to fine both Donnelly and Sartain for their improper methods of question and answer during the cross-examination. It was the Carleton-Clack clash all over again. At the same time Rhoades warned the crowd, saying they would be ejected if any further merriment was demonstrated.

Donnelly asked him to explain how he could follow the trail of one mare over such a distance. He said he first measured the mare's hoof prints with a ruler on the ground at the Clack place, being careful to keep the mare's trail on the right side of his saddle horse. His brother was along, and they both measured the hoof prints often to make certain they were following the right trail, which had led to within 1½ miles of the Crosson place when darkness stopped further tracking. They returned the next morning between 3:00 and 5:00 A.M., looking for a further trail leading north from the south side of the Crosson place to 40 miles north to the Canadian border, but found none.

A big joke among some trial observers, such as Clayton Jolley, was when Sartain became so puffed up about his tracking abilities that he swore he could tell the color of the mare by the hoof prints! People had a good laugh, which upset the judge, and Sartain got razzed plenty over that statement. Of all the statements made at the three-day trial, this one was the most remembered.

It isn't clear why the defense didn't offer a counter tracking expert to explain why you couldn't positively identify a particular horse from its hoof print, especially on the hard, dry prairie ground. If the ground had been wet, that would have been a different matter. Apparently they thought it was too ridiculous to bother with.

Next Stock Inspector Sellars took the stand again. He maintained Welch had signed a statement in Clack's presence. He swore that he and Phil Clack gave their accumulated evidence on the case to County Attorney Griggs at his office, and he and Chief Stock Inspector Lavigne saw Griggs about it another time, too. He testified Clack had consistently told Griggs he last saw the mare in the fall of 1914, not 1915 as Griggs suggested.

The court adjourned until evening, when the main witness was Ed Sartain. The crowds so jammed the courtroom that even standing room was filled. Those standing actually had the best view, as their places at the railing obscured the view of those who obtained seats.

Ed gave practically the same testimony as his brother, and he, too, professed to be an expert tracker, in spite of Donnelly's objections concerning his expertise. He explained how and when he and John had measured the mare's tracks. Although he measured the tracks about fifteen times, he was unable to say how many times his brother measured them because they were occasionally out of sight of each other.

On cross-examination, he said he had run an engine[58] all night on the fourth and fifth, so when his brother had asked for his help in looking for the Clack mare, he hadn't had any sleep. Sartain acknowledged he and his brother had talked over the case considerably, and he had expected that Clack would lose the horse if he didn't put it in a box. He admitted having hard feelings towards Francis since the fight in front of the Havre Hotel (after Redwing's illegal branding trial), but there had been no previous disagreements. Why he switched loyalties from Francis to H. Earl Clack between the two land dispute trials was not explored.

Asked by attorney Carleton to draw the hoof prints on a blackboard and show how he measured them, Sartain demonstrated his technique. He offered that Sheriff Bickle had deputized them to catch a horse thief, but didn't accompany them. Sartain added he hadn't been particularly anxious to take the tracking job. Next Carleton had him draw a map showing their route as they followed the mare. It was consistent with his brother's testimony. No mention was made of whether the Sartain brothers were members of the posse that combed the Milk River area, looking for the mare and finding its mutilated carcass by the Francis rental property fronting the river. Sheriff Bickle followed, and his testimony corroborated that of Phil Clack and the brothers regarding the beginning of the tracking.

Next came a parade of pro-Francis rebuttal witnesses. W. C. Petticord said Andy Avery told him that "they" were framing up Francis. A. W. Morrell said Avery disliked Francis. Ray Ellis stated Avery offered him $1,000 to help frame Francis "if Black Willie didn't go back on us." Interestingly, Floyd Modill, Carruth's foreman and neighbor of Avery's, swore the bay mare Francis traded to them didn't have a white star on her forehead as Clack described, and had only the Pothook brand on the right thigh. R. C. "Doc" Timmons asserted that the horse's skin with the disputed brand on it could have been removed without serious injury to the mare, although it would have left a scar.

County Assessor James Fenton, who had a ranch down the river from Francis, testified he had seen the disputed mare in February of 1917 in Havre—bearing the Pothook brand with two bars lightly drawn through the brand. He thought the Pothook brand did not look like a conventional branding iron was used, more like a running iron imprint. He believed the only fair test would have been to skin the hide, which was now impossible, of course. In cross-examination, Hurd and Fenton reportedly "jangled considerably" over the subject of brands.

More Francis witnesses followed. Jack Mabee testified he couldn't recall Phil Clack asking him about any particular animal in his search for lost or stolen horses.

V. P. Johnson, a farmer from the Simpson area, took the stand and testified Francis had been at his own ranch during the entire time on Saturday,

November 5, when the mare was stolen. Francis's car was out of order, and Johnson was working on it; therefore it could not have been run the entire time.

Orin Selby presented himself as a rancher living near the Simpson area, even though he spent much of his time at the ranches of Francis or Mabee. His testimony concerned working for Francis in November of 1917, and he could vouch for the fact that Francis was on his own ranch the entire time; also the car was on the bum and Francis was helping Johnson repair it. In cross-examination, when asked whether he had told P-Cross foreman Jack Edwards that he had fed the mare to the fishes or that he had gotten blood on his riding boots in the process, Selby denied any such statements, saying the boots in question were presently in a downtown shoe repair shop. Whether the prosecution had a written deposition from Edwards on this matter, or it was hearsay evidence, was not recorded.

Fenton returned to the stand after Selby's testimony. The defense asked if he and Mrs. Fenton had been at the Francis ranch early in November on the Sunday before he heard of the indictment against Francis. He replied they were, and had seen Francis, a man called Shorty Selby, and a man named Johnson. Mrs. Fenton verified her husband's testimony.

And lastly C. C Brundage, H. Archibald, W. B. Pyper, and J. J. Blair all testified to the generally bad reputation of the Sartain brothers, even though they had nothing concrete or specific to offer as to reasons for that opinion.

Actually, they did have poor, but interesting, reputations. Rumor had it that the brothers imported stolen horses from Canada, and Francis's friends believed they killed and planted the mare in the river under H. Earl Clack's orders—but it was never proven. Ed Sartain's wife, Gertrude, sued for and was granted a divorce because of being beaten and abused. Mrs. Redwing didn't like them because they ridiculed her for being a cowboy. She avoided the Sartains whenever they visited Ed at the ranch.

On the civil side, there were negative points that perhaps could have been cited as to their unreliability. The brothers were in debt, and in default, for thousands of dollars to many people and several institutions.

The district court records are filled with litigations against them. In 1910, they were charged with taking money for, but not delivering, hay when acting as buyers for the Hedge Grain Company, J. S. Carnal, Havre agent. A Louise Thompson sued them in 1914 for failing to pay a promissory note to her husband, A. R. Thompson, for $125 at 10 percent interest. The

Thompsons were awarded the full amount plus attorney fees. Ed Sartain was sued in 1916 by A. J. Broadwater (Broadwater-Pepin Company) and the St. Anthony and Dakota Elevator Company for not paying bills. In November of 1917, they were again served for failure to pay a note due in March of 1914 for $375 plus interest to Havre merchant Joseph Gussenhoven. The creditors included Farmers State Bank (later Havre National), B. F. Stevens, Adolph Wieczareck, M. Wick, Hill County for back taxes, Havre Elevator, Ed Redwing, and H. Earl Clack.

In most of these actions, many horses and some automobiles from their businesses were attached by the court. Unfortunately for the bank, most of these assets were supposed to be collateral for the $5,000-plus they owed.

They had problems on the criminal side, too. In 1913, they were charged with the beating of a Neil Tarrey and for the beating and kicking of a Frederick Jones in 1914, being convicted and fined both times.

But the trial went on without any of these facts being revealed, which might have cast some doubts on their veracity.

For the prosecution, Assistant State Attorney General Grorud summed up their version of the mare's short life. She was born on the Clack ranch, branded with the Seven Bar Lazy B after one year, turned loose, and then disappeared. She reappeared on the Francis ranch and was loaned to the Entorf brothers for a season. Francis gave them another horse in exchange when he traded the mare and two other horses to E. C. Carruth for a beaver coat. She stayed briefly at Thomas's Havre livery barn because of illness and was then taken to the Carruth farm, where Phil Clack recognized her. Grorud apparently didn't review the story of the theft previous to her death or the discovery of the carcass in the river.

Continuing the summation, he zeroed in on the relationship between Francis and County Attorney Griggs, pointing out that Francis was both his friend and a private legal client. Grorud said Griggs had compromised his official office by making Francis aware of the evidence presented against him by Phil Clack and the state of Montana. He asked the jury: "Do you think your county is safe with that kind of county attorney?" Grorud appealed to them to fulfill their duty and once and for all put an end to such deeds as had been carried out by Francis.

Defense attorney Carleton's discourse to the jury was rather disjointed. He began by pointing out that Phil Clack was too small (and crippled) to have branded the disputed mare by himself as he had previously testified. Then he condemned the state: first for not presenting several witnesses as

164

promised and second for cooking up the case, making Francis a scapegoat to take the pressure off law enforcement authorities due to widescale livestock thievery and lack of resulting arrests. Surprisingly he finished by eulogizing Francis and speaking disparagingly of Phil Clack's character! Even Francis must have felt embarrassment.

Immediately following Carleton came Donnelly to conclude the defense's case. He tried to convince the jury that the state witnesses' testimonies were rigged in favor of Clack. In perhaps the most impressive argument presented by the defense, he said if Francis was guilty of what the Sartains testified to, then Francis should be tried for insanity rather than a crime. It certainly seems valid to question whether a man with such "talent" and "ability" would have acted in such a reckless and obvious manner: showing himself near the Clack ranch in a noisy, belching Hupmobile; then, after making sure he had been seen stealing the mare, leaving a clear trail—without trying to cover it—back to his ranch; leaving a series of cut fences along the way; and then ditching the animal in plain sight of his ranch. Oh yes, and be sure to cross Shorty Young's property to remind the jurors of their association. This would have been the work of a rank amateur with a suicide complex! And Francis wasn't, and didn't have such tendencies.

Finally George Hurd closed the trial. He declared Francis to be guilty in his opinion, and spoke of the state of Montana's earnest wish to stop horse stealing within its borders by making an example of Francis. Lastly, he posed the question: If Francis was innocent, why did he steal the mare from Clack's barn and destroy it?

Court adjourned, and bailiffs E. A. Darnell and W. B. Hedge led the jury to their overnight courtroom facilities, where the fate of Long George Francis rested.

The Verdict

It was the general consensus of those with an interest in the trial that the jury would have a long and arduous time deciding upon a verdict. Up to a point one could believe there were actually two horses: one born on the Clack ranch, and the other raised on the Francis place; one kept in Clack's pasture, the other in the Francis and Schwartz pastures. The Francis mare had its colt in 1912, but the Clack mare was pregnant when stolen and gave birth at the Francis ranch in 1915. Both had barbed wire scars in the same place, with possibly only one, the Clack mare, having a white star on the forehead. Both horses seemed to have merged into one from the time of the loan to the Entorf brothers.

And of the three brand variations the mare supposedly carried, each man and his witnesses claimed his brand was applied first. The Entorf brothers said one brand was indistinct while the Francis brand was readable; others said it only carried the Francis brand with two scratches for bars across it. Avery said it first carried the Clack brand, but later an indistinguishable one. Others couldn't say whose brand was on her, and so on. Francis claimed Clack destroyed the mare, and Clack vice versa, to hide their illegal branding of the mare.

Surprisingly, a long deliberation by the body of eleven was not the case. The jury took only one and one-half hours to reach a verdict. Judge Rhoades was notified at 8:45 p.m., and court was reconvened. Few were in the courtroom when the jury announced they had reached a decision because the short deliberation was unexpected. Foreman Riley Hadlock read the verdict: guilty as charged. Judge Rhoades then adjourned the court until the next morning at 9:30.

Immediately defense lawyers Carleton and Donnelly filed a notice of motion for a new trial. The hearing on the motion and on the defendant's application for bail and a stay of proceedings was continued until March 4 at 9:15 A.M. The bail, presented the same morning, was to be increased to $5,000 at the request of the court due to the circulation of a rumor that Francis planned to leave the country before sentencing. The postponement came at the request of Francis, so he could arrange his business affairs.

The area newspapers actually had a story that competed with war news: "Francis Declared Guilty," announced the bold headlines. "Sentence to be announced by judge Monday morning," the story went on. "One of the best known ranchers in Northern Montana and president of the Havre Stampede Association . . ."

The *Havre Plaindealer* ran a rather lengthy editorial the morning following the jury's verdict. The editor, Sam Y. B. Williams, must have worked on it all night, probably changing the lead story, too. Williams rejoiced that justice had finally been served:

> Last evening George Francis was declared guilty of horse stealing by a jury of twelve citizens of Hill County.
>
> Francis is one of the most widely known men in Northern Montana. He is a pleasant, likeable fellow with many friends and admirers. However, the verdict of the jury is very much in accord with his general reputation among a large group of people, including many of his friends. He is a product of a certain class of early day ranchers who did not believe or consider it unethical to brand everything found unbranded in order to 'keep even.' In the case closed yesterday the jury decided that Francis's policy pursued even a wider scope.
>
> Yesterday the death knell of such practices and distorted moral principles was sounded. The conviction of George Francis was epoch making in the history of Northern Montana, It would not have been so important if some of the 'smaller fry' had been convicted. He was one of the 'higher ups.' In fact, he had been admired by no small number for his ability to pursue his course and 'get by.' Francis has the ability to make friends. It would be well if some of them would take to heart the fact of their convicted companion. Instead of assuring him of their loyalty, which in a way is admirable, they would have proved their friendship

more if they had advised him to 'lay off' the old game. In reality Francis deserves sympathy. He is the victim of betrayed friendships. But even their position can be appreciated. It is hard for some people to understand that the old Montana is gone and a new Montana has arrived.

There has been too much outlawry going on in this section of the state in recent years. It might be stated in fairness that Francis undoubtedly has not committed all of the crimes of which he has been suspicioned. But he has laid himself open to that suspicion.

There are many others guilty of horse stealing who are still at large. The lightning of the law may land anywhere now that it has finally been made possible to get one major conviction.

This would not be a bad time for some of the other fellows to leave the country. Their game is over. The jig is up. More cases may be erected to be instituted in the near future. County Attorney Griggs, who has been severely criticized for his efforts to save Francis from going behind bars in this case, states that he had nine similar cases in view at the present time that may come to light at any moment. It can be reasonably expected that the state attorney general's office will also carry out further operations. There is a tremendous swing toward a clean-up now that a start has been made. People are going to renew their hopes for good government. Officials are going to wake up, supported by public sentiment. The guilty had better beware!

Past conditions have paralyzed the stock raising industry in this part of the state. Many farmers and ranchers have suffered heavy losses and have found themselves helpless before the onslaughts of organized rustlers. It is a small wonder that many have given up stock raising and others have contracted the friendships of the thieves in order to protect their own herds.

The time is near at hand when they can take heart and feel the results of their efforts will not be in vain.

The jury of the Francis case deserve the gratitude of the citizens of this section of the country for carrying out their duties in such a fearless manner. Their decision was not an easy one to make. Their responsibility was great. They arose to the occasion. Their motives cannot be questioned. Their service to the public cannot be overlooked or underestimated. Not alone that they declared Long George guilty, that is merely incidental, but because they hit a blow at the whole game. This fearless group of farmers are a credit to the country.

The attorney general's office is also to be congratulated for its efforts to remedy evils that have needed adjusting. The organization of the case by Assistant Attorney General Grorud, with the aid of the state stock inspectors and the complaining witnesses deserve creditable mention. The services of George Hurd, attorney, in the prosecution was extremely valuable. It is perfectly proper to compliment attorneys Donnelly and Carleton, counsel for the defense, for the tremendous fight they put up to save their client. In fact, the remarkable strong defense that they put up not only emphasizes the guilt of Francis, but also show up the almost unbreakable net that had been wound around the defendant by the state's witnesses.

Further, Judge W. B. Rhoades deserves unusual credit for the fair and capable manner of performing his duties during the trial.

To many good friends of Francis that are disappointed in the outcome of the trial, we urge that they feel no bitterness, Francis played the game and lost. He took the chance and now must pay the penalties unless the Supreme Court sees fit to reverse the decision of the court. There are others that deserve the same fate as Francis, perhaps. Do not worry, their time may come soon. They will have to take their medicine, too.

It will be very unfortunate if any innocent person is sent to the penitentiary. That is unnecessary if care is taken. But one thing should be clearly understood, and it is that: Stock thievery must cease!

Well, unfortunately, Mr. Editor, in spite of your best hopes, stock thievery didn't stop and still flourished; and very few arrests were forthcoming in Hill County, whether friends of Francis or not. In fact the cowboys, ranchers, and farmers rustling and butchering beef continued without any apparent diminishment, and no one of major note left the country. Jim Massey, a temporary visitor, did return to Texas, but he had left before the trial—and wasn't a major rustler, if at all. Massey headquartered out of Snyder and later Fort Worth and continued to follow the national rodeo circuit and the buying and selling of horses. Premier bulldogging champion Iron Mike Hastings bought a strawberry roan gelding named "Stranger" from Massey. It was considered one of the world's best steer-wrestling mounts.

Coincidentally, about the time of the trial, a major gang was broken up that operated as far north as the Cypress Hills of Saskatchewan and as far south as the Missouri River. The some fifteen-member organization was led by Loren Tolbert and Harry Tescher and had been operating since about 1913. No doubt Francis received credit for some of their work. Part of the group was captured in Chinook by County Sheriff James Buckly and Montana Stock Inspectors, Leslie McCann and James McCoy. McCoy was Francis's old boss from the Y-T ranch. Two Havre-area brothers were tried as gang members in Lewistown; they knew Francis, but were not friends or associates.

The following year yet another large gang of rustlers was captured which operated in the greater Fort Benton-Chouteau County-Bear's Paw Mountains-Beaver Creek Valley regions. Led by Henry Cooch, they set fire to haystacks, range grass, etc., as diversions, cut fences to steal horses and cattle, and took them to Canada. Again Long George surely received some credit for their thieving, although no apparent mention was made of these arrests in the Havre papers. A young man from the Beaver Creek Valley, who was their spotter and later a prominent rancher, turned state's evidence.

One more major gang of livestock thieves was arrested and tried at Chinook in 1928. They had been operating in Hill, Blaine, and Phillips Counties for years. Their membership included recruits from Havre, Chinook, Malta, and Great Falls.

Rustling seemingly became an almost forgotten crime when the reform-based Hill administration took office in the fall of 1918. Their almost singular occupation was arresting bootleggers and eliminating Havre's red-light district. Actually they did a poor job of that, too. In 1923, outside authorities from Canada apprehended another cattle-stealing bunch, this one led by a Ross Voss. They had operated for years along the northern border of Hill County and elsewhere. They killed and butchered the animals and sold the meat to farmers or markets in town.

There was evidence that an organized gang of livestock thieves did operate along the Hi-Line from Browning to Havre, to Chinook, Malta, and Glasgow, and into the Dakotas and Canada. Actually there were several gangs cooperating in the exchange of stolen animals. Some prominent people were involved, including law officers, an attorney, and a banker. Not one shred of evidence ever surfaced that George Francis was a member or led such an organization. In fact, anyone who was very involved in the livestock business knew who they were.

An observer of some of these goings-on was Texas-born and bred cowboy Frank Grable, who settled in the eastern Hi-Line region after he served in World War I. He had taken up and then sold a homestead in the Larb Hills below Malta before the war and worked for various people herding cattle and breaking horses.

There was an oversupply of horses because farmers were buying machinery and turning their horses loose, and they were no longer needed by the Army. Horses were rounded up, sold at $3.00 a head, and shipped to Hansen's Butte packing plant and Chappell Brothers Company in the Midwest, where the meat was processed for shipment to the Orient and Europe. After the war, Grable had a ranch in the Beaverton area and later north of Hinsdale on Rock Creek. He rounded up horses along the Hi-Line from Browning in the west to Poplar in the east. In his travels Frank crossed paths with former Texas outlaws in hiding and several organized gangs of stock thieves and bootleggers. "They would steal anything but a hot stove," Frank said. Grable vividly remembered attending the Havre Stampede and seeing Long George and Tony perform. He was either acquainted with or knew the names of those gang members—and he positively had never heard Francis mentioned as being part of them.

In addition, a stock thief operated close to Francis territory just north at Cottonwood. He was caught in the late 1920s only because a relative turned him in; many of his friends were never caught. And of course Howard Kidman continued to conduct business, although the law was finally closing in on him, but from Chouteau County.

Thus if Francis was judged guilty on the basis of being so well known and "one of the higher ups," it appears to be a bum rap. Granted, he was a livestock thief, but not of the scale presented by the state in his later years. So if anything rang true in the *Plaindealer*'s editorial, it was that Francis didn't commit all the crimes he was suspected of—perhaps far from it. The issue of Phil Clack's allegedly stolen mare seemed to be far from the real issue at hand in the trial. The state wanted a livestock thief in jail at any price, said lawyer Donnelly, and his enemies wanted revenge. If Francis belonged in jail, so did they.

The editor's thirst for justice would not be quenched as soon as he had anticipated, however. When Judge Rhoades' court reconvened on March 4, at 9:15 A.M., Francis didn't show. The judge asked the bailiff to summon Francis: Three times his name was called just beyond the doors of the courtroom as prescribed by law, but Francis did not appear.

He was now a wanted fugitive.

Havre's First Street in 1895, southside. (Windsor Hotel on far left.) Montana Historical Society, Helena

George Francis and friends, circa 1895. Left to right: Ed Sartain, Jack Wallace, George Francis, and Frank Hundley. Al Lucke Collection, MSU-Northern Archives

Hilda Ryan home in the Bear's Paw Mountains, circa 1901. Don Greytak photo

Aldoes Boys, 1903, top row, left corner. Snake Creek-Fort Assinniboine soldier re-burial detail. Al Lucke Collection, MSU-Northern Archives

Ed and Hilda Redwing at the Bull Hook Ranch, circa 1905. DON GREYTAK PHOTO

George Francis and Shorty Young by Francis's 1914 Model 32 Hupmobile Touring Car. MARIAN COUGHLIN PHOTO

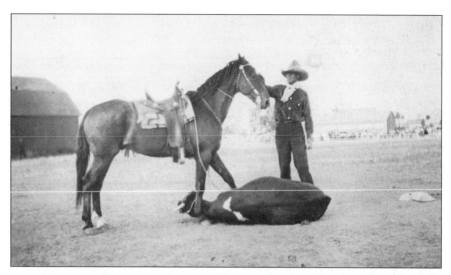

George Francis and Tony at Gildford Rodeo, circa 1915. ART SIMMONS PHOTO

Stampede Rodeo (mounted) band, 1916, in Judge Pyper's office. Standing behind: Orville Berry, Henry Belland, Ed Seifred, W. H. Watson. Standing front row: Andy Darnell, Jack Mabee, unidentified, Ed Timmons, George Francis, Louis Halverson, Loy Ashton, Paul Timmons, Stan Wanazek, unidentified. Sitting back row: John Berry, W. E. Wiltner, A. Wanazek, Prouty. Sitting front row: Vic Whitlock, Shorty Pool, Zeno Wentworth, Waldo Beaudoin. PHOTO FROM THE AUTHOR'S COLLECTION

Postcard scenes from the Stampede Rodeo, 1916/1917. AL LUCKE COLLECTION,
MSU-NORTHERN ARCHIVES

George Francis bull-dogging.

Jack Mabee bull-dogging.

Jack Mabee, circa 1916, studio portrait.
ROY MABEE, JR., PHOTO

Canadian Curtiss Bi-Plane ready to go. – 7/4/19

Jack Mabee at the rodeo, circa 1916. ROY MABEE, JR., PHOTO

Marie Gibson.
NELL BICKLE PHOTO

Tom Gibson (on right) and friends.
AL LUCKE COLLECTION, MSU-NORTHERN
ARCHIVES

Marie Gibson riding bucking bronc in rodeo. NELL BICKLE PHOTO

H. Earl and Margaret Clack. DON GREYTAK PHOTO

A younger H. Earl (left) and Phil Clack. DON GREYTAK PHOTO

Amanda Spears, Farmington, Minnesota, circa 1915. JACK MONROE PHOTOS

Havre's First Street, 1913, looking west from Third Ave. On the left side, fourth building down, is Shorty Young's Mint Saloon, Restaurant, and Apartments, above which George Francis lived. MONTANA HISTORICAL SOCIETY, HELENA

Jack Mabee in Hollywood with (left) Douglas Fairbanks, Sr., and (right) Charlie Chaplin, circa 1925. ROY MABEE, JR., PHOTO

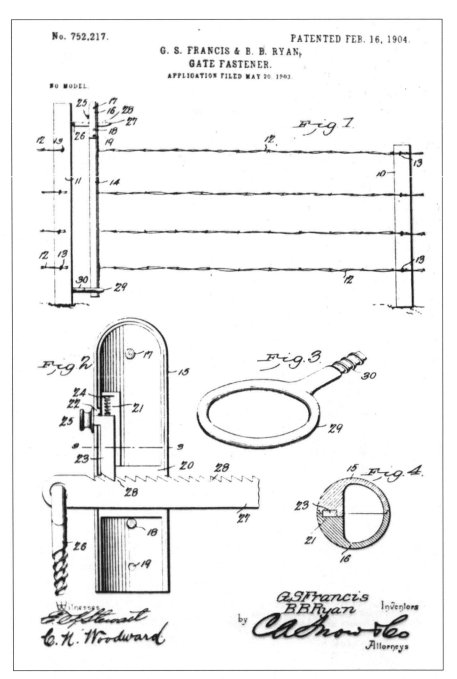

Livestock gate fastener developed and patented by Francis

The Disappearance

IT WAS A DREARY WINTER'S DAY in February of 1918. The scene was a tiny rustic courtroom on the desolate snow-covered plains of northern Montana. Around the single-story log structure stood several horses along with parked buggies and wagons, all belonging to the capacity crowd packed into the tension-filled trial room.

Inside, the hard-fought horse-stealing trial of Long George Francis was reaching its dramatic conclusion. The outcome looked bad for the tall, lean cowboy because of the overwhelming evidence against him. His feeble defense, that Phil Clack's mare followed him to his Milk River ranch, just brought laughter.

The lawyers completed their summaries, and the jury retired to the adjoining room while Francis anxiously awaited the outcome. Shortly the jury returned. When asked their verdict, the foreman announced "Guilty, your honor." "Hell," muttered Francis, drawing a secreted revolver (slipped to him by one of his few friends in the courtroom), and shouted to everyone to stay put. He backed to an open window, called his horse Tony, and jumped out. With one leap he was astride and raced away. At a prearranged secluded spot, Francis turned Tony over to a cohort and sped away in Shorty Young's white Franklin touring car.

For the next year or so Francis reportedly lived or was seen in such diverse places as the Bear's Paw Mountains; the Missouri and Milk River badlands; the Little Rocky Mountains; Butte, Montana; Pueblo, Colorado; Arizona, California, Idaho, New Mexico, Canada, and South America.

But wait! This courtroom vignette occurred only in the imagination of an eastern newspaper reporter and several "eye witnesses" who never saw the trial. The "tiny rustic courtroom" was in reality a three-story masonry building in downtown Havre. There was no revolver, no leap from a third-story courtroom to a horse, or a waiting automobile.

Francis did indeed disappear before his March 4 sentencing date with Judge Rhoades. He stayed in hiding for 16 months.

Because he didn't show for sentencing, the bail supplied by his friends was forfeited, and the notice of motion for a new trial was stayed until the defendant returned. Then, ten days after sentencing, his lawyers could submit a Bill of Exceptions stating their objections to the trial proceedings and an affidavit of motion for a new trial. Also the judge sealed the trial transcript until then, too.

Francis apparently didn't leave because he feared a long prison sentence. Moreover, he was determined to clear his name and he had faith in his attorney's ability to overturn the conviction and procure a new trial. Even if he did go to prison, with such powerful local friends as Young and Ed "Daddy" Marshall, it was likely his incarceration would have been brief; it was a common practice to buy people out of prison or exchange political favors for early pardons.

What he did fear, he claimed, was that while he waited to have his appeal heard by the state Supreme Court, he would be denied bail and be confined to jail , for at least two years, because the court was far behind in their caseload. He further maintained that his friends told him he was not to be granted bond and should leave town. When he heard further bail had been refused, he bolted. He asserted a story that he was to be granted freedom on a higher bond of $5,000 only surfaced after he jumped bail.

In the spring of 1920, Francis supposedly wrote the following in a letter to Guy Weadick of High River, Alberta, organizer of the Calgary Stampede: "I was then considered an outlaw by my enemies, but not in the eyes of the people who knew the circumstances of the case. While I was gone from town a year and a half, and although there was a posted reward of $500 for my capture, no one who really wanted me dared come where I was. If twenty people were taken out of town, I could have returned and no one would have bothered me because I was being persecuted, not prosecuted.

"As far as the matter of right is concerned, it's past and can never be recalled, but I still hate my enemies and love my friends. They were real friends that never quit fighting for me when they saw I was being railroaded for personal spite of my enemies."

It was true no one attempted to capture Francis. He was a fearless man and a crack shot, who wouldn't have submitted peacefully to capture. Besides, anyone who tried would have faced his friends' wrath; no one wanted their ranch or home burned or worse.

The rumor was circulating that Francis planned to leave town before the sentencing date. Worried about this, law officers tried to call on him at his room above Shorty Young's Mint saloon at 222 First Street, but found two men who claimed Francis had just stepped out and would return any minute. They discovered the door open and the room vacant on a second visit. Attempting a third time, they found the room was still empty with the door now locked.

While the law pondered his whereabouts, he had ridden out to his ranch for the last time, packed up his war bag, and headed for the ultimate destination of the Bear's Paw Mountains. He gave Ray Ellis's wife, Nell, his photo album before leaving. He left a quarter of beef on each of Bruce Clyde's and George Herron's doorsteps, along with a framed studio picture of himself to square his debts. A copy of that photo was used soon after for the wanted poster.[59]

Shorty Selby, Albert Thompson, and perhaps others, accompanied Francis to the Thompson ranch near Box Elder, where they stayed until nightfall. Then arrangements were made to remain at Harry Green's ranch near Big Sandy Creek. It was bordered by the new Chippewa-Cree reservation on the southwest corner. They left about 2:00 A.M. for the Green place with a bright moon giving them about ½ mile of visibility. Francis hunched over to prevent recognition, but his head reached the horse's ears, according to Thompson, and he looked even more conspicuous than he would riding upright. At one point, they passed a party of three or four men, yet were not recognized, and they reached the Green ranch east of Big Sandy the following morning.

After resting Francis asked Thompson to ride back to Havre and get a newspaper. Upon arrival, Thompson saw a posse had surrounded a house where "Havre's outlaw" was supposedly hiding in the basement. Thompson was told by the men that the Sartain brothers had tracked Francis there. "When they put the Sartains on the track of a fugitive," someone said, "they sure get him." "You bet," the brothers supposedly answered, "we always get our man." Thompson asked why they didn't go in and bring him out, but no one answered him. Finally it was established that the basement was empty.

Thompson returned to the ranch in the evening with a paper and relayed all the activity he had observed, including the latest scuttlebutt— probably as to Francis's supposed whereabouts. Thompson noticed the ranch hands stayed away from Francis and the windows while in the ranch house. George laughed at the question, saying they didn't want to be mistaken for him and be a target.

In his final trek Francis moved a few miles roughly southeast to a remote wilderness area in the Bear's Paw Mountains in the general vicinity of Black Mountain, on the down side of an unnamed peak surrounded by tall pine trees and reachable only by horseback or on foot. He built a dugout that was about 1 mile back from the nearest country road traversing the mountains. The well-concealed lean-to had a rock face with gun ports and a solid spruce door. Inside he built a fireplace for cooking and heat, a grub box and a homemade table; he stocked his kitchen with a few multipurpose cooking utensils. On one side was his long tarp-covered roundup bed roll with sewn-in mattress and blanket. Other than the bed a rock was his only seating accommodation. Near the dugout was the small year-round trickle of Green Creek, which flowed into the south fork of Big Sandy Creek.

Food, supplies, and mail were brought by a trusted few and secreted by two rocks in a hollow. He hunted deer and sage hens and perhaps a strayed "slow elk" to supplement those staple foods. He sometimes ventured out at night like "a jack rabbit in the brush" to farmers' fields for such treats as a dozen ears of corn. When his Prince Albert tobacco was gone, as a probably pungent substitute, he cut red willows—scraping the sap and drying it out in the sun.

Some days he spent cutting wood until dark and packing it to his shelter. At least temporarily this took his mind off his troubles. The solitary evenings were the worst, lying on his bed, staring into the fire, smoking his pipe, or playing his guitar. Then all the bitterness most likely emerged over how poorly his life had turned out, and perhaps he dwelled on the revenge he'd like to take against his enemies, or in more lucid moments, what to do about his life now. Perhaps he took some solace from hearing the Clacks now had bodyguards. The ranch was gone, back to the bank, and he was separated from Amanda and the rest of the world. He was a true "ridge runner," an outlaw on the run, seeking safety in the high country.

The same New York City reporter who had Francis leaping out of the third floor courtroom window also created for him a pet bird—sometimes a magpie, other times a woodpecker—that stayed awake when Francis slept, ready to give off an alarm at anyone's approach. Actually his only defense consisted of tin cans strung on a rope and his keen hearing. It's very likely that jokesters, like Clayton Jolley and Jack Mabee, helped the reporter with his facts. He did have squirrels and other animals which hung around the camp: some he trapped and kept for a few days in an attempt to tame them. There was even a skunk that came and went at its own leisure, sniffing around the dugout and snacking on the leftovers of bannock. Mice, however, weren't welcome to share his larder, and a few learned of his mechanical expertise when they found themselves caught in his 5- by 8-inch mousetrap made from a tobacco can and wire.

It apparently wasn't any big secret that he was somewhere in the greater Big Sandy area since his letters bore the town's postmark. Supposedly Francis even sent Sheriff Bickle letters with derogatory cartoons, daring Bickle to come after him. One such pencil drawing showed the sheriff stepping on a snake with the reptile warning: "If you don't stop stepping on me, I'm going to get you!" An article appeared in a Havre paper stating: "A messenger of 'Long George' recently complained that George is not receiving his mail promptly. Sheriff Bickle could not be reached for comments."

Yet in spite of this, Frank Lavigne, Chief Montana Stock Inspector, wasn't told of Francis's general location by the embarrassed local officials. Lavigne conducted a fairly extensive search with his limited resources, including a 450-mile trip throughout northcentral Montana and across the border. Even with the state matching the county's reward, not a peep was heard as to where Francis had gone. Lavigne's office even sent letters of inquiry to the Calgary Police Department and Saskatchewan Provincial Police.

Lavigne, interestingly enough, had previously clashed with future governor and then-district judge, Roy Ayers, residing in Lewistown. Investigator Lavigne had managed to arrest several cattle thieves in the Hilger-Winifred area, but Ayers allegedly placed pressure on the county attorney not to prosecute. Ayers and Judge Rhoades later became partners in a Kevin-Sunburst oil exploring operation.

Perhaps the law officers' fruitless search gave Francis something to think about with amusement during his long evenings alone; otherwise working helped kill time. George was careful and never traveled the same path twice except for certain rather inaccessible spots on steep mountain ridges. One day while he was walking through some spruce trees leading into the canyon where the road was located, he heard the distant intermittent revving of an automobile engine. He smiled, thinking someone looking for him had gotten stuck in a mud hole. The engine noises ceased, and two angry male voices drifted up the canyon.

"Hell of a driver you turned out to be. I told you before we started that I ..." [60]

"Shut up, you pot-bellied hunk of pork. Gather up some of that brush to throw under them wheels. All you do is stand around and holler. You idiot, we wouldn't be stuck here in this Godforsaken country . . ."

"Dry up and get busy."

"Can I help?" a third, feminine voice entered the conversation. "Isn't there something I could do . . ."

"You can sit there and keep quiet," said one of the men.

Meanwhile Francis crept closer, crossing the road out of sight and circling back to view the scene from behind a screen of bushes. He saw the car, hub-deep in mud. Behind the wheel sat a tall, thin-lipped, hatchet-faced man, devoid of coat with a cap precariously perched on his thinning hair. While he worked the accelerator pedal and gears, a heavy-set red-faced man huffed and puffed as he put brush under the wheels, received a mud shower for his efforts. Near the front of the machine stood an attractive girl in a gray dress and black hat. It was obvious from her red eyes and flushed face that she had been crying.

Francis started to walk away, all the time worried about the girl's fate, since they might be stranded without food, water, and shelter. Then, thinking he heard her yelp as if she had been hurt and against his better judgment, he turned around and openly approached them.

He saw the tall, thin man climb back into the car, while the heavier man sat on the ground mopping his brow with a large, blue handkerchief. The girl was now sitting close to him on a rock, blood trickling from her mouth. Francis said she looked afraid and presented a miserable picture of dejection. Finally the group noticed his presence. The girl let out a mild cry; the big man growled something and grabbed a shotgun off the car floor. The thin man produced an automatic pistol. Francis ignored them both and walked up to the girl. "You look like you're in some kind of trouble, miss. I'll be glad to help you," he said in a slow, low-pitched and calm voice.

"You can help us get this car out," growled the big man.

"I thought I heard a woman holler for help," Francis said to her, still physically ignoring the two men. "Your mouth is bleeding."

"Oh, she fell down," the big fellow said threateningly, "didn't you, Nita?"

"Yes! Yes! I fell down," she replied.

"Give us a hand here," the tall, thin one directed.

Francis turned to face them, his hand resting on his revolver. "I heard the lady holler for help. If she needs help, she gets it, but not you guys. When you go throwing a couple of guns around, and ordering me to lend a hand pushing a car out of a mud hole, you're wrong, brother. I don't like the way you talk to me."

"There's five bucks in it," said the tall man in a more conciliatory tone.

"I don't need five bucks, mister." Francis then began to half-back, half-walk away.

The big man, in a much nicer tone, asked him to wait, explaining that he and his "daughter" were headed for Lewistown when the "chauffeur" lost the road. Their abruptness was due to their awful predicament and because they were strangers, worried that perhaps he was the outlaw, Long George, they had heard about.

"And finding I'm not, you still have me covered." Then, addressing the girl, he offered her food and shelter at his camp a mile over the ridge while her two companions worked on freeing the car.

"Nothing doing," snapped the driver, "the three of us stick together."

"For a chauffeur," said a smiling Francis to the big man, "he shore gives a lot of orders. I never had one myself, but on a ranch or in a movie it's always the boss that says what to do."

"This ain't no ranch or movies," snapped hatchet face, "I'm a human being and I don't aim to stay here alone and be murdered by Indians."

Francis looked from one man to the other. Finally the girl broke the silence, "I'm afraid there's no other way, but for all of us to stay until we get the car out. It's nice and kind of you to offer help, and I thank you. I think you had better go," she implored earnestly.

Studying her face, Francis asked "Are you sure everything is alright here, miss? Is this man your father?"

"Of course I am her father, you blockhead. I'll pay you well for your assistance."

"A blockhead," said Francis, "is never much assistance. Good evening, miss; if you need me holler loud and maybe I will hear you. I've got a mighty good pair of ears." With those words, he tipped his hat to her and walked away, whistling. The guns of the two followed him until he was out of view. The girl sat on a rock, the picture of utter despair.

Francis knew something was very wrong. The hatchet-faced individual was too bossy to be a chauffeur. The big man acted afraid of him, and George didn't believe he was the girl's father. She looked scared for his safety—as if they might shoot him. He chided himself for being such a damn fool and shoving his nose into such a mess just because of a pretty girl.

Once back to camp, he ate some sandwiches and drank some coffee. Upon reflection, he changed his mind; he prepared some extra food for the strangers and started back down to the road in the dark. Coming down the canyon he could see the glow of the headlights, and hear the occasional roar of the straining engine and the whine of the slipping rear tires. He listened again to their conversation, concealing himself close by.

"Every minute we lose now means more danger. I wish to God I had plugged that wise-cracking cowboy; I didn't like his eyes."

"Why didn't you make him help us?"

"I was just Brown, the chauffeur, and of all the damn fool cracks you made. Oh you worthless tub of lard, see if those chains are tied good . . . we got to get out of this hole."

"I'll drive," said the girl, "you guys push."

Francis watched the girl slip behind the wheel and gun the engine. The car finally was freed from the mud hole with both men pushing, and disappeared down the road. George headed back for camp, vowing not to take another chance with strangers, even if he was certain they weren't lawmen.

Most certainly Francis had been in more danger than they were—perhaps they had been drug smugglers or bank robbers. Yet even they had been a welcome diversion.

Surely Francis felt lonelier after meeting the girl and thought more of Amanda. It is not clear how often they exchanged letters, and it would have been too risky for them to meet. He also became more skittish from the encounter: "Spooky like [Howard] Kidman," as he described it. Anxiousness aside, one night he had reason to be startled. A large boulder fell from the ridge above the dugout, and resoundingly crashed in front of his doorway. Jumping to his feet, half asleep, he picked up his rifle and looked through the gun ports, but his sleep-filled eyes saw nothing. He pulled the bar off the door and called out: "Come in if you feel lucky!" He threw open the door when there was no reply and saw the rock. Much relieved, but being wide awake now, he made some coffee and ate a small bannock cake and a strip of bacon before retiring again.

His imagination went from bad to worse, especially when in the dugout eating meals with a campfire going when his hearing was more limited. Several times he thought he heard someone walking close by. One night, while reading in bed, he was sure he heard someone in front of the door. On his feet, rifle in hand, he called out: "Come in Mr. Law, if you feel lucky!" Hearing nothing but a soft scuffling sound, he ventured a look: his visitor was only Mr. Skunk waiting to come in for a visit and a meal.

This was enough, he decided. Abandoning his lonely fortress, he chanced hiding closer to Havre.[61]

During the winter of 1918-19 Francis stayed at the James Fenton ranch east of the Gibson place on the Milk River. Fenton and his wife testified for the defense at the trial. Clyde Roper, who helped tow Mary Martin's shack back onto the disputed homestead when Clack removed it, was pasturing some cattle there, and Francis cooked for Roper's cowboys to earn his keep. It was easy for the tall cowboy to hide in the thick brush surrounding the house whenever someone rode up. He and Tom Gibson, Marie's husband, spent many hours together over a red-hot forge, using the anvil and hammer to invent various new devices. One apparatus was a bear trap with four jaws. It took over a hundred attempts before they were able to get the jaws to fit and synchronize properly. Tom kept the unpatented model for years, until it and other belongings were stolen from the Gibson ranch house during the construction of the Fresno Dam. They also developed a wagon jack and leather punch, and probably other devices.

One afternoon that winter, the Gibsons received a visit from a stock inspector and deputy sheriff. Naturally they stayed for dinner. Marie called son Lucien, who was sliding on the frozen Milk River with the neighbor boys. She told him to go back to his play, but then to sneak away and warn Francis that the law was close by. Tom, George, and a stranger were in the ranch's blacksmith shop when Lucien arrived. Not wanting to speak in front of the stranger, Lucien told Tom that mother wanted him to come right home. Lucien explained to him of Marie's warning message once he was outside with his stepdad. In appreciation Francis thereafter called Lucien "Little Close Mouth."

Francis may have ventured out further at times because one day Bruce Clyde saw three "Indians" ride by their house on west Second Street. One of them, tall and lean, waved at Clyde. If it wasn't Francis, it was his twin brother, Clyde said. Whether he was able to see Amanda or not is not known, but it was likely the law was watching her.

Finally some unrecorded friends promised him he would now get a square deal and would be allowed freedom on bond if he turned himself in. Following their advice, Francis had Joe Lucier drive him in a green Essex to the front of the courthouse for an 11:00 A.M. appearance on Tuesday morning, the eighth day of July, 1919. He wore a neat-fitting blue serge suit, dark brown glasses, and had a nice short haircut, according to a *Chinook Opinion* article. A large crowd soon gathered, once the word of his presence circulated. The rumor mill had correctly predicted his return; County Commissioner Crosson had wanted to rescind the county's reward based on the story of his impending return.

The same Tuesday morning, Assistant Attorney General Grorud, County Sheriff Matt McLain, and his deputies raided Shorty Young's Parlour House adjoining the old Montana Hotel/Honky Tonk. Eighteen men and eleven women were arrested. Was this a coincidence? Or was it meant to further embarrass Francis about his friendship with Shorty Young?

District Judge W. B. Rhoades was notified and immediately opened court. J. P. Donnelly was in attendance to represent Francis. Except the "square deal" he expected wasn't to be. The defendant was denied bail of any kind and sentenced to a term of not less than six years or more than twelve years for grand larceny. Donnelly argued the court had previously granted bail to an accused felon pending an appeal to the state Supreme Court; however, Rhoades replied he had only done it once, and the party had not been a fugitive from justice. The largely pro-Francis courtroom crowd showed both surprise and disappointment at the results of the proceedings. They had all been led to believe he would be allowed out on bail. He no longer had any friends in the county government, as of the fall election of 1918; it was now controlled by the Nonpartisan League farm vote. They were a strictly reform-minded group who had no use for gamblers, whore-mongers, prostitutes, barmen, or wayward cowboys.

So Francis was now in the county jail. A reporter for the *Havre Promoter* asked Francis for a statement about his whereabouts during his absence from Havre, but he declined any comment. The reporter was able to write that Francis had visits from many friends and that they were confident he would be granted a new trial. He probably also observed that Francis received home-cooked meals from the likes of Mrs. James (Mary) Auld.

While Francis sat in jail, another complaint for grand larceny was filed against him by Phil Clack; this time for the theft of the mare's colt. A hearing was scheduled in Justice Court for July 29.

Meanwhile, the Francis attorneys filed a 320-page Bill of Exceptions for a new trial. In addition to the transcript of the evidence, it contained several affidavits. They also filed a certificate of probable cause action to prevent the defendant from going to prison, pending the decision of the new trial motion. The 17th District Court Judge, John Hurley, then granted both bail and a stay of proceedings until such time as the district and state courts ruled on these matters. The judge also gave the county attorney additional time to file affidavits rebutting the defendants.

The bail, for $12,500 plus $1,000 for the new charge, was put up by 13 people: Ed Marshall, bar owner; Sid Hirshberg, theater owner; Lou Lucke, clothing store owner; Dr. J. Almas; F. F. Bossuot, architect and builder; Pat Yeon, pool halls owner; John Lamey, former bar owner and Young associate; C. C. Brundage, pool hall/cigar store owner; J. Auld, rancher; H. Archibald, store owner; Shorty Young and Frank Keple; and A. J. Edwards, rancher and P-Cross foreman.

Jack Mabee wasn't on the list for good reason. First, he and Young's associate, George Colter, had furnished the original bail forfeited when Francis fled. This they only paid after being sued. Now Mabee faced a lawsuit from Bond Lumber for the non-payment of $235. The lumber was purchased to build a hangar for his ninety horsepower, former Canadian Armed Forces Curtiss biplane, situated on Zeal Pepin's property, 1½ miles north of town on Shepherd Road. Luckily, his help wasn't needed this time.

Additional help came from individuals who made formal statements in the Francis case for a new trial. Reverend L. J. Christler asserted that about the time of the Francis trial he was in Guy Hockett's barbershop and overheard a conversation between two district court jurors. One later identified as Riley M. Hadlock, jury foreman, said to the other that he hoped to sit on the Francis case because he believed Francis was a cattle thief and he wanted to get rid of him. The Reverend later saw both of the men on the Francis jury. His affidavit was corroborated by barbers H. A. Smith and Art Dollard.

An A. J. Hoolihan stated that while he was at the Embleton Feed Barn, he overheard H. M. Reams, another Francis juror, say to J. J. Smith that it wasn't necessary to try Francis because there was no question as to his guilt and everybody knew it. August Kiehn corroborated Hoolihan's sworn statement.

Next, former juror Carl E. Sorenson avowed that he believed Francis was innocent and had voted so, but he finally changed his vote out of fear when another jury member threatened to throw him out of the window. Ex-juror Oscar F. Harvey backed up his statement.

A third former jury member, Tony J. Alex, swore that while at dinner juror Andy Darnell said Francis had stolen a three-year-old colt from him and charged $30 to get it back.

C. C. Brundage, Havre businessman, stated that prosecution witness Andy Avery confessed to him that he had not told the truth on the witness stand, "not by a damn sight." John Auld claimed to have heard the same conversation.

Cowboy Frank Hundley swore he had a conversation with Avery three weeks after the trial in which Avery told him he hadn't gotten the money promised for testifying as the Sartains had, who were paid by "Ed Redwing and them fellows."

The preliminary hearing for the second theft was held on July 29, with these motions in the works. Phil Clack, the only state's witness, claimed Francis admitted to him that the mare had a colt, promising if Clack could prove he had stolen her, he would give him the colt. Since Francis was convicted, he wanted either the colt or remuneration for it. Assistant County Attorney A. Lee Golden represented the State, and the district court records from the first trial were introduced.

Donnelly contended the most Francis could be charged with was petit larceny because Montana statutes provide the value of the animal must be established as a sufficient amount to maintain a grand larceny charge. Incredibly, Golden denied such a statute existed, but Donnelly secured a copy and submitted the section for the consideration of the court. Donnelly emphasized to Golden that it did matter to the defendant what the laws of Montana provided, and it was the right of the defendant that such laws would receive consideration by the court.

Justice of the Peace Kirkland ordered the case transferred to district court with a November trial date. County Attorney C. R. Stranahan issued subpoenas for fifteen people.[62]

At the same time Francis's appeal for a new trial continued, Attorneys Donnelly and Odell McConnel of Helena presented arguments as to why a new trial should be granted, based on the evidence they had presented.

Near the end of the hearing, long after the Bill of Exceptions had been presented, State Assistant Attorney General Grorud asked to have the affidavits accepted that he had spent a week gathering on the Hi-Line with a stenographer. This brought laughter from visiting attorneys watching the case. Counsel for defense quickly objected, protesting the time had long since passed for this. Grorud also tried to submit a hefty bill for his efforts, which didn't go over well, either.

Judge Rhoades denied Francis a new trial on August 22. An appeal was then filed with the state Supreme Court. On September 22, the high court granted a stay of sentencing until the court could rule on the appeal. Along with this positive action, the second criminal charge was dropped on December 8. Chief prosecution witness Andy Avery was in bed with cracked ribs and other injuries—it wasn't public knowledge how he received those injuries: by accident or by friends of Francis. The other prime witness, James Massey, still could not be found; he was probably on the rodeo circuit, operating from his Texas home. This was information Hill County most likely didn't possess. The state had no case since no one else could or would testify to the colt's birth.

Francis was glad to be back, although he was tired of being the center of controversy. He needed a place to stay out of the public's view, yet close to his friends—and especially Amanda. So he pitched a tent on land about 30 miles northwest of Havre near the east bank of the Milk River. The land belonged to Louise Kolvert, sister of Amanda Spears. Approximately five miles to the northwest was Amanda's homestead near the junction of the Lost and Milk Rivers. The terrain was rough with many coulees and was used mainly for grazing sheep and cattle. His camp on the main coulee was secure from view in any direction.

Louise's ten-year-old son, Alvern Arno, stumbled on to George's camp one day while on the way to fish at the Milk. Arno became quite attached to Francis, spending many happy hours at his campsite. From George, he learned how to make camp dishes and a coffee pot complete with lid and handle from tin cans, by using only a jackknife and pliers. He even once fired George's pearl-handled, nickel-plated Colt .45 single action Peacemaker revolver. (Once was enough.) Arno said he carried a second plain work gun with rubber grips.

Arno, like others, said Francis was a good shot, yet wasn't blood thirsty and killed only for food, not pleasure. He said Francis liked animals, and they instinctively liked him. This is why he believed Tony worked so well

194

with Francis, "because they were pals and a team." And he said of Francis: "He was a boy's pal type and a man's man."

It's sad that Francis never lived long enough to have children of his own. Amanda and George were engaged and hoped to marry once the trial and sentencing ordeal were over. Sometime in mid-1918, Amanda became pregnant with George's son and took a year's leave from teaching.[63] But sadly, the baby died at birth, believed to have been by strangulation from the umbilical cord, when Amanda was alone in the cabin during wintertime. Just after the birth she is believed to have rushed over to the Ernie Simpson ranch for help, but the baby was already dead. There, the sad little grave mound lies in a pasture near a small stream with rocks still encircling its top. A Mason jar with a note identifying the parents was buried with the body. Near there supposedly was buried John Amos Smith, patriarch of the large Smith family that Amanda knew well.

In addition to this tragedy, besides a prison sentence hanging over his head, Francis had money problems. He needed to support himself and pay his mounting lawyer bills. So the "over-the-hill" forty-five-year-old cowboy cashed in on his notoriety and returned to the rodeo arena. His first re-entry was a big one: the 1919 six-day Calgary Stampede held August 25-30. The event was staged by his friend Guy Weadick, a High River, Alberta, rancher, and the sponsors were the same backers of the 1912 version: George Lane, "one of the world's biggest farmers and stockgrowers"; Pat Burns, "the Calgary packer"; A. J. McLean; and A. E. Cross. One hundred thousand dollars in prizes were being offered. It was only the second Calgary Stampede. Yet other major rodeos had been held in Winnipeg and Saskatoon. It was to be called the "Victory Stampede" in honor of the (few) returning World War I Canadian soldiers.

Along with the attraction of the many top topers and riders from around the world, Charlie Russell held an exhibition of his works in a specially built gallery. Opening the ceremonies in Victoria Park was the Prince of Wales and party, courted by the scarlet-tuniced men of the R. N. W. M. P. The arena could accommodate 25,000 spectators since the addition of a new concrete grandstand.

Although Francis hadn't been a rodeo participant in about two years, he wasn't forgotten. In fact his notoriety as "the Montana outlaw, Long George," increased and expanded his popularity. The Gibsons and Steve Adams of the Empire ranch near Harlem were apparently the only other local contestants.

Marie Gibson rode with him in the parade in which large crowds lined both sides of the street. In her remembrances she wrote: "The people stared at him. You'd hear once in awhile someone saying, that's Long George Francis. George would laugh and look at me." Of course, Francis was at his best, in his purple sateen shirt with white buttons and deluxe pure beaver Stetson, and was decked out in silver-plated spurs, ornamented chaps, and perhaps belt buckle, plus the nickel-plated revolver. Tony was wearing the silver-mounted saddle, bridle, taps, martingale, saddle skirt, et. al. with the "V" brand prominently stamped on the other leather gear. After the parade they rode to the rodeo barns and fed their horses. Then it was time to get ready for the 2:30 show.

Weadick wrote that Francis made many friends while in Calgary, describing him as "a quiet, courteous, unassuming man, a genuine cowboy of the old open range days."

The show began with the introduction of the contestants, representing nearly every western state, province, and British Empire country: the trick riders, Indian chiefs, artists Charlie Russell and Ed Borein, the organizers, and lastly Guy Weadick. Much of the stock and performers came directly from a rodeo herd in Bozeman, Montana, located in the Gallatin River Valley.

In the roping and bulldogging contests, Francis was up against championship-caliber younger men who weren't rusty from a two-year layoff. "Iron" Mike Hastings, old friend Jim Massey, Ed "Yakima" Canutt, Ed Burgess, Ed McCarty, Joe and Clem Gardiner, Jesse Stahl, J. O. Banks, Walt Stirling, Roy Kinnet, Roy Knight, and Johnny Mullens.

There were no complete results available, but Marie Gibson is believed to have done quite well on the bucking horses; as did Tom Gibson on the bucking bulls and Francis in the calf-roping contest. Experience won out for Long George when he roped and tied a large range Texas steer that none of the other well-known riders were able to do, although he didn't make it into the over-all top steer ropers or bulldoggers. That feat probably meant as much to him as any win of his career. And how could the crowds forget the spectacle after Francis roped, threw, and tied a steer? Once he raised his hands, Tony walked up to the tied animal, placed two hooves on the animal's side, and took his own bow; and then turning and standing to one side as the judge inspected and ordered the steer freed, Francis took his bow, too.

The Lou Lucke and Rocky Klinger families of Havre attended the Stampede while on vacation. They ran into Francis, and they said he looked the worse for wear. He had a bandage around his middle from being gouged by a steer's horn and a cut-up mouth and loosened teeth from a steer's kick.

After the rodeo, Francis went home to mend and rest his weary bones and Marie Gibson went on to a Dillon community rodeo in southwestern Montana. Next on the schedule for Francis and the Gibsons was the September 17-18 Hinsdale (Montana)[64] Milk River Stampede. Besides the usual rodeo events and car and horse races, the "Catch 'Em Cowboy" show featured a hot air balloon, night shows, dances, and big feeds at the cafe in "Slippery Gulch." The Glasgow and Saco community bands added music to the show. While Francis was the star attraction, he was not the promoter. Locals Art and Frank Seeley and Morris Denham put on the show. Newspaper ads for the rodeo read: "See Long George Francis, the premier cowman of Montana featured in bulldogging and other hazardous stunts. Long George Francis, Havre's best known range rider, making the Stampede Association a permanent feature, returned from the Calgary Stampede bringing down big prizes for roping and bulldogging."

Francis lived up to the glowing publicity by winning the bulldogging contest, taking only third in the steer roping. In one event, he gave the crowd a thrill by catching one steer between two of the autos parked in the circle around the arena, as witnessed by young Richard Eaton.

Next, Francis was to join Mabee at the Poplar (Montana) Indian Fair on the Fort Peck Indian Reservation. Mabee had been 60 miles down the road to the west at the Phillips County Fair at Dodson. Along with participating in rodeos, Mabee and his former Army pilot, Lt. C. R. Innes, had flown their biplane to many fairs in northern Montana with the Clack Oil banner streaming behind. They gave both flying exhibitions and rides and established or broke many air speed records.

They had engine trouble on their return trip from Poplar, however, and had to land just south of Malta. They thought the problem was well enough corrected to get them home, but in their attempted take-off, they crashed on a rocky bank near the town's water tower.

How either Francis or Mabee (if he made it) fared in the Poplar rodeo, or whether that was their final rodeo of the year, is not known. However, they may have participated in a St. Paul, Minnesota, show with the Hinsdale promoters.

Francis earned his keep in 1920 by working as deputy collector (now called a custom officer) for the U.S. Customs Service under Chief Inspector

Frank Wiles of Great Falls. Presumably he worked out of a Havre office in the Masonic Temple along with other federal agencies, since there were no border stations. His job was to help apprehend bootleggers along the border.

Reportedly Francis arrested few, yet did confiscate many loads of liquor. On one unofficial excursion, he accompanied some Havre police officers (and one future police chief) who were hijacking loads from independents competing with the Havre bootlegging bunch in which Shorty Selby was involved. In this instance the bootlegger recognized his robber and was killed. Francis confided in George Herron of the experience, since he was shaken over this unexpected turn of events and was against senseless killing. Francis knew he couldn't do anything against such a powerful organization; and besides, most of them were his friends. He never accompanied any of them on any illegal seizures again.

In later years after his death, Francis was credited with having been the head of the major Havre liquor smuggling and hijacking organization that operated along the Hi-Line from Canada throughout the West and Mid-west. He was given the blame by some for the death of Lewistown (Montana) bootlegger Jack Hardin, who was killed north of Havre in December of 1920—even though the killers' names were actually widely known. These accusations came from either careless historians or his enemies. The names of those who led the Havre Bunch were not a secret: Shorty Young and Daddy Marshall were always in the news. They were soon joined by the likes of Pat Thomas, Pete Weyh, Ed Jacoby, Mike Lewis, and Clair Dow.

Inaccurate stories about Francis have been published as late as the 1960s. One author tells us: "He was secretly involved with a gang of men who ran liquor across the nearby Canadian border." Another goes even further: "His second side was one of a rustler, thief and bootlegger. Many a night was spent running liquor across the border into Canada. His bootleg mob was known as one of the largest operating across the border at the time. The first shovelful of earth excavated at Fresno Dam destroyed one of the bootleg hideouts of Francis." (Yet this "bootleg hideout" was his Milk River ranch, which he abandoned before the state prohibition or federal laws were enacted.)

Fortunately Francis would never be aware of the extent to which his life would be distorted and exaggerated.

A month before attending the Glasgow (Montana) Stampede rodeo, he wrote home after receiving letters from sister Fran and youngest brother Henry. In his letter he said he had been dreaming of his enemies so often that he had to pray to dream instead of his mother and sisters, Ella and Fran. As in the past, he promised to come home—but didn't. He did hint of worrying about his mother dying before he could see her, but ended his comments jokingly about his own aging problems. He ended on a note wishing Ella would write to him. (At one point he was trying to get at least one sister to come out and teach at Simpson.) The letter was written on stationery from the Havre Hotel, where he may have been living.

In his only recorded rodeo appearance of 1920—although he may have performed in several—he competed in the Glasgow Stampede, staged by the Milk River Stampede Association of Hinsdale. The rodeo began on Saturday, July 3, and ended on Monday, July 5. The "We're Wild" rodeo was joined by a Wolf Point-Glasgow baseball tournament. "World Champion Bulldogger" Long George Francis was again the star attraction. His $1,000 saddle, won at a Pendleton Roundup for steer roping, would be on display, it was announced in the pre-rodeo publicity.

Other Havre participants were Tom and Marie Gibson, Jack Mabee, Byron Connelly, and Shorty Selby. Ed Sartain, then of the Great Falls area, was scheduled to appear, but was gravely ill. Recording the event was a *Minneapolis Tribune* reporter.

Unfortunately it didn't go smoothly for Francis during the Glasgow rodeo. During one calf-roping competition, he stubbed his finger on the saddle horn and broke it. Another time his rope broke after the animal was thrown, but he repaired it and still managed to come in second behind a Frank Drabbs. He managed only third overall in the bulldogging, having to throw an extra steer because in one try he was disqualified for "hoolihaning" it. This was the outlawed method of jumping on the steer's neck to bring it down. Francis did win the steer roping off a loose horse and one stage of the "Catchum Cowboy" race. Marie Gibson won the Cowgirls Race and Bucking Horse Championship for girls, and Tom Gibson won a segment of the Wild Horse Race. Either Jack Mabee didn't show as scheduled, or he didn't place in any event. The association's next rodeo was to be held at Brush Lake, North Dakota, and possibly on to Minneapolis.

A competing one-day, July 4 Wild West Show—sponsored by the local Elks club—was held in Havre. Ray Ellis was one of the promoters, along with Bob Ingersoll and Bert Wanazek. It also featured the ever-increasingly popular sport of baseball with a game between the Hi-Line Red Sox and Great Falls Smelters. No results were published since the national Democratic convention in San Francisco monopolized the papers. It was the last major rodeo in Havre for several years. The Stampede rodeo grounds was thereafter used by the high school football teams. It wasn't until later years the games were played at the natural amphitheatre on the west end of town where previously the circuses had performed.

In addition to the rodeo's demise, the Havre Flax Mill was destroyed by a violent storm, and there was drought, crop failure, and insect infestation to add to the Milk River Country residents' feeling of foreboding.

A small rodeo promoted by Ray Ellis and friends was held the following summer at St. Joseph, a small farming community north of Havre. It also featured a community baseball game between Cottonwood and St. Joseph. Again, no results were published. There was no magic without a performance by Long George Francis and Tony.

The Hill County fair was discontinued until 1928 when eighty acres were acquired from Shorty Young on his ranch west of town on the hill overlooking the city. At the same time, Young put the former Stampede grounds up for sale, divided into 212 lots. To further replenish his diminishing bankroll, he sold his downtown office building, behind the Hill County Bank, to E. C. Carruth. The now poorer and less powerful, tarnished vice king moved his office into a former tailor shop.

Young and Francis were not the only ones involved in conflicts: The range battles continued between the last of the big ranchers and the homesteaders.

Simon Pepin had died in 1914, leaving assets of over $1 million in cash, real estate, livestock, and investments throughout north and central Montana and Alberta. His Canadian Bear Creek ranch property was sold to the Wallace and Ross ranch, and the Shepherd and Pearson Company bought the north-of-Havre horse ranch from Pepin's daughter, Elizabeth Meyer. The Broadwaters operated the P-Cross ranch in the Beaver Creek Valley. Among those working for the ranch were Francis's friends: Ray Ellis, Pete Brower, Frank Stirling, Clayton Jolley, and Martin Nobel.[65] Texan Jack "Daddy" Edwards was probably foreman. The 5 feet 7 inches, ever-pipe-smoking Edwards was also known by his friends as "Lyin' Jack" because he loved to tell tall stories. For instance, upon passing a friend on the trail, he would say: "Ain't got time to talk; I got bit by a rattler." One of his favorite stories was that he once shot an elk in this locality, so large that the antlers were at least 6 feet across, and that he kept the antlers in the attic of his Beaver Creek Valley cabin. He knew his stories were getting to him when he actually looked in his attic for them! He and Harry Broadwater operated the last local roundup association in the Milk River rangelands. His former wife and two daughters lived in Chinook. Edwards previously worked for the Coburn ranch near the Little Rockies.

In the spring of 1919, a certain homesteader named Thompson moved in with a widow who lived near Black Coulee in the Bear's Paw Mountains. He decided he was tough enough to run the P-Cross off the range, so he organized the other settlers with the intention of rounding up the P-Cross cattle and running them across the Milk River. At the same time some of the "nesters" were to cut the ranch's fences and drive away the riding stock.

But unbeknownst to the puffed-up interloper, one of the farmers was keeping the P-Cross men apprised of his schemes. The night before the raid, the cowboys each caught a horse and put the animals in the barn.

At daybreak the thirteen P-Cross cowhands rode out. From atop a hill they spotted the thirty-two thieves and swooped down on them with much yipping and whooping through a stand of thick timber. The ensuing scuffle must have resembled a wild scene from an old Western movie. Some of the surprised riders were rudely unseated and felt the sting of ropes whipping them as they regained their feet and fled. Within ten minutes they had all disappeared over the hill—some mounted, others chasing their own runaway horses. Although some were carrying concealed pistols, they dared not draw them against the more heavily armed and proficient cowboys. Thompson tried to get away on his pregnant mare, but Clayton Jolley caught up with him and jumped from his horse onto Thompson's and pulled him off.

Needless to say, the ranch had no further problems with that bunch, and the boys had enjoyed chasing off the interlopers.

The sheep disputes continued also. About a year later, two P-Cross men surprised a sheepherder and a band of sheep trespassing on the ranch property north of Havre through a cut fence. One moved the herder and his sheep off the pasture while the other put a rope on his wagon and pulled it down a hill, smashing it into pieces.

The next year the same man, either through bravado, stupidity, or necessity, ran sheep across the ranch's land again to get water, resulting in several of his woolies being trampled by the cowboys' horses for his actions. There were other instances of more ruined wagons, some burned.

Both the P-Cross ranch and George Francis were struggling to survive against the fates and the encroachment of civilization.

The Death of George Francis

FRANCIS HAD WRAPPED UP THE 1920 RODEO SEASON, performing with the Hinsdale Stampede Association, still not certain of what the future held for him. At forty-six he knew he had been pushing his luck, and many more rodeo performances could result in him becoming an arthritic cripple or worse. But the lawyers' fees for two trials and his current appeal had to be met. If the appeal was successful, he needed money to support a bride and buy land, possibly an extension of Amanda's place. And hopefully he planned to build up the new ranch by legal means only. After all hadn't he angered some of his friends by not allowing them to keep their stolen livestock on his ranch (presumably) once the Stampede rodeo began? Also, life had become too dear to him to risk any further thievery; there was no reason he couldn't be a successful promoter of rodeos. The Stampede could be revived in Havre again.

The fall weather, wet and cold, must have ended his camping days, and he may have moved in with Amanda at the Lost River homestead, and stayed with the Gibsons while in town. It should have been far enough away from Simpson and her place of work and the school-supplies house to minimize any scandal. These were probably the happiest days of George's life, even though a prison sentence hung over his head. Amanda shared some of the same qualities that Hilda possessed: She was a strong-willed, hardy, outdoors-loving woman with a farming background, who enjoyed hiking, horseback riding, berry-picking, vegetable-raising, and wildlife-watching. She likewise shared his enthusiasm for music—playing the piano, reading the classics and poetry, besides dabbling in oil painting. Amanda, with her hint of a German accent, was about thirty-two years of age at the time.

Their time together came to an abrupt halt much too soon, when the state Supreme Court denied his appeal for a new trial. Montana Supreme Court Justice Matthews expressed the following in support of their opinion: "The situation in which the defendant found himself on July 8, 1919, was brought about solely by his own wrongful, voluntary and contemptuous act in defying the authority of the court . . ."

Thus the appeal was dismissed because he had been a fugitive from justice. The evidence introduced at the trial concerning the second offense of the mare disappearing from Clack's barn was ruled admissible because of evidence presented of Francis being seen in the area, and the tracks followed to near his ranch. Since the high court's action seemed to rest on his flight from sentencing, it had been a bad move to flee even if he would have had to remain in jail awhile until the bail situation had been straightened out. It would have been better if he had left the area permanently and taken Amanda, since he hadn't been willing originally to tough it out in Havre.

The court's decision came about December 15, and at the time County Attorney Stranahan was in Helena. Even before a writ for Francis's surrender was received from the court, Stranahan immediately ordered the sheriff to apprehend Francis. Stranahan claimed that one state justice had told him to arrest Francis immediately. There wasn't any basis for this action since Francis was already under a legitimate bond. However, Francis received advance warning and hid at the Gibson place in Havre until the sheriff realized the county attorney's action wasn't official and told the local press: "If Francis walked in and announced that he would go to Deer Lodge now, as far as I am concerned there would be no necessity to send a man along with him as I know Francis would do just as he said."

While Francis "hid out" at the Gibsons, he left his Hupmobile parked behind the house, plainly visible. Many visitors came by wondering if Francis was living there, but he remained in the bedroom until they were dispatched. Once this legal wrangle was settled, he again returned to the Lost River ranch. On about Friday, December 17, he returned to Havre so Amanda, nephew Alvern Arno, and stepfather "P-Bell" John Kolvert could Christmas shop. Francis headed through the snow to the Gibsons while

Kolvert put his car in a downtown garage. The house was full of company when he arrived, so he tapped lightly on the frosted-over back door glass. She closed the door to the living room and put Francis in the bedroom after going out back for a load of wood.

Tom ("Slim") then left with the company, and Marie locked the door and put the blinds down. Lucien and Andrew ("Buster") discovered his presence and said, "Hello Uncle." [66]

"Hello, children," replied George, "have you been good since Uncle left?"

Lucien said, "Yes."

George explained why he was in town and who was with him. He put his hand on Marie's shoulder and said how much he missed her. At her suggestion, he hid when Tom returned. The family told Tom they had a surprise for him; when he couldn't guess—or pretended so—Buster told him who was there and led him back to the bedroom, where the two friends conversed. Then supper was served. Lucien poured the coffee. Tom passed George the butter, which brought some playful kidding from Francis, since he only used lard on his bread.

Amanda soon arrived. Apparently the family had never met her before, at least according to Marie Gibson's memoirs. George asked her where "P-Bell" and Arno were. She replied that she got tired and decided not to wait for them. They adjourned to the living room, gathering around the stove. Francis took out his big pipe and filled it with Prince Albert tobacco, settled in a chair with another chair as a footstool, and puffed contentedly. Looking at Amanda, he said, "There's no place like home, is there honey?" The subject next turned to the weather. Amanda said the snow was really coming down. "Well we are under shelter, let it come," said Francis laughingly. "Well here we are poor cowboys and almost snowbound—and it's near Christmas too. Amanda, you'll have to stay here with me till I go to the Deer Lodge jail."

She said she would like to, but couldn't—she had to teach school on Monday. George argued about the long lonely trip on hazardous snow-filled roads, yet she was adamant. Therefore, the following morning, after telling George Herron of his plans, he, Amanda, John, and Alvern drove out to his old ranch and harnessed his old gray horses, which had been running loose.

Before she departed, they spoke of their love for each other. Amanda promised she would wait for him, even come visit at the state prison. He held her in his arms and promised to marry her once he was out of prison. And he kissed her goodbye, tucking the blanket around her on the wagon seat.

That was the last time she ever saw him alive.

About Wednesday, the December 22, Sheriff Matt McLean and Deputy Sheriff Herron came to the Gibson house after supper, and they discussed when Francis should leave for prison. They evidently decided it would be best for parole purposes that Francis should begin doing his time in 1920, and a date was chosen after Christmas.

Apparently Francis worried for his safety even though he was headed for prison. He kept his knife, pipe, and revolver on a table in the spare bedroom. In the past, Marie told George she objected to the presence of the pistol because of the children, but he said it was okay where it was.

One day he was talking to Marie about the stolen mare and the witnesses who had framed him. "We were punching cows together, then they turned state's evidence against me. We've been hungry and thirsty together, cold and wet for days at a time. We had squatted in rock holes and against boulders till morning came so we could move our stock. We went through anything together that make men shore as hell pardners under the hide, and then some of these would-be friends turned state's evidence against me."

After those words, he got up with an angry look in his eyes, left the room, and returned with his revolver. "Take my gun and put it away. Don't ever give it to me even if I ask for it. I might hurt somebody. If I am sent up for any length of time then you give the gun to Harry Green to put in his safe." He said Harry would know what to do with it. Marie locked it in her trunk along with his field glasses.

Francis didn't venture from the house, apparently fearing an incident—accidental or planned—or foolish questions he didn't want to answer. Tom and Marie ran errands for him, and sometimes George and Tom whiled away the hours playing guitar and fiddle and no doubt sharing a few rough-sung tunes.

The Reverend Christler visited Francis several times; the last was probably Thursday, December 23. The two had lunch together, discussing the latest aspects of the case. When the meal was over and the minister was ready to leave, Marie brought his coat and hat. He said, "Well George, Merry Christmas to you and your lady friend. I'm trying my best to get you a pardon. I think it will go over."

"Thanks, Merry Christmas to you too, I'll see you when I get back."

The next day, while making plans to drive out to Amanda's house for a Christmas party, he tried to convince Marie to go along. "You can drive the car if we get stuck and I'll push. Then I won't have to shovel much."

"I'd love to George, but I can't. I would lose my job." [67]

Finally they agreed to flip a coin. "I'll match you," said Francis, "tails you go, heads you don't." Francis lost, in more ways than one.

"Well," she said, "two is company and three is a crowd. I have to be here for Christmas anyway."

The following Friday morning, Marie fixed breakfast. Francis kiddingly asked why Marie hadn't brought him coffee, so she did. Hence Tom had to have coffee brought to him, too. Francis went outside for a load of wood after breakfast since Tom was not feeling well. As he threw the load into the woodbox, he told them, "It's quite cold."

"It's only 15 degrees below," Marie replied.

He playfully responded by sticking his cold fingers down her back to make her shiver.

Marie got ready for work after breakfast and at the door said, "Well George, I won't see you until you get back."

George gave her a hug and kiss, saying: "Sis, you take care of yourself and don't take any wooden nickels, or rubber ones because they spring away." "Bye, dear," were his last words to her. There was a strong kinship between them. She was like his sister and Tom, his brother—as close as a family could be.

After Marie left, Tom and George sat around smoking their pipes and exchanging small talk; then they cleaned the house. Francis went outside to start the car, but it was just too cold. First they tried pouring hot water from the tea kettle over the radiator.[68] When that didn't work, they made a torch and tried heating it from underneath. The two worked on it quite awhile before finally getting it started. They put a large blanket over it and let it run, while they ate dinner.

Francis drove downtown after eating, filled up the gas tank and got a shave and haircut at Guy Hockett's barbershop. During the time at the barbershop, Police Chief Dave Osborne supposedly walked by, noticed Francis's car, and went in to say hello. He later claimed he overheard Francis tell Hockett he had to go to Deer Lodge, but he would not go alone.[69]

Having been in isolation so long, Francis must have enjoyed the bustle of Christmas shopping and the decorated stores. Ranchers were loading cars and wagons, and cowboys tying sacks of goodies behind their saddles, all anxious to get home for Christmas before another storm hit.

Francis went to Granieri's grocery store on First Street across from the viaduct; there he bought candy, a box of apples, nuts, Christmas presents, etc. At the store he met Nell Ellis, Ray Ellis's wife, and exchanged pleasantries. He gave her a bag of candy to give to the kids who always crowded around him on the street whenever he was in town. She watched him drive away under threatening skies.[70]

Tom was hauling wagon loads of coal cinders from the Havre Hotel to bank his foundation against the winter's cold. Francis was at the house when he returned with the first load. They parted company about 1:30 after a last smoke together, but not before Francis had Tom break the lock and get his revolver from Marie's trunk. George asked him to tell Herron or McLain he had gone up to Amanda's place, and he would return Sunday night or Monday morning. He wished Tom and his family a happy Christmas, thanking him for having been such a good friend. His last words to Gibson were, "Take care of Sis and the kiddies."

Perhaps singing, humming, or whistling such songs as "Oh, bury me not on the lone prairie," [71] as much a prayer as a song, Francis pointed the 1914 Hupmobile roadster west out of town up Second Street onto the hill road, along the south side of Shorty Young's ranch, the Mount Hope Cemetery, and on to the dimly outlined wagon road that paralleled the railroad tracks. The rangeland glittered with its deep blanket of snow while dark storm clouds overhead indicated more snow was imminent, but he thought he could beat it. The winds kicked up and the temperature dipped to twenty-two degrees below zero.

He soon reached the railroad flag stop of Burnham and may have stopped for coffee. No doubt by this time he had misgivings about continuing the journey, yet knowing that Amanda was waiting and they had so little time left together must have spurred him on. Somewhere west of there, he turned north, taking a shortcut on an old seldom-used wagon trail which went through the Chain of Lakes and skirted the west side of the frozen Milk River.

Francis was about 20 miles, as the crow flies, northwest of Havre when he hit the edge of the severe blizzard; its wind-driven snow and intense cold struck with all its fury. Darkness made the situation even worse as he battled the deepening snow and the trackless prairie. Even though the river was some 30 yards to his right, he probably could no longer see it, only sense its presence. The cracked, yellowed side curtains of the car obscured his limited vision, and the manual windshield wipers were now worthless. He had to stop quite regularly and wipe the ice crystals from the windshield with rock salt and, at the same time, try to keep in visual touch with the river. He had to rely on his cowpuncher's instinct of direction since he was all but traveling blindly. The bitter cold was also playing havoc with the steering and shifting of gears.

"A fine place for a feller to be, all by himself on Christmas Eve," he must have muttered as he strained his eyes to see ahead. Finally his struggles with the vehicle came to an abrupt halt. He found himself on a curve to the left, on a 3- to 4-foot incline, stuck in a snowdrift that had blown across the trail. The exhausted cowboy put the Hupmobile in reverse and backed up slowly, probably intending to drive around the impasse. But unknown to Francis, the car was only a few feet from the edge of a 12-foot cutbank on the water's edge. By the time he realized what was happening, it was too late to react and put it into first. The car slid backwards down the bank, and in the process, the right front wheel dug in, causing the vehicle to roll over and slamming it onto the ice on its cloth top. Having received quite a blow to the head from the crash, he may have lost consciousness initially.

Dazed and in pain, but alive, Francis realized he was pinned under the car. In the impact Francis had sustained a compound fracture of his right leg. He soon saw the blood oozing profusely through his layers of clothing and could feel the bone protruding. His chest and stomach hurt from being thrown against the now-broken steering wheel and his head throbbed from being bounced off the car's interior. He was covered with broken glass and he had some cuts.

"I gotta get outta' here," he must have thought to himself. He finally managed to force the right-hand (and only) front door open, dragging himself free. He started crawling north and tried to get to his feet, but the crippled leg wouldn't hold his weight, so he returned to the car and huddled against it for shelter from the storm. Realizing he wasn't going anywhere without fixing the leg, he fashioned a splint from the sides of the apple box and tied it with strips from his flannel-lined coveralls. He could do nothing about the bleeding without removing several layers of clothing, which wasn't practical. The splinting was slow going, not only because of the numbing cold, but also because of the sluggish thinking caused by the concussion, shock, and pain from his wounds and oncoming hypothermia.

Surrounded by the debris of candy, celery, apples, and nuts, he decided to stay with the car until the storm's intensity abated, and commenced a search for firewood.[72] Fighting off panic when he found none, he began to figure his options. No one else would be foolish enough to be out in the storm, so help wasn't imminent. He needed shelter and the warmth of a fire to work on the bleeding leg. He knew his approximate location and that Percy Wilson's abandoned dugout was across the river, about one and a half miles to the north, that the Emil Paul house was about two miles north, and the Ernie Simpson house about four.

There was an abandoned house somewhere near to the southwest, but his chance of finding it was nil. He apparently chose the dugout since it was the closest. There he could wait until the weather broke or a rider came by.

Francis began his desperate journey northward, using the left bank of this river as his guide. He progressed a few feet at a time, sometimes hopping, sometimes crawling on the good left leg and knee; he occasionally stopped to rest, leaving a tell-tale pool of blood wherever he paused. At some point it must have occurred to him that firing his revolver might have attracted help if anyone was near—except he had left it in the car. Next he turned eastward across the frozen waterway, thinking perhaps it wasn't that far: He could make it. He lost a mitten, and later his flashlight, but didn't turn back for them—maybe he didn't even know he had lost them. Wait! He could now see the opposite bank. just a little further. With a landmark visible, he rested and commenced a slow, painful northward journey. How long his struggle went on is unknown. Weakened by excruciating pain, hypothermia, and serious blood loss, the completely exhausted Francis now could only count his progress in inches.

He must surely have despairingly thought, "I'm not going to make it . . . Amanda, Mother . . . I'm sorry, I tried . . ." He gave out nearly three-quarters of a mile from his goal—about half way—his great strength was gone, and his iron will broken. No shame. A younger man could have done no better. Even his enemies had to admire his courage.

He probably wondered how long it would be before death set in, and would he be alive yet unconscious if any predators came for him? He would rather be dead than senseless. Therefore, he would choose his own moment of death. Knowing his gun was gone and with the last of his strength, his frozen hand fumbled for his small pen knife, willing numbed fingers to open the blade.

Hopefully his bitterness subsided as he prepared to meet his maker. After all, the Lord had spared his life twenty-two years earlier in the hotel fire. The faith of his youth, combined with the Scriptures read often by Amanda, hopefully helped him gain peace as he may have prayed for friends and enemies alike.

Once the blade was open, he held it poised at his throat, summoning his courage and strength to plunge it deep into his neck. Then the deed was done.

It was about 1:00 P.M. on the day after Christmas. The storm had moved on during the night; all was calm and peaceful. Local farmer K. L. Ackerman took his sleigh out to check on some of his coyote traps and gather some wood on Percy Wilson Flats near the river. Ackerman lived five miles to the northeast of there. He particularly wanted a pole he had previously seen in the river.

Traveling on the frozen riverbed, Ackerman spotted something unfamiliar about 100 yards distant and reined in the horses, trying to determine what the strange mass was ahead. He continued towards it, unable to see clearly, and finally determined that it was a car resting upside down on the iced-over river.[73] He pulled alongside, dismounted, and made a closer examination, seeing the mangled cloth top, a broken steering wheel, the splintered right front wheel, oil pools from the broken crankcase, and frozen water puddles from the cracked radiator. He saw that the right front door was open and the right rear one was sheared off. Lastly he crawled under the car to see if anyone was trapped. He found no body, but he saw a pearl-handled, nickel-plated .45 revolver under the front seat. Tools were scattered about and the ground was crimson by a broken apple box whose contents were strewn on the ground.

He got back in the sleigh and followed the bloody trail on the ice, first north, then east across the river. The astounded farmer first thought he was following the tracks of two men, one dragging the other because of the separate hand prints and marks made by the leg being dragged. The tracks led across the frozen expanse to a figure lying partially covered with snow. He shouted, "Hello," but no response came. For a moment Ackerman hesitated before finally walking up to the man: speaking to him, questioning him, but still getting no reply. The tall man in a sheepskin coat was lying slightly on his right side with his head resting on one hand. Ackerman reached down and lightly shook him, but received no reaction. Finally he noticed the neck wounds, and saw the small pool of blood under the head and a larger quantity under the body.

The shaken farmer hurriedly got back in his sleigh and urged his team on to Havre in the -15 degree clear, icy air. Arriving in town, he went straight to Sheriff McLain's office and notified him of the accident and death. McLain gathered Judge W. Pyper, acting coroner, and Funeral Director James Holland. They couldn't take the funeral ambulance because it was too heavy and cumbersome to drive on the snow-choked roads. Together, they followed Ackerman's sleigh in Holland's Hupmobile.

At the Coroner's Inquest, Holland testified: "With the farmer leading the way, he piloted us down and around, some 15 miles to the location of the body lying on the ice in the middle of the Milk River and frozen completely solid." They wrapped Francis's body in a canvas and tied it to the right front fender of the car for the return trip.

While this was all taking place, Tom and Marie were sitting in their living room by the fire in the evening. Marie wasn't feeling well and Tom brought her a blanket. It was 10:00 P.M. when someone knocked at the front door. The two men, met by the sheriff, told the couple that a dead man had been found up the river on the ice. One asked: "Did Long George have his six-shooter?" They affirmed he did. "Are you sure?" Tom repeated he was, and related he had gotten it for George out of Marie's trunk. They then asked if he was wearing his (famous) fur coat. She replied no; it was in her trunk. She said he was wearing the sheepskin coat, and left the fur for her to wear.

"That's Long George all right," said one. "That answers the description of this man. The man that found him wasn't sure that it was Long George."

Marie, near collapse from illness and grief, asked if his body had been brought in yet. "No, they were getting ready to leave. They should be here by five in the morning."

The Gibsons went to the funeral parlor when the body was returned. The coroner had him lying on a table, with his arms folded over his forehead, and his eyes wide open. They observed his injuries: the right leg broken in two places below the knee with the bone protruding, the knife gashes on both sides of his neck, and the various other cuts and bruises.

They wired George's mother living at Inkom, Idaho, concerning her son's death. Mrs. Francis replied she would come for the funeral, and meanwhile, Tom persuaded the Sathre brothers to bring Amanda to town.

An inquest was held at 11:00 A.M. at Pyper's office in city hall. The main witnesses were Ackerman, the Gibsons, Holland, Pyper, McLain, and Doctor Stewart McKenzie. Assistant County Attorney C. Lee Golden represented the county. The jury consisted of Ed M. Allen, foreman; E. T. Trump, C. C. Bronson, R. G. Linebarger, Chas. C. Graw, and Orville C. Perry. Ackerman gave the first testimony. He told of sighting the car, described the accident scene and of following the bloody path on the ice and finding the body, and further recounted the hurried round trip to Havre with the corpse. Ackerman said Judge Pyper had found the jackknife under Francis with blood and snow frozen on it. One of Francis's mittens was lying next to the body; the other mitten and a flashlight were discovered on the trail from the car. The group examined the wounds on the jaw and throat, finding a large gash on the right side and a smaller one on the left side of the throat. The men examined the splint and afterwards noticed the good leg on his blanket-lined coveralls was worn smooth from crawling. After re-examining George's tracks, they concluded the imprints were made by only one man: The outside marks he made by dragging his leg and the inside with his hand and good leg. Ackerman said they found no evidence of any kind of struggle or fight. Mr. Holland had gone up the bank from which the car had plunged, but couldn't tell much. Although there had been two blizzards since the accident, the night was clear and the moon bright. No other vehicle tracks were found.

The farmer recounted to the jury that he went back the next day with Charles Graw, the county surveyor, and Mr. Sathre. At the scene they found a clean, broken knife blade and about 16 inches of rope near where the body had been, but the items turned out to be the judge's and were used to wrap the body in the canvas and put it on the car. The two righted the car and examined the contents. Nothing new was found except a few revolver cartridges.

He was asked other miscellaneous questions regarding where he lived, the road itself, where various houses were located, the weather conditions, etc. Other testimony added nothing new.

Next, Dr. MacKenzie reported the results of his official autopsy at the Holland funeral home as directed by Coroner Pyper. His examination of the body revealed the two stab wounds, a bruise over the left eye, bruised fingers, and the open compound fracture of the right leg. The stab wounds under the ears had severed the jugular veins on both sides and facial arteries on the left side. After his analysis, he concluded that death had been immediate from the stab wounds and that considerable blood had already been lost from leg wounds. The doctor was asked several questions by the jury and Assistant County Attorney Golden:

Would Francis have left a trail of blood from crawling over the ice with his broken leg? He answered yes.

Was Francis in good health other than his wounds? Again, yes.

Any other signs of violence? No.

In his opinion, had the auto accident caused the broken leg? Yes.

Cause of death? From the neck wounds, he reiterated.

Could Francis have made both stab wounds? Yes, probably with one hand, then the other.

And lastly he was questioned in more detail on the stab wounds. McKenzie said that, with Francis's knowledge of anatomy from butchering cattle, he knew how to cause his own death and there was enough time to cause both cuts—although the second one was delivered with less force.

Marie and Tom concluded the testimony with a reconstruction of the last day of George's life in Havre.

The official cause of death was then given: death by loss of blood from hemorrhages, caused by injuries from a knife severing his jugular veins—all occurring on or about December 24, 1920, approximately 30 miles northwest of Havre, Montana.

Amanda arrived with Alvern later in the day, driven to town by Elmer Sathre, who left her off at the Gibson house. Once Amanda was inside with Marie, she broke down. Marie tried to comfort her, saying it was God's will, and his time had come. Amanda told Marie how highly George thought of her and Tom. Amanda said she was even jealous of Marie until she had met her just before Christmas. They adjourned to the kitchen where Marie's friend Marita B. had made some biscuits and coffee.

Once Amanda had partially recovered from the grief she expressed to Marie, they walked over to the funeral home and were met at the door by Mr. Holland. He said the preparation of the body for viewing wasn't complete, but he allowed them in as a favor to Marie. Amanda looked at the body for a few moments before breaking the silence, speaking words of love to George and kissing him. Turning to Marie, she said, "What on earth have I done to be punished like that? Why, he looks so real—like he is lying down resting. He always puts his arm like that."

Marie agreed, but wanted to leave. She wondered aloud whether, if she had accompanied George, he would be alive now or if she would be dead, too?

The following night, Mrs. Francis and a son arrived on the train, although Marie and Amanda were too far away on the crowded platform to catch her. They followed them to a nearby hotel; they were admitted to her room by son Warren. Mrs. Francis was dressed all in black and wore a veil and was sitting on the foot of the bed. Mrs. Francis said George was her third oldest, "while this son is my thirty-year-old baby. He was a kid when his brother left home." She said, "George never could get along with his father so he decided to leave. I pleaded with him and so did his sister, but he said goodbye and left. I knew when he left that something would happen. First I buried his father, now him."

The group left the hotel by taxi to the Gibsons for supper, visiting for a while before retiring. The following day, they arranged for the funeral, before which Mrs. Francis had her long-awaited but very sad reunion with her son, as she viewed the now-prepared body. She said, "Son, I never expected to live to go to your funeral." She kissed him on the forehead, then broke down and kissed him several more times until Warren took her away.

The funeral was held on a cold and snowy Friday afternoon, December 31, at St. Mark's Episcopal Church of Havre. The pioneer Reverend J. M. Chestnut of Fort Benton and the Reverend L. J. Christler of the home parish conducted the service. Beforehand, Tony was led from the funeral home to the church by Lucien Gibson. The horse wore an empty saddle decorated with silver and black ribbons; his former master's chaps and spurs were attached to the saddle. He was tied to the bumper of a car during the service. According to the *Havre Plaindealer*, "the whole service, which was simple and impressive, lasted one hour. Both the church and choir room were filled to the doors and people stood in the guild room. The male quartet consisted of messrs. Funk, Nelson, Lindsay and Abraham, and sang two songs."

Marie said the church was filled with flowers, and people were lined up a half-block down the street. The pallbearers were George Aldous, Harry Green, John Auld, Thomas Gibson, Jack Edwards, and Chouteau County Sheriff Merrit Flanagan of Fort Benton. Other Francis brothers would have been present, if they hadn't been prevented by a blizzard in the Jackson Hole (Wyoming) area. Jack Mabee wasn't able to attend either; he was believed to have been in hiding over the theft of some beef.

Among the "mourners" were Phil Clack and John and Charles Sartain; though they weren't welcomed by Francis's friends, who wanted to drag them out and beat them up, they refrained from any violence out of respect for Mrs. Francis. The boys did get in some glaring at them, however, as the Reverend Christler gave his sermon extolling the innocence of George Francis, shaming a system of law that could oppress the innocent. While preaching, Christler stood beside the casket with his hand on it and spoke directly to George:

George Francis has fallen before the only foe he could not meet. We feel with the cold which benumbed and listen with him to the winds which pierced, till our own blood almost freezes. Minutes and hours passed, the sun rose and set, winter snows deepened, but they brought him not the long wished hour of help and rescue. Tell me, men, with all combined to blast the last bud of hope, who could have mastered such a melancholy fate? It may not have been with the rose of Heaven upon his cheek, nor with the fire of Godliness in his eyes that he died, but there was none the less the charm of invincibility stamped upon the tragedy. I would not say one word which would wound the feelings of friend or foe, but as I stand here on this bit of Montana soil, my mind filled with tradition of early days and sturdy hearts, I bear record of one recollection, namely, the Spartan chivalry kindred with fair play, and men abided by it with eloquent homage. It could not be bought or sold in any market, nor at any price. It was the language of the western heart, felt and understood over plain and mountainside.

His voice reached us a few days ago, but cannot now break the silence, and was not accorded that coveted valor in his last days. I speak these words in sorrow.

Is it not expected that free men will patiently bow down and kiss the sod? Why, men, anyone who bears the form, visage and name of man—nay a beast, dog, a sheep, a reptile that wants discourse of reason to comprehend the injustice of its injuries, would bite, bruise or sting the hand by which they are inflicted. It is then for a human being to fold his arms and stand still in submissive apathy? Press not ugly delusion to your bosom.

They cry these days, 'the law'! I too reverence the law and bow to the majesty of the obligations, but the law executed in truth, in righteousness, and in equity. Satan himself could not devise a system which would more blaspheme the name of justice than too much of the system of law today, so infected with the essence of the Nebuchadnezzaran practice that whom it would slew and whom it would spare. It sends forth neither the flaming sword of justice nor the convictive rule of the Nazarene teacher. George Francis fell victim of this oppression. We would not rob him of his deserved need of praise.

This was Christler's eloquent way of saying Francis was framed and betrayed by people who were supposedly his friends and railroaded by the court. Author Walt Coburn's eulogy would have been considerably shorter: "Game he lived, game he died." Right after the speech of praise, Clack and the Sartains left quickly.

After the service, the long procession started for the Highland Park Cemetery, 1¼ miles southwest of the downtown on a hill overlooking the city. Tony followed the horsedrawn hearse, again led by the young Gibson boy, as Mrs. Francis had especially requested. Unfortunately, the steep hill was too slippery for wagons or cars, so Tony was returned to the stable and the pallbearers helped push the hearse up the hill. Mrs. Francis, Warren, Amanda, and Alvern returned to the Gibson home. Amanda and the boy had to stay there a week because of a major snowstorm.

Reportedly, Redwing later stood on the grave site and said: "That's where you belong, you s.o.b.!"

Whether Mrs. Francis and the family were meant to receive George's possessions, or simply refused them, is not clear. The revolver and Tony were given to Harry Green. Although there are several stories to the contrary, Green said he let Tony loose from the Big Sandy Creek ranch to roam the mountains for his remaining years. When others asked what happened to Tony, he just acted dumb on the subject. Flaxey, one of Francis's other personal horses, was found roaming in the north Milk River country with his leg badly crippled by barb wire cuts. Cowboy Art Pederson put Flaxey to rest.

Other personal effects of the cowboy just vanished. A diamond ring he was said to have been wearing supposedly disappeared after the body was brought to Havre. The suspected culprit was neither connected with the funeral parlor nor the county, however. Livery stable proprietor, Ed "Dogey" Thomas, was said to have put George's silver-mounted saddle out in the sunshine to dry the day after the funeral, and it was stolen. Francis's friends felt that Jack Mabee had taken it and sold it to help alleviate his pressing money problems. Francis probably wouldn't have minded anyway, since he owed Jack money. The saddle reportedly later turned up in the possession of a Lewistown (Montana) merchant. His silver bedecked chaps, spurs, bridle, martingale, and extra-long stirrup tapaderos also became scarce, although they were said to have been in the possession of Roscoe "Doc" Timmons. The current owner has some of these items on display in Hill County's Clack Museum. Others whose parents knew Francis claim to have riding equipment of his, too. The beaver coat was eventually given to Lou Lucke by Johnny Auld to display in his clothing store. It finally disappeared (or fell apart). Lucien Gibson buried the wrecked Hupmobile for riprap on the river side of the Gibson homestead.

Thus, Mrs. Francis went home with little to remember her son by: his "library, financial records, and books of instruction, guitar and violin music instructional books, etc." Sarah returned the following year on Memorial Day to decorate her son's grave, but she was not well enough to continue the yearly vigil after that.

The true nature of George Francis's character was seemingly a matter of controversy to some family members—they felt an embarrassment over having an "outlaw" in the family. Since they were such a distance from him and never knew all the facts surrounding the trial, this is understandable.

The morning after Francis's body was brought in, many legends were born. In every barbershop, pool hall, and restaurant, people recounted many tales about him—some previously unheard, many well-worn, some imagined and others exaggerated. Of course, his enemies told stories that contained little or no truth, many of which survive today.

Speculation as to whether or not he was murdered dominated many conversations. One rumor widely circulated claimed Jimmy Moran (the next police chief) murdered him. A story perhaps started because Moran was allegedly involved in clandestine businesses with Police Chief Dave Osborne, who said he had heard Francis make threats against unnamed people that last day in the barbershop. One tale held that Francis was really alive in Mexico and a dummy had been placed in the coffin; another, that he was killed in Glacier Park while stealing cattle. And then there was the one that he and Tony froze to death during the storm—they were found like an ice statue with Francis in the saddle. And lastly, that a suicide note was found in his gun barrel . . . after he shot himself! Oh, well.

It appears George Francis's early years of thievery, coupled with tall tales and outright lies told after his death, made him a larger-than-life outlaw who, in reality, was at best a petty criminal—looked down on by the likes of Harvey "Kid Curry" Logan, Leroy "Butch Cassidy" Parker, Harry "the Sundance Kid" Longabaugh, "Dutch" Henry Yeuch, "Long" Henry Thompson, and the other genuine gunmen-outlaws of Montana.

If Francis had not died in such a dramatic fashion and had served his time (which probably would have been short), no doubt this part of his life—like his contemporaries'—would have been forgotten, only brought up among friends at card games or during an intermission drink behind the Cottonwood community hall dance. He then would have been remembered as a married rancher and a first-class rodeo performer and promoter. His Stampede rodeo probably would have survived and became a major attraction, and it might still be on the rodeo circuit today.

Another thing made Francis memorable: He represented a dying breed—the cowboy on the open range. Here in northern Montana, that way of life vanished, replaced by hired hands using mowing machines, hayrakes, and ditching tools. Even the outlaw on horseback officially disappeared in February of 1921 with the killing of Oklahoma's Henry Starr during a bank robbery, replaced by gangsters with fast cars and machine guns.

Ironically, his conviction and death were connected to the modern device of barb wire—which the mare's body was identified by—and the automobile that led to his death. A man on horseback wouldn't have attempted the trip. Conversely, the drought and collapsed post-war farm commodity prices that began just before his death ended the homesteader's invasion, and much of the land they occupied reverted to rangeland or became part of large combination farm/ranches. Except for his accusers many of the reform-minded farmers who wanted his conviction were gone soon after his death, driven out by hard times.

A March 21, 1921, article in *Jim, Jam, Jems* sums him up this way: "He was a genuine son of the open, wise to nature's ways and disdainful of civilization's veneers."

As a friend, writer Walt Coburn concluded in his article about Francis: "The saga and legend of the colorful life of Long George Francis has been told and retold (getting it more incorrect all the time) countless times at roundup camps and bunkhouses and winterline camps; and is still recounted, after nearly half a century of time, by old timers wherever and whenever they meet. Nothing in the eventful, adventurous, brave life of George Francis became him like the leaving of it."

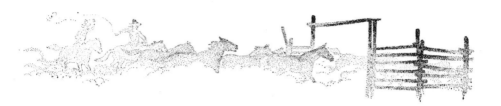

Mabee Goes South

ANY FURTHER DREAMS AND AMBITIONS Jack Mabee may have had for himself in the Milk River Country didn't work out. With the poor economy, population loss, and intermittent droughts and insect infestations, northern Montana's impoverished citizens couldn't support major rodeos. His airplane exhibitions, promoting Clack's Hi-Power gasoline, apparently hadn't been lucrative either, with having to pay a pilot's salary and maintenance costs. Then the plane was demolished in a non-casualty crash that occurred on the hill south of Sacred Heart hospital. Mabee may have been piloting it himself with J. A. "Doc" Wright, a local dentist, as his passenger. He also had to sell his share of the cattle on the Big Sandy ranch to Jim Kipp, whose ranch was at the junction of the Missouri River and Cow Creek at Cow Island,[74] to satisfy bank debts. With no major sources of income other than bartending at illegal speakeasies, he turned to the currently lucrative, but hazardous vocation of bootlegging. He acquired a few cars, probably with the help of certain Havre businessmen in the entertainment business. Recent war veteran Verne "Chip" Brader and a partner worked on Mabee's cars at a small garage located near the old phone company building at 319 Second Street. Young Brader also drove for Mabee on occasion

Mabee had only one reported local scrape with the law when, in 1922, he was arrested along with several associates for hauling illegal whiskey near the town of Box Elder, but the charge was dismissed. He didn't fare as

219

well in his next clash with the law, however. The confrontation occurred on the Wyoming portion of old Highway No. 87, once part of the secluded paths of the old outlaw trails extending from Canada to Mexico. Here, outlaw gangs rode fast and hard, led by the likes of Butch Cassidy, Kid Curry, "Big Nose" George Parrot, "Flat Nose" George Curry, and their countless followers as they traveled between their established hideouts from roughly 1870 to 1910.

Mabee and driver-mechanic Brader were ferrying liquor from Regina, Saskatchewan, to the booming oil refinery town of Casper, Wyoming. Riding shotgun were Frank Keple and Shorty Selby. They pulled into a safe ranch stop for gasoline, food, and rest near Buffalo, Wyoming, about 70 miles south of the Montana border. The Johnson County seat, Buffalo had been the scene of the 1892 invasion of cattlemen and their hired guns from Cheyenne. They had intended to kill about seventy small ranchers, farmers, and county officials, claiming the area was a protected hub for rustlers. But more likely they were interfering with the large ranchers' illegal domination of the open range. Further south, about 45 miles from their present location and west of the small cowmen's community Kaycee on the middle fork of the Powder River, was the narrow entrance through the red-stone canyon walls to the Hole-in-the-Wall ranch, once a principal outlaw hideout. Many times Mabee, Brader, and their cohorts had carried booze throughout this country.

This time the stop wasn't restful, though. They drove into a trap. A greeting committee of lawmen was in wait. Luckily both drivers had enough warning, and they escaped under a hail of bullets. While fleeing, Brader went through an irrigation ditch too fast and lost power due to a loosened battery cable. He temporarily repaired it, risked a trip into town for fuel, and then continued on his way south separate from Mabee. It is believed that Brader took a west yet parallel road to the highway through the deserted village of Barnum in the Hole-in-the-Wall country, and later rejoined the main road. After crossing the south fork of the Powder River and a high, dry plateau, they descended into the broken, rocky alkaline flats, passing the derricks of the Salt Creek oil fields and the oil-bearing Teapot Dome formation. The narrow roller-coaster road with blind curves crossed the largely empty sagebrush flats with a rare farm among the low pine-crested hills. They finally reached a plateau overlooking Casper and the North Platte River. Once there, they were reunited with Mabee at the drop site.

In the next trip, destined to be their last, the boys evidently detoured further west through the more mountainous country traversed by U.S. highways 310 and 20 to avoid meeting up with the Johnson County sheriff again. Unfortunately, they still met trouble on the Wind River Shoshone Indian Reservation located just west of Riverton in sugar beet country. They were fired upon by tribal police when they drove through a roadblock and again had to flee to Casper. Fearing a description of their Montana-licensed vehicles had been sent out, they cached the alcohol in a coulee before entering the city. Sure enough, Natrona County sheriff's officers were waiting. Their incarceration was short because of lack of evidence, and the cars had to be returned because they were registered in their sponsor's name. The disillusioned and shaken Mabee decided there must be a better and less troublesome way to make a living. Not so the rest, who continued running booze. Brader ignored the judge's admonition that he was too young to be in this business, and survived it. He later worked many years for the city of Havre's engineering department.

Jack's marriage to Clara was at an end, too. His attention had strayed to Cecilia "Cis" Gaston, who worked as a cashier at Sid Hirshberg's Orpheum Theater along with her sister, Jorene. Clara had left with their daughter, Edith, and returned to her parent's home in Great Falls, and she was granted a divorce in about 1921. She eventually married a man who was in a more stable line of work: carpentry. After moving to Colorado, she lived out her final years on a ranch neat Willets, California. Clara is survived by a granddaughter, Joanne.

Cis lived at the Havre Hotel (as had the Mabees) along with her sisters, Jorene and Sue. Sue worked as a stenographer at the Havre Commercial Company (department store). Their oldest sister, Nell, was married to Hirshberg, and the couple lived above the theater.

Nell had met Sid in Conrad (Montana) where they ran competing department stores. Nell Salisbury was a widow from Kalispell, about 100 miles to the west. Hirshberg was from a Fort Benton business and ranching family. When they married, the couple sold out both businesses in 1912, moved to Havre, and bought the Orpheum Theater building. Her sisters had followed from Eau Claire, Wisconsin.

Meantime, Jack was in a quandary as to what to try next, although his thoughts were turning more and more to southern California. His brothers, Roy and George, had previously moved to the Los Angeles-Anaheim area in 1915, and in 1918 brought out their mother, Emma, and half-brother and sister, Frank and Florence Brown. Roy owned an orange grove at Anaheim and later operated a deep-sea charter fishing and flying service. George worked for the U.S. Customs Service, but after acquiring further education, relocated to Hanford (California) to teach school.

As further encouragement friends Henry "Hank" Loranger, former (and first) Hill County sheriff, and his son, Hubert "Hugh," moved to Burbank in about 1923, where Hank had an automobile dealership. Later both worked for Warner Brothers Studio security. And Mabee's growing interest in Hollywood's Western movie business no doubt increased when fellow cowboy Ed Timmons was drafted to Hollywood by film maker Art Staton, another former Havreite. Timmons had been featured in a documentary filmed during a Havre Stampede rodeo. Often wearing Long George's fancy duds, Timmons had played trombone while riding a bull in the Havre Stampede Mounted Cowboy Band. He also had broken horses for Francis—not knowing for sure if Francis had obtained them legally or not.

Nothing major came of his career as an actor, although Timmons did do stunt work and play bit parts as a cowboy, soldier, knight, or whatever else involved riding horses. Besides movies Timmons participated in rodeos—like one in Los Angeles sponsored by Hollywood celebrities—and worked on the gigantic Miller-Lux ranch near Bakersfield, also performing in his uncle Herman's dance band around California. During his brief movie career, he did get to closely observe such big stars and directors as Pola Negri (who was engaged to Rudolph Valentino), cowboy Tom Mix, Erich von Stroheim (known as the "Dirty Hun"), and Douglas Fairbanks, Sr., etc.

Championship riders that Mabee most likely met on the western rodeo circuit—particularly at the Pendleton Roundup—who became well-known Hollywood stuntmen/actors included fellow Oklahomans Ed "Hoot" Gibson and Art Accord; also there was eastern Washington's Enos "Yakima" Canutt, who acted and later directed as well as becoming known as the greatest cowboy stunt man of all.

Surely Mabee, Francis, and the boys had watched on the Orpheum theater's screen the romantic-adventure (silent) Westerns of the first top cowboy star, "Broncho Billy" Anderson, who played smiling-noble-hero types who fought and rode (clumsily) to glory, and the more realistic blood, dust, and sweat melodramas of deadpan, good-badman, William S. Hart. And the slick, polished newcomers: Harry Carey, Neal Hart, Jack Holt, Al and Jack Hoxie, Buck Jones, Ken Maynard, Tim McCoy, Fred Thompson, Tom Tyler, and others.

Yet the "rhinestone and neon" cowboy picture king who inspired hundreds of would-be actors to pour into Los Angeles-Hollywood was Tom Mix. Mix and his horse Tony[75] first gained attention in 1914 playing "Chip," a character from Big Sandy author B.M. Bower's *Chip of the Flying U.* In his zenith at Fox Studio, the husky 5 feet 11 inches star commanded a yearly salary of about $750,000. No wonder the $30-a-month cowhands left the ranches for greener pastures.

Mix built a Spanish mansion overlooking Hollywood and the Pacific Ocean in the then mostly empty prairie of Beverly Hills, The house had nine marble-lined bathrooms, a rainbow-colored fountain in the dining room, and a butler who dressed in a powdered wig and knee pants. He and wife Victoria had "his" and "her" drawing rooms: his in "cowboy" and hers in 18th century French. The beautifully landscaped grounds had an Olympic-sized pool, tennis courts, and garages full of custom-built sport cars. For water-going recreation he had a 96-foot yacht called "The Miss Mixit." On the home's roof was a personalized neon sign that read "TM" in brand form. (It probably became a convenient beacon for aircraft.) If that wasn't enough, every door had a 14 karat gold "TM" inset on it.

But wait, there's more: His long limo's hood was decorated with a leather-tooled saddle and steer horns. His elaborate, mostly white personal cowboy outfits were just as gaudy: topped by a horsehair belt with a diamond-studded buckle. For "dressup," he wore flamboyant purple and white tuxedos.

Soon, Jack Mabee would be knocking on the film companies' doors, hoping to become a movie star too, along with the other estimated 500 cowboys yearly seeking stardom in Hollywood.

To make the south-going group complete, Sue Gaston married a Malta (Montana) man, and they moved to Burbank. Jorene and Cecilia soon followed, finding employment as cashiers at a Loew's theater in downtown Los Angeles. Nell moved there, too, to watch over her younger sisters. The Hirshberg family, with children Helen and Sid, followed suit. Not only were they saying goodbye to the theater they had sold to Jack Moore, but to their lodge near Lake McDonald in Glacier National Park. Reportedly Mabee had spent his share of time there, too, getting to know their lake neighbor, Charlie Russell. Hirshberg's new business in Los Angeles was the Brooks Restaurant at Eighth and Olive; it reputedly had the longest bar counter in town.

When Mabee arrived, he went straight to the top dog himself, Tom Mix. How he met Mix, or who introduced him, is not known. At least they

had a common denominator in having been cowboys and rodeo performers in Oklahoma. Mix, in turn, may have introduced Jack to his Beverly
Hills neighbors, dramatic-action actor Douglas Fairbanks, Sr., and top
comedian Charlie Chaplin, because Mabee had his picture taken with
them. Or perhaps Fairbanks was the link, since he had quite a Charlie Russell painting and illustrated letter collection.

It is doubtful either Chaplin or Fairbanks could have directly helped
Mabee, since Chaplin's studio made comedies, and the husband-wife team
of Fairbanks-Pickford—et al.—United Artists was into Mary Pickford,
America's Sweetheart: movies of young, simple, and wholesome characters
such as *Rebecca of Sunnybrook Farm* and *Pollyanna*. And Fairbanks made
adventure spectaculars such as *Thief of Baghdad* and *Robin Hood of Sherwood
Forest*, although the latter used lots of cowboys as extras in period costumes.
At this point in time, Westerns were less popular at the box office.

In the end Mabee is believed to have temporarily settled for stuntwork
at MGM, where Tim McCoy was to become the big star. This work, as he
discovered, was dangerous, causing endless injuries, and for perhaps $7.00
to $10.00 a day, he placed himself even at the risk of death. Granted, this
was better than a ranch hand's monthly wage, but Mabee had intended to
do better. He was most likely sickened by the brutal treatment of horses in
those times, which were often crippled and maimed by front leg wire-trip
devices used in the deadman's fall scenes.

Just prior to Mabee's sojourn in southern California, the massive white
wooden letters spelling out "Hollywoodland" were placed on the side of
Mount Lee. The Cahuenga Valley area was "civilized" in 1887 by Kansas
prohibitionists Harvey Wilcox and his wife, Daeida, who established a
120-acre ranch subdivision dubbed "Hollywood." It became a quiet,
respectable, alcohol-free suburb dotted with fig and walnut orchards, vegetable gardens, and orange groves. On the surrounding foothills of the
Santa Monica mountains grew thick chaparral, lupine, yucca, cactus, apricots, and holly berries. In the valleys, oranges and lemons flourished along
with alfalfa, melons, strawberries, cantaloupes, guavas, figs, mustard, and
sage. Sheep, horses, and mules grazed peacefully throughout the bucolic
countryside and sleepy village. Incorporated in 1903, it became part of Los
Angeles in 1910 with a population of 5,000. By then, the open fields of
Wilcox Avenue had begun to give way to a business district and residential
section, with the Hollywood Hotel as the centerpiece.

It was certainly quite a contrast from the wide-open plains of northern Montana.

A dramatic change was in the making, though, when Eastern film makers, like Cecil B. DeMille and Jesse L. Lasky, not legally licensed by Thomas Edison's patent-controlling camera company, discovered both a safe haven and a warm, sunny climate and unspoiled landscapes perfect for making "flickers."

In 1911 the Nestor Film Company leased the vacant Blondeau Tavern and former stage stop at the village's crossroads—later named Gower Street and Sunset Boulevard—to film Al Christie Westerns. The barn behind the tavern was used for developing the film. Later, this area was to become the world's film capitol: "Tinseltown" or the "Dream Factory." Thus, Hollywood became more than just a few businesses surrounding a post office, a bunch of frame houses with little old ladies sitting on white porches, or a remote station on the L.A. inter-urban Big Red trolley line.

Early on, the Western movie was king, and the king of Western movie making was Thomas Ince. Ince's "West" was located at the end of Sunset Boulevard at the south of Santa Ynez Canyon near the ocean. Here he had Western townsites, a ranch, and buildings to house his large crew of cowboys and horses. He later built a studio in the new Culver City development on land donated by Harry Culver. It had become MGM when Mabee worked there in 1924.

Tom Mix also had a sixty-acre filming headquarters between Hollywood and Santa Monica beach called "Mixville." It was a huddle of shacks, indoor and outdoor sets, a blacksmith shop, cookhouse, and bunkhouses. His props included wagons, buggies, stagecoaches, and corrals filled with horses and Longhorn cattle.

Mabee probably saw both, but he didn't stay around Hollywood very long once he had given up hopes of an instantaneous movie career. At the time the Western was making a comeback with such epic "A" productions as *The Covered Wagon*, *North of 36*, *The Iron Horse*, and *The Pony Express*. Though the comeback meant his employment chances might have increased, he instead moved south to adjacent Orange County and its county seat of Santa Ana, the major citrus-fruit-growing region of the state, especially known for Valencia oranges.

Mabee wasn't interested in raising fruit, vegetables, or nuts, however. At first, he may have worked as a land development salesman. Then, one morning, he walked into the local Hudson-Essex auto agency, obtained a salesman's job, and moved into the nearby Elks Club. When leaving that day for lunch, he met a gentleman who was also looking for a good place to eat. They dined together at the Good Fellow Grotto, and in the process, Jack sold him a Hudson; reportedly that began a stint as their top salesman. But Jack preferred to be his own boss and soon left the dealership.

He hocked his diamond jewelry and obtained his own Moot auto agency for Santa Ana. He had no funds to rent a showroom, so he parked his demonstrator curbside. It wasn't long before Mabee could afford to lease his own building on Main Street across from the courthouse. His half-brother, Frank Brown, came to work for him. Mabee sold a number of brands: Rickenbacker, Marmon, and Graham-Paige, but finally settled on Oldsmobile. Jack sold the franchise in the latter part of 1927.

Perhaps partly from his desire to rub elbows with show business people and partly because Cis was now living in Los Angeles, Jack returned to the Hollywood district and the bootlegging business. At the time, Hollywood was in transition to "talkies." A major Western production called *The Big Trail*, starring a then-unknown actor, John Wayne, brought the Western into the sound era. Other box office hits were *In Old Arizona* starring Warner Baxter, and Gary Cooper in *The Virginian*. There were no speaking parts for Yakima Canutt, whose voice was once described as having the range of a hummingbird, yet he became John Wayne's number-one double.

By this time Hollywood had grown to a metropolitan center of 36,000. The main thoroughfare of Hollywood Boulevard ran east and west, with the business center of stores, taverns, small hotels, movie theaters, beauty shops, bungalow courts, apartment houses, etc., intersecting at Vine Street.

The business district's wide avenues were lined with green parkways of palm, pepper, and eucalyptus trees. The small, mainly white stucco bungalows with red tile roofs of the residential area had neat lawns, hedges, and flower gardens. This was the other Hollywood, as opposed to the rich camelot of Beverly Hills with English manors, Spanish haciendas, Italian villas, and French provincials. In 1919 Douglas Fairbanks and Mary Pickford became the first celebrities to move onto its then-scrubby, barren alkaline hills that had most recently been beanfield, and into Fairbanks' two-story hunting lodge that later became the Pickfair estate. Charles Chaplin, Tom Mix, and many more followed suit. It evolved into 5.6 square miles of moviedom with its exclusive shops, restaurants, apartment houses, and mansions surrounded by pine trees and colorful flora.

Between Beverly Hills and the downtown on Sunset Boulevard was a section called "the Strip" with movie colony night spots, high-priced shops, couturiers, salons, and theatrical agencies, most of which were housed in white modified Georgian-colonial buildings with green shutters.

Mabee's speakeasy was located on the east end near the small, independent studios of "Poverty Row," mostly housed in two-story pseudo-Spanish-type buildings, that ground out cheap, quickie-dramas, Westerns, and comedies. Located roughly between Sunset Boulevard and Hollywood on Gower Street, these studios included at one time or another about twenty now-forgotten studios, with Monogram and Republic lasting the longest next to Columbia, which survives today.

Here it was not an unusual sight to see cowboys in their chaps, vests, and ten gallon hats, stuntmen, extras, actresses, and actors hurriedly exiting the studios and crossing the streets to have lunch at the corner hot dog and hamburger stands. The would-be cowboys and other actors called it "Gower Gulch," where extras and bit players dreamed of becoming stars. The Gulch consisted of some Western clothing stores, a bootmaker, and several bars. Their headquarters was the Columbia Drugstore; meals were cheap and a pay phone was available for picture job calls. By 1923 the drugstore had been replaced by a central casting office at Hollywood and Western that had 17,000 registered film extras.

It is not clear whether or not Jack's first illegal bar was the same one he opened legally in 1933 at the northwest corner of Santa Monica Boulevard and Lillian Way, one block off Sunset. The business was about midway between the Poverty Row Studios and the more prestigious Paramount and newly built R. K. O. studios. Paramount was a major producer of Westerns, including Zane Grey's books. Jack called his business the Roundup. (One of his old Havre rumrunner cohorts, Jack Blake, also ran a bar by the same name on the west end of Havre by the fairgrounds.) The bar was a small hole-in-the-wall, narrow and long. The building had a long bar counter on the right side and a mirrored back bar with stools and a hot food section at the end.

The kitchen was in a small back room shared with a storage area. On the opposite wall of the bar counter were three booths with a jukebox in front. On the back area wall were exhibited Jack's cowboy hat and chaps, perhaps rodeo trophies and other Western paraphernalia. One such was a large set of Longhorn cattle horns—once in Bachini's bar on Havre's First Street.

So many old friends and acquaintances came to have a drink with Jack—either from Montana or now-transplanted Californians—that the bartender had to give him nonalcoholic drinks on the sly. The Roundup was mainly patronized by a middle-class clientele, including Western actors, stuntmen, and bit players; some were helped financially by Mabee.

Jack spent much of his time telling of his Montana and earlier experiences, including many references to Long George Francis. Perhaps this is why some movie production people were said to have made a trip to Havre in an attempt to gather more information about Francis for a possible movie, but were run out of town by his still-present enemies. Too bad: Mabee could have at least been a one-time film consultant.

The bar did well, causing him no major problems . . . until one evening when Mabee was away and a state inspector from the California Board of Equalization came by. Normally that would have been okay, except this particular night the cook was sick and didn't come to work. The inspector closed the bar because the law read: no food, no liquor served. Undaunted, Jack reopened immediately, selling soft drinks along with food. Jack's lawyer arranged a meeting a few weeks later with district "Mr. Big" of the state office and had his license reinstated for a $15,000 payoff—considerably higher than Havre's rates.

Mabee sold the bar and bought another he called The Backroom, perhaps further west on Santa Monica Boulevard near the Paramount Film Studio.

On the social side of life, Jack and Cis saw each other frequently, eventually marrying and living in a two-story stucco house at 3212 DeWitt Drive. They lived in the upper five-room apartment and rented out the bottom floor. The building was located northwest of Hollywood on the southern edge of Universal City, an 800-acre parcel of unincorporated county around the Universal Motion Picture Studio. Besides residential lots, it contained 16 sound stages, enclosed lots, and a back ranch with a 300-horse-capacity barn and outdoor sets where Westerns were filmed. Hence, perhaps it was no accident he moved there.

Along with visiting friends and relatives, the Mabees may have attended the L.A. Philharmonic Symphony orchestra under the stars at the Hollywood Bowl just to see Montana's former Copper King and California railroad magnate, William Clark, play "second fiddle." His $150,000 yearly contribution probably helped guarantee his orchestra seat. If they went nightclubbing, Ciro's would have definitely been on the list, and the Ambassador Hotel's Coconut Grove. And the Friday night fights at the Legion stadium may have attracted him. For less formal entertainment they may have been attracted to the Vernon Country Club and the Sunset Inn.

While Jack's life should have been happy, in many ways it wasn't. He had a drinking problem, and his temper hadn't improved. He apparently stayed bitter because of never accomplishing his dream of cowboy movie stardom. Perhaps, along with the other romantics, he wanted to pretend the Old West hadn't ended.

Another problem area was his daughter, Edith. She came to L.A. and attended high school there, although she saw more of Uncle Roy than him, while staying at their Anaheim home. She married and moved to Denver. In a case full of conflicting facts, she was murdered. This made Jack feel even worse, and he drank more because he felt he had neglected her.

Cis finally separated from Jack to live with her widowed sister, Jorene. They reunited sometime after World War II.

Mabee acquired another bar-restaurant in the small desert town of Niland, California. In the rear was a legal poker game operation. Niland is located on the northern end of the Imperial Valley, with the Cuyamaca Mountains to the west and the Chocolates to the east. It is southwest of the below-sea-level Salton Sea, which has several recreation areas. The Imperial Valley has large farms, growing citrus fruits, cotton, and vegetable crops made possible by irrigation canals flowing from the Colorado River. There was definitely wealth there to tap at the card tables.

He planned on branching out with other establishments, but he became discouraged when this one wasn't successful. Jack couldn't spend enough time there, and the business wasn't being run properly. Whatever future business plans he had were called to a halt by his death in 1948 at the age of 59. His liver finally failed. Cis died soon after.

Today all that remains visibly of the Mabee family's California legacy is the two-and-one-half-acre R.V. park in Anaheim on the remains of the orange grove; it is run jointly by Roy Mabee, Jr., and his sister Virginia. They both inherited their father's interest in flying: Roy is a licensed pilot and Virginia is an airline flight attendant.

While Jack's life wasn't the success he contemplated, at least the family name survived. This was something he could hold over Francis when they met again at the final roundup, across the big divide—looking for a new range with good water and plenty of grass.

Epilogue

THE GREAT NORTHERN STAMPEDE RODEO of Havre is all but forgotten, except for the same logo on the Havre High School student newspaper—until 1993. That year the Hill County rodeo became the Great Northern Stampede, bringing back a nostalgic memory of Havre and the Milk River Country's short, but wild and untamed cowboy era on the last frontier of the American West.

One thing that would bring smiles to the old-timers good and bad, who have mostly passed over the great divide, is the possible return of Longhorn cattle. The breed fell from grace when range conditions improved and the faster-growing British breeds of Herefords and shorthorns/Durhams became popular, producing fat marble beef. But now that the American public is more conscious of eating lean, low-fat meat, some modern cattlemen are taking a new look and rediscovering the species.

The Longhorn is much superior in hardiness, stamina, fertility, and resistance to disease and is fearless of any enemy. They lick worms off and will stand for hours in water to drown the one they can't reach. The other breeds could have not survived well on the range.

Thanks to the creation of a 1927 federally protected Oklahoma herd in the Wichita Mountains, which was comprised of the last pure breeds and once consisted of only twenty cows, three bulls, and four calves, a part of the Old West has survived and may make a comeback. Perhaps the western movie will as well.

And lastly, Havre's remaining Clack family members have all left Havre. Thanks mainly to Mrs. Clack, the Clack money did good things for the Havre area. And they still support the ever improving Clack-Hill County Museum. According to one family member, "We know he (H. Earl) was a scoundrel, but he dearly loved his family."

Perhaps "Long George" and H. Earl Clack were made to stay in Purgatory until they became friends.

Endnotes

1. Observation given by Harrison Lane, Ph.D., Professor Emeritus, Northern Montana College.
2. Also spelled Bearpaw or Bear Paw(s).
3. This was more likely true earlier; most were now camped along the Milk River near Cree Crossing by present-day Malta.
4. Also called Mitchif.
5. Actually son Little Bear (also called Immassees) was in control of his father's band at this point
6. 6,916 feet above sea level.
7. Now called Phelan's Divide.
8. Hill County records inaccurately give his date of birth as September 20, 1872.
9. His father, Robert Coburn, had a 30,000-acre ranch in the long shadows of the Little Rocky Mountains.
10. The cattle ranch was located in the northwest corner near Harrison in Sioux Country. The country was described as "barren and worthless as anything that could be conjured up." The flatlands were broken up by conical mounds. To the north were the white buttes of the Pine Ridge. A thin trickle of water ran through the "sandy, good for nothing soil." It was called Hat or Warbonnet Creek.
11. Many, many claimed this honor, although three primary sources give this combination of ten names.
12. What really happened to him will be the subject of a book by Larry Pointer, author of *In Search of Butch Cassidy*.
13. An 1884 bounty resulted in the death of 568 bears, 146 cougars, and 7,224 wolves and coyotes. In Chouteau County in 1906, the June kill report was a total of 1,280 combined wolves and coyotes, most of which were pups.

14. They were Exor Pepin, Tom McDevitt, Gus Decelles, Joe Demars, and Charles Goutchie.

15. The Sioux War was precipitated by the loss of the Black Hills and the advance of the Northern Pacific Railroad. The various Indian bands were finally subdued by the Army units under Colonel Nelson Miles.

16. Some of the Francis letters have been lost, and there may have been earlier ones.

17. Spoken of earlier by Bob Anderson and Andy Avery.

18. Originally called Sioux Butte.

19. According to local folklore one such girlfriend was Goldie Moses. She lived with her parents and brothers, Henry and Lawrence, near Mount Baldy. Her brothers later had a place on Clear Creek, and she married a William Wingfield. They had a grocery store for years in east Havre.

20. One Francis acquaintance said he had several of those hideaways.

21. See Appendix A for complete text.

22. The Havre Senior Citizens Center is now in that general location.

23. The Gussenhoven home was later known as "The Castle," a name it received when it was a boarding house.

24. See Appendix B.

25. The first Honky Tonk, which burned down in 1905, may not have been as elaborate as its replacement, built the following year.

26. From a copy in the possession of Lee Grant, Grant's Trading Post, Havre.

27. Ella, Bill, and Jim were brothers and sister of George Francis.

28. Wigen was married to Dade Thomas, sister of Pat Thomas, the Havre bootlegging kingpin.

29. More adequately described as a primitive log saloon with cribs or "hog pens" behind for the prostitutes.

30. See page 181.

31. Young may have torched his own business so he could move further west out of city limits. Years later, he positively did burn the second one down when law officers closed it during prohibition.

32. Believed to have been established in 1912.

33. Said to have held about 200 horses.

34. He now also owned the Northern Pacific and Chicago, Burlington and Quincy railroads under the United Securities Company.

35. They got their wish in February of 1912 when Havre beat out Chester as the county seat of newly established Hill County, and Chinook

bested Harlem in Blaine County. Later Chester seceded from Hill to form Liberty County.

36. It's not clear whether the sheriff was Henry Loranger or his 1916 successor, George Bickle, since no date was given.

37. Perhaps this reaffirms that the fight with Redwing was over him not paying a young boy his promised horse for one winter's work.

38. This individual was a renegade member of a prominent local family, living on the upper road in Beaver Creek Valley.

39. Eight hundred thousand cattle were said to have been lost in Montana Territory alone.

40. Horn was a famous Army scout during the Apache wars, a Pinkerton detective, and a professional gunman for the Wyoming Stockgrowers Association. He was hanged at Cheyenne, Wyoming, in 1903 for one of several killings.

41. Between 1909-1919, wheat was the number one farm crop in Montana and fifth in production in the U.S.

42. It contained 5,266 square miles before the loss to newly created Toole County in 1914.

43. Havre Land office record No. 0259, final patent No. 551424.

44. H. Earl Clack Homestead application No. 034565. Mary J. Martin No. 035861. Hugh B. Elliot No. 035874. Department of the Interior; U. S. Land office, Havre, Montana; Contest No. 6098.

45. In later years, during Prohibition, Reed was the convicted leader of a gang of bootleggers and bank robbers who operated in western Canada and Montana.

46. The only rodeo event that can be traced to its origins.

47. The Board of Trade or the Mint are mentioned in all versions.

48. Three years later, in a less-than-honorable public display, Mabee knocked down a smaller, local reform minister, E. J. Huston, in the Havre courthouse. Mabee was angry about an article Huston had written. Huston escaped further injury when his sister and a janitor intervened.

49. Although listed in the newspaper pre-publicity, he was not shown on the program.

50. Brinkman, like other Francis friends, had an old Army-type spur and bit that Francis had coated with silver. They eventually were given to George and Leah Brown at Havre.

51. Simpson came into being when the store and post office at Oldham closed down.
52. Where the Senior Citizens Center is now located.
53. See Chapter 14, "The Enemy Within."
54. This seems to conflict with the Entorf brothers' statement. They said no other brand was discernible.
55. There is an unsubstantiated story that Avery was shot while trespassing on Acison's ranch. Perhaps he blamed Francis.
56. In the Redwing altered-cattle-brands trial, the defense argued that the state's method of clipping the hair around the brands wasn't sufficient to prove ownership, and only removing the skin would be conclusive proof!
57. This was a strange question since the state claimed the mare was tracked by its hoof prints from Clack's barn to near the Francis ranch. Nothing was ever mentioned about tire tracks. Besides it wouldn't have fit very well.
58. Perhaps this refers to some aspect of the auto livery business they had in Havre.
59. See page viii.
60. All dialogue written by Marie Gibson.
61. The shelter and its abandoned furnishings and utensils were left there by the Green family for nature to consume. In the late 1980s the author and Lawrence Green, Jr., removed the last of the cooking and eating utensils.
62. One of those was Albert Thompson, who immediately decided to visit in Miles City for a while.
63. The author has linked the facts of pregnancy and a leave of absence from school together, since no other time frame works out.
64. A farming and ranching community of then about 500, located about 130 miles east of Havre on the Hi-Line.
65. Martin Nobel is believed to have been the last living member of the P-Cross and Francis bunch. He died in November of 1988.
66. All dialogue written by Marie Gibson.
67. It is believed she worked as a hotel maid or restaurant cook.
68. Lucien had to wait an extra half hour for more warm water to do dishes before going skating.
69. The Gibsons knew of no such conversation or plan to get even with anybody even though Doc Timmons apparently believed it genuine.

70. According to Nell's memory, Francis crossed the viaduct after leaving the store. This could be, yet he had to have recrossed to have returned to the Gibson house. What he did or where he might have gone is beyond speculation.

71. "The Dying Cowboy" by George N. Allen, 1850.

72. An unsubstantiated report held that he had tried unsuccessfully to burn the car's upholstery for warmth.

73. The spot is about six miles west of Cottonwood and about one mile south of the present Cottonwood bridge.

74. Site of the September 1877 Nez Perce attack on the steamboat cargo landing.

75. Mix's sorrel horse had a white diamond mark on his forehead and may have inspired George Francis to name his later horse the same, since Mix first appeared on the Silver Screen in about 1911.

Acknowledgments

I deeply thank those pioneers of north central Montana and their descendants, local and throughout the United States, whose shared oral and written recollections have substantially contributed to this text.

My thanks to Signe Sedlacek, who as chairman spearheaded the publication of the 1976 *Grit, Guts and Gusto*, and to Janet Allison, who authored *Trial and Triumph: 101 Years in North Central Montana*. These books were prime sources and provided a scope and depth of this country that is rare in a local publication.

I am grateful to those who helped me with the (physical) lay of the land in the Milk River Country: Nell Bickle, Mabel Blackwood-Dehlbom, Rose Faber, Lucian and Marian Gibson, Frank Grable, Lee Grant, Lawrence Green, Jr., Don Greytak, Hugh Loranger, John "Blacky" Lofgren, Alvin "Al" Lucke, Robert "Robbie-Mr. Bear Paw-Howdy Beaver" Lucke, Bill Lumpkin, Jim Magera, Esther and Martin Nobel, Tom "Dock" Reese, Wade Reese, Gordon Sands, Art Simmons, Vina Stirling, William "River Web" Thackeray, and Floyd Whaley. (And to whomever I left out.)

My gratitude to the very professional personnel of libraries; historical societies; archives-museums; local, state, and federal governmental agencies; and newspaper offices—primarily in the West, who provided such generous assistance. And a special thanks to the past and present staffs of the Havre, Hill County, and now, combined libraries: Mary Almas-Antunes, William Lisenby, Dorothy Armstrong, Bonnie Williamson, Mary Leamer, Betty Peck, and my Person Friday, Francine Brady.

Further praise is due Louise Thomas, former Northern Montana College assistant librarian, Mary Ellen Haberger and her staff at the 12th Judicial Clerk of the Court's office, and Dianne Mellem and her staff at the Hill County Clerk and Recorder's office.

Special gratitude is expressed to Sharma Nieser, deputy clerk (1981), City of Inkom, Idaho, whose research found the Francis family; Rena

Moore, associate editor (1981) of the *Willets* (California) *News,* who helped find the Mabee family; Jeanne Taylor, associate editor (1981) of the *L.A. Times,* who also helped with Jack Mabee; and James Muhn, historian (1981) for the B. of L.M. at Billings, Montana, who found the Clack-Francis-Martin land dispute record; of course, to my wife, Donna, for her editing and proof-reading skills; and again to Jim Magera, local and regional historian and Fort Assinniboine Preservation Association's archivist, for reading the manuscript, offering valuable suggestions, and providing valuable information. Last, but far from least, to Harrison Lane, Professor Emeritus, Northern Montana College, for sharing the important information in selected term papers from his former Montana history classes.

While I have many, many people to thank for assistance, the ultimate responsibility for the facts and interpretation of history developed in this book rests with me.

Gary A. Wilson
Bull Hook Siding (Havre), Montana
February 1989

Appendices

Over the Big Divide

1.

The thieves of the mountains
Are all in a stir,
And old Lord Alex McLoughry
They are going to transfer
For branding some calves
That he never could hide.
he is now on his way
Over the big divide.

2.

For old Mr. Ed Lawler
Was the first one to holler.
And when the news got
To Old Archie B. Smith,
He said what a bunch
I surely have missed.
And the Canadian Kid
Took to the woods and hid.

3.

And when Inspector Hall
Got wise and started to scout,
Henry McKinley and Griffen
Got scared and jumped out.

And Mr. Young Brooks
Thought it a shame
That he had no chips
In such a smart game.

4.

And Old Mister Cheyenne
Is branding his cattle
With a frying pan.
But he had better be true
Or he'll have his hoofs
Mixed up in it too,
Tho' he's a poor man
And uses a frying pan.

5.

And old Mr. Kid Casey
Is a cowpuncher by trade,
And he would steal cattle
If he wasn't afraid.
He lives on his gall
And his ignorant cheek,
And every one says
He's a dirty low sneak.

6.
And old Mr. Jack Ryan
is howling all the time,
And says he never steals.
But the people all say
His head is full of wheels,
For he's killing stray beef,
And every one knows
he's a dirty old thief.

7.
And old Mr. Redwing,
If he had his just dues
To a tree he would swing,
Tho' he crows like a cock.
Now he's stolen all he's got,
But he's nothing but lies
And he'd steal copper cents
From his dead mother's eyes.

8.
Still Old Mr. Redwing,
"Stop thief," he bellows,
and sings.
You can tell by his slang
That he's a disgrace to his gang.
To his dirty low tricks
They will always refer,
And every one says
He's a dirty low cur.

9.
Now all take my advice
And never try it twice.
Don't burn any hay
When your foe is away.
Don't brand any calves
Nor burn up a hide,
And avoid a long trip
Over the Big Divide.

　　　　　　　—*COW THIEF*
　　　　　　　(GEORGE FRANCIS)

Coolie, Montana, November 1, 1904

Havre Fire 1904

Havre burned like a torch
While the men were drinking
Whiskey by the quart.
For it was an awful sight
The booze that they did fight
For there was Mr. Judd
Who fought it by the tub.
And there was Captain White
That killed a barrel that night.
There was little Shorty Young
They say he killed it on the run.
There was R. X. Lewis
Who hadn't much to lose
So he kept on fighting booze.

The mayor went around and said
That all must close their door
For I don't like whiskey any more.
And he hollered like a loon
Cause Hinote wouldn't close his saloon.
So they took old Hi to jail,
While the mayor was drinking
His whiskey from a pail.
So when they let old Hi out,
They had him charged with
Drinking whiskey through a spout.
Though he never went to court,
For he was only drinking whiskey
    by the quart.

There was Barber Green
The drunkest fool you ever seen,
And little Barber Bud,
Crying for just another jug.
And there was Charley Chase,
Drinking whiskey by the case.
And there was Charley Carroll,

They say he drank it by the barrel.
And there was little Willie Auld,
He never had a drink at all.
And there was Jim Kinsella
Who was another sober fella.
And so by four o'clock
The fire had burned another block.

And at twelve o'clock the fire
    broke anew,
And burned Joe Gussenhoven too.
It took the drug store out of sight
And left the little bank for spite.
It took the Hotel Havre pretty quick
And took the Cheney pretty slick.
But it made the Maverick kick.
The Buffalo went very slow,
But the Chinks, they all had to go.
Old Hinote had gone out and
was still drinking whiskey from his
little spout.

So by four o'clock, the fire
had burned another block.
And you bet I was there
And saw it burn the Fair.
It was an awful mess,
To see the bums trying to dress,
I am nothing but a bum,
But I surely love my rum,
I had an awful jag,
Drinking whiskey from a keg,
They say old Hinote has
another stand
Where he is selling whiskey
made by hand.

—GEORGE FRANCIS

Bibliography

Interviews

Part of this manuscript was based on local and regional oral history, and the majority of those who contributed wished to remain anonymous (even though few are living today)—hence no individuals are credited. However, the following material did provide background information, whether general or specific.

Books

Adams, Ramon F. *Charles M. Russell, The Cowboy Artist*. Pasadena: Trails End Publishing, 1948.

——. *The Old-Time Cowhand*. New York: MacMillan Publishing Company, 1961.

Allen, Frederick L. *Only Yesterday: An Informal History of the 1920s*. New York: Perennial Library, 1964.

Allison, Janet S. *Trial and Triumph: 101 Years in North Central Montana*. Chinook. The Chinook Opinion, 1968.

Anonymous. *Progressive Men of Montana*. Chicago: A.W. Bowen and Company, 1901.

Autry, Gene. *Back In The Saddle Again*. New York: Doubleday & Company, 1978.

Bard, Floyd C. *Horse Wrangler: Sixty Years in the Saddle in Wyoming and Montana*. Norman: University of Oklahoma Press, 1960.

Beal, Merrill C. *A History of S.E. Idaho*. Caldwell: Caxton Press, 1942.

——. *History of Idaho*. Volume 1. New York: Lewis Publishing Company, 1959.

Berry, Gerald. *The Whoop-up Trail.* Edmonton, Alberta: Applied Art Products Ltd., 1953.

Branch, Douglas. *The Cowboy and His Interpreters.* New York: Cooper Square Publishing, 1976.

Brown, Mark and W. R. Felton. *Before Barbed Wire: The Frontier Years.* New York: Henry Holt & Company, 1955.

Bryan, William Jr. *Montana Indians: Yesterday and Today.* Helena: Montana Magazine, 1985.

Burlingame, Merrill G. *The Montana Frontier.* Bozeman: Big Sky Books, 1980.

—— and K. Ross Toole. *A History of Montana.* Three volumes. New York: Lewis Publishing Company, 1957.

Carey, Diane S. *The Hollywood Posse.* Boston: Houghton Mifflin Company, 1975.

Cheney, Roberta C. *Names on the Face of Montana.* Missoula: Mountain Press, 1984-Revised.

Clancy, Fred. *My Fifty Years in Rodeo.* San Antonio: The Naylor Company, 1952.

Coburn, Walt. *Pioneer Cattlemen in Montana, The Story of the Circle C Ranch.* Norman: University of Oklahoma Press, 1968.

Cushman, Dan. *The Great North Trail, America's Route of the Ages.* New York: McGraw-Hill Book Company, 1971.

——. *Plenty of Room and Air.* Great Falls: Stay Away, Joe Publishers, 1975.

Dawson County Bicentennial Committee. *Montana Stockgrowers 1900 Directory of Marks and Brands.* Glendive, 1974 reprint.

Dempsey Hugh A. *Big Bear, the End of Freedom.* Lincoln: Bison Press, 1986 reprint.

Dobie, Frank J. *The Longhorns.* New York: Bramhall House, 1982.

Eigell, Robert W. *Cows, Cowboys, Canners and Corned Beef and Cabbage.* New York: Vantage Press, 1988.

Federal Writers Project. W.P.A. The American Guide Series.
California. New York: Hastings House, 1945.
Idaho. New York: Oxford University Press, 1960 reprint.
Los Angeles. New York: Hastings House, 1941.
Montana. New York: Hastings House, 1946 reprint.
Wyoming. Lincoln: Bison Press, 1981 reprint.

Fenin, George and William Everson. *The Western: From Silents to Cinerama.* New York: Orion Press, 1962.

Fletcher, Robert. *Free Grass to Fences*. New York: University Publishers, 1960.

Friesen, Gerald. *The Canadian Prairies: A History*. Toronto: University of Toronto Press, 1984.

Furlong, Charles W. *Let 'Er Buck, A Story of the Passing of the Old West*. New York: G. P. Putnam's Sons, 1921.

Giegel, Doug, Editor. *In Print, Havre, Mt., Volume One: 1887-1904*. Big Sandy: The Performing Arts Group, 1987.

Gray, James H. *A Brand of Its Own*. Saskatoon, Saskatchewan: Western Producer Prairie Books, 1986.

Grey-Chaplin, Lita. *My Life with Chaplin*. New York: Bernand Geis Association, 1966.

Halseth, James A. *Cowboy Ways: On or About the E-Y*. Havre: Bear Paw Printers, 1975.

Hill County Bicentennial Commission. *Grit, Guts and Gusto*. Havre: Bear Paw Printers, 1976.

Hollingshead, Lillian. *Life As It Was*. Havre: Bear Paw Printers, 1975.

Horan, James D. *The Gunfighters*. New York: Crown Publishers, 1976.

Howard, Joseph K. *Montana: High, Wide, and Handsome*. New Haven: Yale University Press, 1943.

Kelly, Charles. *The Outlaw Trail: A Story of Butch Cassidy and the Wild Bunch*. New York: Bonanza Books, 1959-Revised.

Lane, Harrison. *The Long Flight: A History of the Nez Perce War*. Havre: H. Earl Clack Museum, 1982.

Lavigne, Frank C. *Crimes, Criminals and Detectives*. Helena: State Publishing Company, 1921.

Lucke, Marly E. *Margaret* [Faber]. Havre: privately published, 1983.

Lucke, Robert C. *Historic Homes of North Central Montana*. Havre: Hill County Printing, 1977.

Madsen, Betty and Brigham. *North To Montana!* Salt Lake City: University of Utah Press, 1980.

Malone, Michael P. and Richard B. Roeder. *Montana, A History of Two Centuries*. Seattle: University of Washington Press, 1976.

Martin, Albro. *James J. Hill and the Opening of the Northwest*. New York: Oxford University Press, 1976.

McGinnis, Vera. *Rodeo Road, My Life as a Pioneer Cowgirl*. New York: Hastings House, 1974.

Merriam, Harold G., editor. *The Recollections of Frank B. Linderman.* Omaha: University of Nebraska Press, 1968.

Miller, Don, and Stan Cohen. *Military and Trading Posts of Montana.* Missoula: Pictorial Histories Publishing Company, 1978.

Mix, Paul. *Tom Mix, Life and Legend.* San Diego: A. S. Barnes, 1972.

Nesland, Levin. Homestead Locations, Hill County Ownership Map [1915-19171. Havre: Susie's Copy Shop, 1988.

Nicholas, John. *Tom Mix: Riding Up to Glory.* Kansas City (Missouri): Lowell Press, 1980.

Nobel, Martin. *Looking Back.* Great Falls: privately published, circa 1975.

North Havre-St. Joe Residents, The. *Always the Wind.* Havre: Hill County Printing, 1979.

Noyes, A. J. *In the Land of Chinook.* Helena: State Publishing Company, 1917.

Price, Con. *Memories of Old Montana.* Hollywood: Highland Press, 1945.

Raymer, Robert. *Montana, The Land and The People.* Three volumes. New York: Lewis Publishing Company, 1930.

Robertson, Frank C. *Fort Hall: Gateway to Oregon Country!* New York: Hastings House, 1963.

Rollins, Phillip A. *The Cowboy: An Unconventional History of Civilization on the Old Time Cattle Range.* Albuquerque: University of New Mexico Press, 1979 reprint.

Russell, Austin. *C. M. Russell, Cowboy Artist.* New York: Twayne Publications, 195 7.

Sandoz, Marie. *The Cattlemen.* Lincoln: University of Nebraska Press, 1978 reprint.

Sanders, Helen F. *A History of Montana.* Three volumes. New York: Lewis Publishing Company, 1913.

Sharp, Paul F. *Whoop-up Country, the Canadian-American West.* Norman: University of Oklahoma Press, 1973 reprint.

Stout, Tom. *Montana, Its Story and Biography.* New York: The American Historical Society, 1921.

Thackeray, William, editor. *The Metis Centennial Celebration Publication, 1879-1979.* Lewistown: Central Montana Publishing Company, 1979.

Toole, K. Ross. *Twentieth Century Montana, a State of Extremes.* Norman: University of Oklahoma Press, 1977 (4th printing).

Watts, Peter. *A Dictionary of the Old West.* New York: Promontory Press, 1987.

Whetstone, Dan. *Frontier Editor.* New York: Hastings House, 1956.

Wilson, Gary A. *Honky-Tonk Town, Havre's Bootlegging Days.* Havre: High-Line Books, 1986 reprint.

Woodson, Warren. *Pioneer Tales of Montana.* New York: Exposition Press, 1965.

Other Sources

Anonymous. "A Day's Drive With Montana Cowboys." *Harpers New Monthly Magazine.* New York: circa 1886.

——. "A Short History of Havre." Havre Group of the Montana Institute of the Arts. Typed handout, circa 1954.

——. "Battle of the Bears Paw-Blaine County-Chinook." Chinook Businessmen's Association. Printed handout, date unknown.

——. "Beaver Creek Originally Part of Military Post." *Great Falls Tribune:* June 6, 1943.

——. "Blaine County History Clear Creek Years." *Chinook Opinion:* jubilee edition, 1964.

——. "Golden Spike Utah Centennial Issue." *United Transportation News.* Cleveland: April 26, 1969.

——. "Sees Buildings of Fort Assinniboine." *Great Falls Tribune:* November 17, 1935.

——. "Story of Old Fort Assinniboine." *Big Timber* (Montana) *Pioneer:* circa 1930.

——. "That Big Cattle Steal." [Boise] *Idaho Daily Statesman:* January 27, 1891.

Beal, Merril C. "Rustlers and Robbers: Idaho Frontier Days." *Idaho Yesterdays.* Idaho State Historical Society, Boise: date unknown

Bell, John T. "Ne-Cot-Ta." Volume One. Unpublished and undated manuscript.

Bosley, Donald R. "A Montana Town That Is No More: Coberg, Montana." *Montana: The Magazine of Western History.* Helena: October 1975.

Broadwater, Kathlyn. "Early Days of Fort Assinniboine." Three parts. *Havre Daily News:* January 1933.

Bronson, Earl. "An Area History of Havre and Hill County." History column in the *Havre Daily News,* 1960s.

Bryant, Karen, editor. *Fort Benton in Historic Chouteau County.* Forward. Fort Benton, 1988.

Cheney, Elizabeth. "Lonely Winter Death of a Cowboy." *Montana: The Magazine of Western History:* January 1967.

Clark, Sam H. "The End of Crimson Trail." *Jim, Jam, Jems* magazine. Bismarck: March 1921.

Coburn Walt. "Good Hearted and Unlucky." *Old West* magazine: Spring 1968.

Cook, Ed. "The Laredo Community." Havre: undated manuscript.

Costello, Gladys. "A Frontier Marshall Turns in His Star." *Great Falls Tribune:* March 4, 1954.

——. "Former Stage Driver Recalls Little Rockies Boom," *Great Falls Tribune:* November 22, 1959.

——. "Malta Country." *Montana Magazine.* Helena: Spring 1977.

Cowan, William. Letter to Earl Wooldridge, Rocky Boy Reservation superintendent, referencing Chippewa-Cree-Box Elder history; April 10, 1934.

Davis, Karen E. "Your Guide to Northern Montana." *Bear Paw Sentinel:* June 15, 1983.

Entorf, John F. "Long George Francis (Horse thief?)." Montana history term paper, Professor Harrison Lane, Northern Montana College: circa 1956.

Estell, Ruth. "Early Ranching and Cowboys in the Bear Paw Mountains." Montana history term paper, Professor Harrison Lane. Northern Montana College: circa 1960

Eudy, Martha A. "Havre, Montana—Its Historical Development." Montana history term paper, Professor Harrison Lane. Northern Montana College: March 1960.

Faber, Rose, family historian. Ryan-Redwing-Faber history collection. Sucker Creek: various dates of unpublished papers and clippings.

——. George Francis-Matilda-Ryan-Redwing letters. Sucker Creek: 1902-1914.

Federal Writers Project, W.P.A. "Western Range Cattle Industry Study, Montana Livestock History Collection for Havre area, 1940-4l." Montana Historical Society Archives.

Ferris, Robert, series editor. "The National Survey of Historic Sites and Buildings." Volume XI. *Prospector, Cowhand and Sodbuster.* National Parks Service, 1967.

Freedom, Gary S. "Military Forts and Logistical Sufficiency on the Northern Plains, 1866-1891." *North Dakota History Journal of the Northern Plains.* Bismarck: Spring 1983.

Gibson, A. Marie. Unpublished autobiography. Havre: circa 1925.

Gibson, Marian. "Long George Francis." Montana history term paper, Professor Harrison Lane. Northern Montana College: circa 1960.

Gunderson, Carl. "The High Line." Chapter XX; Burlingame and Toole, *A History of Montana.*

Hagener, Antoinette (Toni). "Index of Havre Newspapers, 1893-1953." Reference section, Havre-Hill County Library.

——. " Hill County Celebrates its 70th Birthday." *Bear Paw Sentinel:* February 24, 1982.

Hardeman, Nicholas P. "Brick Stronghold of the Border: Fort Assinniboine, 1879-1911." *Montana: The Magazine of Western History:* Spring 1979.

Havre City Library Scrapbook. Articles on George Francis by Andy Avery, Jean Carruth, and Mike O'Neal, circa 1933.

Havre-Chouteau County-Havre-Hill County directories. Polk's, Butte-Helena, 1909-10. "EB and JH Fenton." *Havre Promoter:* 1915-16.

Hodgen, C. W. "Idaho Range Industry: Early Cattle Days in Idaho." Classroom handout, University of Idaho: circa 1948.

Inman, Francis. "Cattlemen, Homesteaders; Puncher and the Plow." *Havre Daily News:* December 24, 1984.

Jenks, Theodore. "Mrs. Mabee-Brown family history." Balboa: unpublished; May 1982.

Johnson, Sonja, "A Short History of Havre." Montana history term paper, Professor Harrison Lane. Northern Montana College: 1961.

Jones, Lee A. Mrs. "Reminiscences of Early Days in Havre." Unpublished, undated paper.

Kaiser, Louise. "Rocky Boy Reservation." Montana history term paper, Professor Harrison Lane. Northern Montana College: 1959.

Kannberg, Elizabeth. "Kremlin: the early years." *Havre Daily News:* October 17, 1988.

Kardell, Lloyd. "George Francis." Montana history term paper, Professor Harrison Lane. Northern Montana College: 1961.

Larson-Clack, Elinor. "A Bit of Havre History." *Havre Daily News:* June 4, 1986.

——. "Interview with Mrs. Lohman." Unpublished paper: 1953.

Larson-Clack, Elinor and Alvin J. Lucke. "Beaver Creek." Unpublished paper: 1954.

Havre, Hub of History." Unpublished paper: 1954.

Lawrence, Lou. "History of Big Sandy." *Big Sandy Mountaineer* booklet: circa 1963.

——. "The Pioneer Days." *Big Sandy Mountaineer* booklet: circa 1961.

Lucke, Alvin J. Untitled paper and map on early Beaver Creek-Cow Creek-Fort Belknap-Hayes and Little Rockies. Handout, 1954.

Lucke, Robert C. "Fort Assinniboine." *True West* magazine: July 1983.

——. Selected "Howdy Beaver" newspaper columns. *Havre Daily News:* 1980.

Lusk, Bryon D. "Golden Cattle Kingdoms of Idaho." Unpublished master's thesis, Utah State University: 1978

Lux, Mabel. "Honyockers of Harlem; Scissorbills of Zurich." *Montana: The Magazine of Western History:* Spring 1969.

Lumpkin-Bentley, Cecelia, coordinator. Martin-Lumpkin family history (Letters to author; 1982-86.)

Mercier, Laurie. "Recording Montana Hi-Line Memories." *Montana Post* (M.H.S.): Summer 1987.

Mierau, Doreen. "Rustlers and Grain Thieves." *The Leader-Post.* Regina: September 13, 1974.

Miller, Fred, 111. "Sands family homesteaded in 1904." *Bear Paw Sentinel:* December 23, 1981.

Miller, Robert E. "Montana's Enterprising Colonel Broadwater." *Montana Magazine:* May-June 1981.

Montgomery, Curtis. "Long George—Hill County Anti-Hero." *Milk River Press:* July 9, 1975.

Newell, Kathie. "1989 Sees Fresno Dam Mark its 50th Year." *Havre Daily News:* April 24, 1989.

Oliphant, J. Orin. "The Range Cattle Industry in the Oregon Country to 1890." Unpublished doctoral dissertation, Harvard University: 1930.

Overholser, Joel F. "World's Innermost Port, Fort Benton." River Press Publishing Company: October 22, 1980.

Parrish, Michael, editor. "100 Years in the Life of a Town." *Los Angeles Times Magazine:* January 1, 1987.

Porter, William H. "Iron Mike Hastings." *True West* magazine: August 1986.

Reichelt, Clyde. "Pepin-Broadwater Founded P-Cross Ranch." *Great Falls Tribune:* December 13, 1959.

Ross, Karen. "The [Clear] Creek." Montana history term paper. Montana State University: 1967.

Stiffler, Liz and Tony Blake. "Fanny Sperry-Steele, Montana's Champion Bronc Rider." *Montana: The Magazine of Western History:* Spring 1982.

Scott, J.D. "Texas Longhorns on Comeback." *Reader's Digest:* January 1987.

Snedecor, Marie. "The Homesteaders: Their Dreams Held No Shadows." *Montana: The Magazine of Western History:* Autumn 1963.

Stirling, Vina. "Beaver Creek-Bear Paw Mountains." Havre: unpublished paper, circa 1958.

———. The Life of Louis Shambo (Chambeau)." Havre: unpublished paper, circa 1958.

Wallace, Carol, editor. "The 100th Birthday of Hollywood." *People Weekly:* February 9, 1987.

Weadick, Guy. "Long George." *Canadian Cattleman:* May-June 1982.

Weed, Donna. "The Philanthropies of Shorty Young." Montana history paper, Professor Harrison Lane. Northern Montana College: 1962.

Wessell, Claudia. George Francis-Francis family letter collection, 1892-1920. Arizona.

Wilson, Gary A. "Along the Milk River." *Montana Magazine:* May-June 1982.

———. History articles on northern Montana. *Havre Daily News-Bearpaw Sentinel:* 1980s.

Newspapers

Bear Paw Sentinel
Billings Gazette
Box Elder Valley Press
Calgary Herald
Chicago Tribune
Chinook Opinion
Chouteau County Independent
East (Pendleton) *Oregonian*
Glasgow Courier

Great Falls Tribune
Havre Advertiser
——*Daily News*
——*Herald*
——*Independent*
——*Plaindealer*
——*Promoter*
Hi-Line Herald
Hill County Democrat
Hill County Journal
Hinsdale Tribune
Laredo Tribune
Los Angeles Times
Malta Enterprise
Milk River Free Press
——*Eagle*
Seattle P.-I.
The (Fort Benton) *River Press*

Rodeo Programs

Glasgow (Montana) Stampede, 1920.
Great Northern Montana Stampede, Havre, 1916 and 1917.
Milk River Stampede, Hinsdale, 1919 and 1925.

Governmental, Public, and Private Organizations

City of Inkom, Idaho.
Department of Montana Institutions, Warm Springs/Galen State.
Fort Harrison, Montana Veterans Administration.
Havre City Library (now combined with county).
Hill County:
    Clerk and Recorder's office.
    Clerk of the District Court.

Library (now combined with city).

School Superintendent's office.

Idaho State Department of Law Enforcement, Boise, Idaho.

——Historical Society, Boise, Idaho.

——University, Pocatello, Idaho.

Los Angeles Times, News Department.

Montana:

Department of Livestock, Chinook Brand Inspection Office.

Historical Society, Helena.

State University, Roland R. Renne Library, Bozeman.

National Cowboy Hall of Fame; Oklahoma City, Oklahoma.

National Archives and Records Service, Washington, D.C.

North Dakota Historical Society, Bismarck.

Northern Montana College, Vande Bogart Library, Havre.

Oregon State Department of Agriculture, Livestock Division, Brand Recorder, Salem.

U.S. Department of Commerce, Patent and Trademark office, Washington, D.C.

U.S. Department of Interior, Bureau of Land Management, Billings, Montana.

Utah State Historical Society, Salt Lake City.

Utah State University, Merril Library, Logan.

Willets (California) *News*, News Department.

Wyoming State Livestock Board, Cheyenne.